Gender and Romance
in Chaucer's
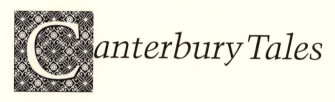anterbury Tales

SUSAN CRANE

PRINCETON UNIVERSITY PRESS · PRINCETON, NEW JERSEY

Copyright © 1994 by Princeton University Press
Published by Princeton University Press, 41 William Street,
Princeton, New Jersey 08540
In the United Kingdom: Princeton University Press,
Chichester, West Sussex

Library of Congress Cataloging-in-Publication Data

Crane, Susan.
Gender and romance in Chaucer's
Canterbury tales / Susan Crane.
p.   cm.
Includes bibliographical references (p.) and index.
ISBN 0-691-06952-2 — ISBN 0-691-01527-9 (pbk.)
1. Chaucer, Geoffrey, d. 1400. Canterbury tales.
2. Romances, English—History and criticism.
3. Man-woman relationships in literature.
4. Sex (Psychology) in literature.
5. Sex role in literature.   I. Title.
PR1875.R65C73   1993
821'.1—dc20   93-32421 CIP

This book has been composed in Adobe Trump Mediaeval

Princeton University Press books are printed
on acid-free paper and meet the guidelines
for permanence and durability of the Committee
on Production Guidelines for Book Longevity
of the Council on Library Resources

Printed in the United States of America

1   3   5   7   9   10   8   6   4   2

1   3   5   7   9   10   8   6   4   2

(Pbk.)

CONTENTS

❧❦❧

ACKNOWLEDGMENTS

I T IS A PLEASURE to acknowledge the many debts I have incurred in the course of this project. The early stages owed much to Georges Duby's kind invitation to attend his seminar on medieval women at the Collège de France. Larry Benson sponsored my year as a Visiting Scholar at Harvard, where the Department of English Medieval Colloquium and the Seminar on Medieval Literature at the Center for Literary and Cultural Studies provided invaluable conversations. Drafts of various parts of the book became talks at Brown University, Columbia University, the University of Connecticut, Harvard University, Princeton University, the University of Rochester, Susquehanna University, the Modern Language Association, and the New Chaucer Society. For these opportunities and for warm hospitality I thank Peter Awn, David Benson, John Ganim, Thomas Hahn, Frank Hoffman, William Jordan, Elizabeth Kirk, and Jan Ziolkowski.

For helpful comments and criticisms on parts of the text I am grateful to Larry Benson, Howard Bloch, Carolyn Dinshaw, Sheila Fisher, Louise Fradenberg, Elaine Hansen, Monica McAlpine, Anne Middleton, Charles Muscatine, Lee Patterson, Derek Pearsall, A. C. Spearing, and Winthrop Wetherbee. Throughout the project I have received encouragement and advice from John Fyler, John Ganim, and Paul Strohm. Many colleagues at Rutgers, particularly Ed Cohen, Elin Diamond, Cora Kaplan, Elizabeth McLachlan, and Bruce Robbins, have contributed bibliographical suggestions and their lively intellectual engagement to my efforts. I owe debts reaching far beyond this project to the friendship and the critical acumen of Susan Gal, Sam Hamburg, Barry Qualls, and Dick Foley.

A Fellowship for University Teachers from the National Endowment for the Humanities and grants-in-aid from the Rutgers Research Council have substantially aided my work. Thanks are due for permission to print revised versions of articles appearing in *The Arthurian Yearbook*, *The Chaucer Review*, *PMLA*, and

Studies in the Age of Chaucer. For access to the library of the Ecole des Chartes I am indebted to Jacques Monfrin. The staffs of the Bibliothèque Nationale, the British Library, and the libraries of Rutgers, Harvard, and Princeton Universities have been unfailingly helpful. Peggy Knapp and Paul Strohm provided valuable suggestions as referees for Princeton University Press. The Camargo Foundation offered a residence and time for rewriting. Robert Brown's editorial guidance and the superb copyediting of Lauren Lepow have generously sustained me through the final stages of the project.

Gender and Romance

in Chaucer's

Canterbury Tales

• INTRODUCTION •

HE THESIS of this book is that gender is crucial to Geoffrey Chaucer's conception of romance in the *Canterbury Tales*. In Chaucer's works, as in those of other poets who engage romance, gender provides a way of reading aspects of the genre beyond courtship alone. Social hierarchies, magic, adventure, and less salient preoccupations of romance are so intimately involved in gender that their operations are unclear in isolation from it. My concern is not with identifying specific sources and analogues for the *Canterbury Tales* nor with encompassing in my discussion every aspect of romance. The many studies that illuminate these issues provide a context for investigating more specifically how Chaucer understood the place and meaning of gender in the history of romance.

Gender and genre have phonic and etymological but also more substantial bonds. Both are systems of distinction that are susceptible to hierarchization; both have an informing relation to specific persons and works. They can be conceived as the inspiring potential that generates intelligible identities and texts; they can also become measures that constrain and evaluate. Gender and genre can make claims to transhistorical permanence, when they ground their claims in nature in the former case and art in the latter, but both categories prove to be subject to negotiation as they are mobilized in particular identities and works. Finally the historicity of both categories must be accepted: both are persistent over time but also reperformed and reinterpreted in their every instantiation. For Fredric Jameson this link between recurrence and reinterpretation makes a concept of genre necessary to literary history: "Only the history of the forms themselves can provide an adequate mediation between the perpetual change of social life on the one hand, and the closure of the individual work on the other" ("Magical Narratives," 136). It is equally evident that a concept of gender can clarify the relation between the shifting social functions of gender and particular gestures, literary or

historical, that are meant to distinguish gay from straight or masculine from feminine behavior.

Gender and genre are not simply analogous but intersecting
constructions in romance. This is the medieval genre in which
courtship, marriage, lineal concerns, primogeniture, and sexual
maturation are most fully at issue. In plots that dramatize the
establishment of gendered identity, romances raise questions
such as: What differentiates men's values and comportment from
women's? How rigid is the binary contrasting masculine to feminine? Can same-sex relations persist within heterosexuality? So
rich are the implications of gender for romance that my discussion only begins to indicate the questions gender can illuminate
in the five *Canterbury Tales* most indebted to the genre, the
Knight's, Wife of Bath's, Squire's, and Franklin's tales and the
Tale of Sir Thopas. I am concerned not to find the edges and sub-
divisions of romance but instead to discover in Chaucer's tales
what aspects of the genre are invoked there and to what effect.
The range of Chaucer's reference is wide, encompassing Breton
lays, Middle English metrical romances, late medieval composite
romances, the *romans antiques*, and more. What focuses his response to these disparate kinds of romance is a concern with how
the genre imagines gender. In the *Franklin's Tale*, for example, a
narrator drawn in part from romance, the hospitable vavasour, attempts to revise the genre that defines him as a passive domestic
figure, an anomaly among men. Canacee's encounter with the falcon in the *Squire's Tale* recalls other women's adventures in both
its miniaturized resemblances to chivalric adventure and its suppressed difference from that dominant model. These tales stage
the authority and durability of concepts of gender and romance
but also the interrogation to which each concept is subject in
every new enactment. The brief overview below argues that this
tension between ideological consolidation and particular destabilizations generates the historicity of gender and genre.

A first way of conceiving gender is to contrast it to sex. In that
contrast, gender is the exterior, social interpretation of sexual
practices specific to a particular culture. Sexuality, broadly understood as the generation, expression, and organization of desire, is
the ongoing behavior that informs gendered identities. Deriving

gender from sexuality risks referring all gendered traits to physical differences between female and male. Insofar as they are said
to be verified by biological sex, the gender distinctions a given
culture elaborates may appear more stable and fundamental than
other distinctions such as those of estate or national identity. But
the permutations of gender over time and place suggest that biological sex does not constitute its unchanging natural foundation.
Judith Butler argues against treating sex difference as the verifi-
able basis for gender, noting that humans experience their bodies
through the conceptual processes that have elaborated ideas of
gender. "Bodies cannot be said to have a signifiable existence prior
to the mark of their gender. . . . There is no recourse to a 'person,'
a 'sex,' or a 'sexuality' that escapes the matrix of power and discursive relations that effectively produce and regulate the intelligibility of those concepts for us" (8, 32). Even the most directly
physical phenomena such as giving birth or losing virginity immediately partake of cultural formulations that give meaning to
physical changes. For humans, as Denise Riley puts it, "in a strong
sense the body is a concept, and so is hardly intelligible unless it
is read in relation to whatever else supports it and surrounds it"
(104; see also Laqueur). Better than conceiving gender to be the
complex of meanings assigned to sexuality is conceiving sex to
be subsumed within a gender system that makes it available to
consciousness.

   If sexuality is positioned within gender as a socially negotiated
and defined status that does not itself determine gender, then a
binary gender division is not the only possibility. A third gender
occurs in some cultures; same-sex and mixed sexual orientations
proliferate and overlap in others. For reading Chaucer one implication of this sense in which gender is arbitrary should be that the
sex of an author is not a completely reliable predictor of a work's
perceptions concerning gender. Taking seriously the idea that sex
and gender are both constructed and continually renegotiated
through an array of social forces entails untying the bond between, in the case of Chaucer, a historical man and masculine
discourses. The sex of an author fixes discourse no more securely
than sex fixes gender. To be sure, critics have traced conventionally masculine orientations in Chaucer as they have traced conventionally feminine ones in Marie de France (e.g., Huchet, "Nom

de femme"; Freeman). Chaucer's and Marie's more predictable alignments, however, should not obscure for us certain sensibilities that are less obviously consonant with their sex.

Far from being natural, then, the sex-gender system is inherently and intensely ideological. Convictions about gender underlie choices in every social context, from the public and private behavior of a young knight to the ground plan of a nunnery, the law of primogeniture, and the sacrament of marriage. This is the quality of gender that helps to situate romances in their historical moment. Romances place themselves in their time less through the referentiality of their representations than through their participation in forming, playing out, and disputing interrelated beliefs that have meaning for their authors and audiences. The romance genre is a particular vehicle among many for the expression, perpetuation, and critique of gender in the culture as a whole. Considered as social forces, genders and genres partake of ideology in their capacity to constitute social identities through powerful appeals to imagination.[1] Thinking of gender and genre as instances of ideology at its work of establishing and revising consciousness involves the particular instance of "gender in romance" in the culture's wider negotiations.

That gender speaks through conventional discourses such as romance does not displace it from its equally powerful involvement in the gestures of everyday behavior. Written and enacted instances reinforce one another; in Teresa de Lauretis's formulation, "the construction of gender is both the product and the process of its representation" (Technologies, 5). Conceiving gender as a representation encompasses texts and gestures in one register of meaning that is subject to historical fluctuations. Gender emerges not as the fixed expression of binary sex difference but as a socially instituted construct that interacts with other constructs of class, faith, and so on—very differently, for instance, in the experience of a provincial countess and a London alderman.[2] Like all

[1] De Lauretis proposes the analogy between gender and ideology (Technologies, 6–11). It is probably clear from my discussion that I am not considering ideologies to be false consciousness that makes oppressions bearable but instead to be genuine attempts at the broadly social level to understand and justify the social order from the perspectives of differing interests.

[2] Foucault, History of Sexuality, excludes the medieval period from the social

social representations gender has a history, and literature has a prominent role in that history of asserting and modifying what it means to live in gendered identity.

Over all these reconsiderations hovers the inadequacy of the terms *men* and *women*, inaccurately universalizing, indeterminately referring to persons and to ideas of gender, and differently specified even in compatible theories of gender. Meaghan Morris writes that "we seem to be sliding on our signifieds, and the scare quote stalks in to fence off the space of a disaster zone: 'woman,' 'women,' 'Woman' are the warning signs of an increasingly unposable problem, all of a heap, wrong from the start" (24). My deletion of the wary scare quotes is a typographical convenience that does not claim determinate meaning for gender terminology. To attempt to simplify the problem by declaring, for example, that I use "woman" to refer only to the literary idea of woman in one set of texts would be to deny my conviction that there is a constitutive relation between ideas and historical identities. Nor does labeling a behavior "masculine" evade in my view the important complication that masculinity is differently resisted and mobilized in different persons. But I recognize that the place of gender in identity and in social analysis is heavily contested. In terminology as in conceptions, the burgeoning diversities of gender theory challenge each position within it while generously sustaining new possibilities.

One indication that gender holds greater social power than genre is the ease with which recent critics have resisted genre's coercive classifying function, so congenial to earlier literary study. Gender is more than a concept and exerts substantial control in the world; genre is a conceptual tool that can be refashioned without significant repercussions for society at large. Currently, then, genre has come to provide a context for reading particular works rather than a standard against which works are measured. So conceived, gen-

---

articulation of sexuality, tracing that articulation to the eighteenth century (e.g., 103–5), but much of his argument on sexuality's social function as "an especially dense transfer point for relations of power" (103) fits the late medieval period better than his own characterization of that period as monolithic, without competing discourses on sex, would suggest (e.g., 33).

res do not have a fully constitutive relation to texts; their hold over texts is relatively slight, as is their capacity to explain specific texts. Jameson suggests not only that we distinguish consistently between the facilitation or potential of genre and the concreteness of particular works, but further that generic categories "are ultimately to be understood (or 'estranged') as mere ad hoc, experimental constructs, devised for a specific textual occasion and abandoned like so much scaffolding when the analysis has done its work" (*Political Unconscious*, 145). Adena Rosmarin concurs that for the purposes of critical explanation genre should not be taken as a preexisting category but as an implement for reading. We would then not assume that *Lybeaus Desconus* should instantiate a definition of romance; we would instead read it as if it were a romance, with the aim not of accounting for its deviance from a norm but of discovering its meaning through the aid that a generic perspective can provide. Genre study so conceived resists the taxonomic impulse and imagines genre to be less a pigeonhole than a pigeon—mobile, organic, and subject to time.[3]

The case of medieval romance makes particularly clear how provisional and protean a genre can appear. The breadth of features illustrated in romances Chaucer uses or cites, such as *Guy of Warwick*, the Breton lays, and *Cleomadés*, is compounded by time: Chaucer stands relatively late in the course of romance, when other genres can briefly invoke it as a mode. In these conditions "romance" can refer to a few lines or an entire tale, a familiar resonance or an innovation that departs from and even contradicts the genre's past. Conceived as a historical genre, romance draws together measures of scale, style, structure, and content that inform entire works; conceived as a generic mode, romance is a register or moment that calls features of the historical genre to mind within any number of other genres.

For some scholars the capaciousness of romance makes it "doubtful whether the romance can be indeed regarded as a genre at all," in Pamela Gradon's judgment; "it seems preferable to talk

[3] The image is from Fowler: "Some have concluded that genre theory, being unhelpful in classification, is valueless. But in reality genre is much less of a pigeonhole than a pigeon, and genre theory has a different use altogether, being concerned with communication and interpretation" (37).

of a romance mode" (269–70).[4] Even if lays were excluded from
affiliation with romance, which would in my view falsify their
place in the genre's history, romance would resist definition according to recurring expectations of form, subject matter, or narrative technique.[5] Yet Chaucer and his contemporaries did attribute generic meaning to the term *romaunce*. In the fourteenth
century, the term could designate works written in French and
sometimes any written source, or secular works that were not rigorously historical, or a generic category of narrative fictions concerning the deeds of chivalric heroes.[6] The *Book of the Duchess*
uses the term in the first or second sense in attributing the story
of Ceyx and Alcioun to "a book, / A romaunce" (47–48), probably
to recall Chaucer's French sources, Guillaume de Machaut's *Dit
de la fonteinne amoreuse* and the *Ovide moralisé*, as well as
Ovid's *Metamorphoses*.[7] Paul Clogan argues that "romaunce" has
more generic force in *Troilus and Criseyde*, where Criseyde so
designates a book whose contents tally with those of the *Roman
de Thèbes*, in contrast to the *Thebaid* material that Pandarus then
invokes. In *Sir Thopas* "romances that been roiales" and "romances of prys" designate works that Thopas describes as "Of
popes and of cardinales, / And eek of love-likynge" and that the
narrator specifies as the stories of Horn, Ypotis, Bevis, Guy, Lybeaus Desconus, and Pleyndamour, all less fine than the tale of Sir
Thopas (VII 845–50, 897–902). The popes, cardinals, and holy Ypotis would seem to be comic violations of a generally accepted idea
of romance, since the narrator's promise to tell "of bataille and of

[4] Barron, 4, and Jordan concur with Gradon; see also Parker. I will not be concerned with genre as a mode that transcends genre altogether, as in Frye's use of
the term to denote "the structural core of all fiction"(15).

[5] Hernadi responds to this difficulty by proposing that genre can manifest itself
in a number of registers, some of which evade measures of form, others of content.
He suggests four kinds of similarity that might be described in generic terms: a
mental attitude expressed within works, verbal and stylistic similarity, a shared
imaginary world or view of the external world, and a shared effect on readers.
Accepting multiple registers for romance permits the genre to encompass long
works and short ones, a subtle poetic of *conte* and *conjointure* and straightforward
storytelling, verse and prose, chivalric exploits or courtship or both.

[6] See Strohm, "*Storie, Spelle*" and "Origin and Meaning"; Thompson argues that
an awareness of romance as a genre can be discerned in the Thornton manuscript.

[7] All quotations from works of Chaucer and from the *Romaunt of the Rose* are
taken, unless otherwise noted, from *Riverside Chaucer*.

chivalry, / And of ladyes love-drury" (VII 894–95) resembles medieval and modern accounts of the genre.

Chaucer's references to romance indicate a doubly low status
for the genre that helps explain why and how Chaucer took his
distance from it.[8] First, that one of its subjects is "ladyes love-
drury" oddly but appropriately associates the foundational fictions of heterosexual courtship with one sex only. Romance is a
feminine genre according to medieval writers. The scene of reading in *Troilus and Criseyde* sustains this connection. When Pandarus finds Criseyde reading with her women, she explains, "This
romaunce is of Thebes that we rede," and describes a sequence of
events peculiar to the *Roman de Thèbes*. Pandarus's reply that he
knows its "bookes twelve" refers to the Latin *Thebaid* despite
Criseyde's designation of the vernacular "romaunce." Clogan
notes Pandarus's pedantic display of knowledge; the genre gap di-
viding Pandarus's allegiance to classical epic from Criseyde's to
"romaunce" instantiates a gender gap as well. Adenet le Roi asserts that two ladies have commanded him to write *Cleomadés*
(ll. 17–66), and Chrétien de Troyes claims that the matter and the
sense of *Le Chevalier de la Charrette* were provided to him by
Marie de Champagne (ll. 1–29). Denis Piramus notes that "les lais
solent as dames pleire" (lays are pleasing to the ladies) but that
they "ne sunt pas del tut verais" (are not at all true) (*Vie Seint
Edmund*, ll. 38, 46). The association between untruth and a
feminine audience recalls the Nun's Priest's asseveration "This
storie is also trewe, I undertake, / As is the book of Launcelot de
Lake, / That wommen holde in ful greet reverence" (VII 3211–13).
Literary histories have invoked such claims to argue for women's
patronage of romance, but they refer more directly to the doubtful
validity of the genre, to a hierarchy of genres that matches the
relatively low credibility of romance's lies and wonders to feminine identity. Romance has the name of a feminine genre, although its historical audiences were surely mixed.[9]

---

[8] It is virtually a critical commonplace that Chaucer eagerly seized on such genres as the fabliau, saint's legend, and dream vision but "felt less easy with the very
genre which we regard as most characteristic of his period, the knightly romance"
(Burrow, "*Canterbury Tales*," 109; see chapter 5, "Adventure and the Feminine in
the *Knight's Tale*").

[9] On gender and the audiences for romance see R. F. Green, "Women"; Hanning,
"Audience"; Krueger; Strohm, *Social Chaucer*, 58–62.

Romance is not only feminine but outmoded in Chaucer's milieu. The pastness that earlier conferred dignity on the genre—the
"olde dayes of the Kyng Arthour" (III 857), the "olde gentil Britouns" (V 709), the "Whilom, as olde stories tellen us" (I 859) of so
many prologues to romance—becomes a mark of obsolescence in
the later fourteenth century. As Chaucer's youthful work indicates, romance writing did not dominate literary production at
English and French courts in the later fourteenth century. Lyric
poetry, *dits amoureux*, and dream visions were in ascendance, in
part for their suitability to occasional commissions and to oral
performance during the decades when poetry writing was becoming an important social accomplishment for courtiers. To such
poets the metrical romances may well have seemed but "drasty
speche" (VII 923) and Arthurian material as remote as in the
Squire's Tale. There the narrator refers to Gawain and Lancelot as
models of behavior respectively "olde" and "deed" (V 95, 287),
invoking their excellence but locating it in a past inaccessible
even to rhetoric: in both cases the citation of the hero's name
marks with hyperbole the absence of an account of courtly behavior. Chaucer's literary experience stretched far beyond the poetry
of Machaut and his compatriots, but their influence is great in his
milieu and early works. As its authority and source of motifs,
their poetry declares its debt to the *Romance of the Rose*, in
which Guillaume de Lorris reorients the courtship narratives of
romance toward allegory and lyric autobiography. The *Romance
of the Rose* made romances in the generic sense unfashionable,
yet Guillaume's work is obviously dependent on the genre despite
its allegorical mode and dream-vision form. The *dits* of Machaut
and Froissart and Chaucer's *Book of the Duchess* perpetuate such
features of romance as its dramatization of courtliness and courtship, its melding of lyric and narrative impulses, and its use of
allegory to unfold moments of emotional turmoil. The *Squire's
Tale* illustrates the contiguity between romance and the more
modern *dit* as it moves from narrating the arrival of Cambyuskan's adventure-provoking birthday gifts to the falcon's lyric lament based on *Anelida and Arcite*. The generic shift is virtually
imperceptible because the narrative component of the falcon's lament and its concern with the vagaries of courtship incorporate it
into the generic frame of romance. Here as in the *dits* of the later
fourteenth century, conceiving romance to be outmoded seems to

be a strategy for remobilizing it, just as declaring the genre to be feminine licenses its production and reception beyond women's circles alone.

The parallels between gender and genre move in two directions. One line of connections to investigate would be how historical men and women "perform" romance—how their behavior imitates or inspires romance's representation of gender and how they receive, interpret, and circulate particular romance texts.[10] My question in this study is how romances "perform" gender rather than the reverse—how they construe masculinity and femininity, how they work out the paradigm of difference and the challenge of intimacy, and how they relate gender to other expressions of social identity. I seek out the most visible and repeatable ways in which the genre configures gender, with the goal of illuminating both the durability of gender ideology and its mobile instantiation in Chaucer's response to romance. I am not concerned to establish whether Chaucer was familiar with each text to which I refer; it is evident that he knew the genre and that it holds an important place in the *Canterbury Tales*. Rather than attempting to provide a history of romance, I treat resonances between Chaucer's works and others as part of Chaucer's moment, features of his context and his response to the literary history he experiences. My premise is that romance assigns gender a high degree of motivating and explanatory force. Romance implicates the dichotomy between masculine and feminine in a range of other oppositions between authority and submission, familiarity and exoticism, justice and mercy, public and private, with which the gender dichotomy suggestively interacts. The insights drawn from gender theory that are most important to my readings are roughly four: that the conceptual power of difference strongly characterizes romance's depictions of gender; that difference is innately hierarchizing in romance; that the gender hierarchy is related to other systems of

[10] R. F. Green, *Poets and Princepleasers*, and Poirion usefully situate poetry writing in court culture; the theoretical work of Jauss, e.g., *Aesthetic of Reception*, particularly sustains audience-oriented studies. Wimsatt has made many contributions to the study of literary influences in the *dits* of Machaut, Froissart, and others, most recently in *Chaucer and His French Contemporaries*. See also Krueger; Fewster, 104–28.

distinction; and finally that despite the dominance of a hier-
archized conception of gender difference, romance also represents
gender contrarily as unstable, open to question, and in danger of
collapse.

The first chapter considers how romance imagines masculine
identity. In the paradigm of difference, polarizing male and female
traits does not confer equivalent status on masculine and feminine identity. The social position occupied by those gendered
male becomes conflated with that of humanity at large, exiling
those gendered female to the position of difference, otherness, and
objectification.[11] The process is central to romance's depiction of
masculine maturation and courtship. Striving suitors establish
their identity in meeting and overcoming resistance from the
objects of their love. However projected and predetermined by
masculine desire that resistance may be, its difference marks it
feminine and announces romance's particular engagement with
gender. As for the male protagonist, his centrality in romance criticism attests to the self-determination romance plots seem to
place in his charge. But Chaucer's use of the genre recognizes that
the heroic subject is first of all part of the social unit, and only
by its consensus is he distinguishable and self-determining. As
masculinity strives for definition in courtship, heterosexuality
works to exclude the threat of homoeroticism, which persists in
plots that make courtship analogous to and involved in relations
among knights.

Intrinsic to masculine identity in romance is the concept of a
fundamental difference between self and other. In the dominant
paradigm of courtship, women attest to their suitors' deeds and
reflect back to them an image of their worth. The resistance
women may put up to suitors is compatible with the masculine
desire for a complex experience of affective subjectivity. However, certain distortions of the paradigm can speak against it.
Chapter 2 treats a feminine mimicry by which women attempt to
resist the scripted position of the other. Their mimicry is not

[11] The locus classicus is De Beauvoir; Cixous articulates the more recent corol-
lary that otherness risks or amounts to absence: "The paradox of otherness is that,
of course, at no moment in History is it tolerated or possible as such. The other is
there only to be reappropriated, recaptured, and destroyed as other. Even the exclusion is not an exclusion" (71).

merely the echo of masculine speech but an ironic repositioning of it that makes its premises available to criticism. Physical distortions extend the effects of verbal mimicry for women by loosening the bond between the feminine and the bodily that contributes to defining gender difference.

The third chapter examines how gender in romance is related to other hierarchical social arrangements. The hierarchical ordering of gender difference is so nearly universal in medieval articulations as to appear natural and unproblematic. From Aristotle a dominant theoretical tradition has conceived the original social differentiation to have been gendered, based in the different capacities and natures of men and women (Allen, Maclean). Modern theorists attribute gender's hierarchies to its subsumption in wider power negotiations. "Feminism is a theory of how the eroticization of dominance and submission creates gender, creates woman and man in the social form in which we know them to exist," writes Catharine MacKinnon, "Gender here is a matter of dominance, not difference" ("Desire and Power," 107–8). In romance, gender difference is implicated in hierarchies of gentility, estate, and degree (roughly, of moral worth, social duty, and achievement). Chaucer particularly exploits the overlap of gender and social hierarchy through the relation of narrators to tales. For example, in a crossgendered comparison of marginal gentility to femininity, the *Franklin's Tale* aligns Dorigen's incapacities with those of the narrating Franklin to express the restrictions of their respective social statuses.

Magic is a familiar generic feature of romance whose workings are closely involved with gender. Chapter 4 argues that in association with masculine characters and concerns, magic expresses desires for achievement and completeness that are denied to masculine identity in romance. The magic of learned clerks promises Aurelius and the children of Cambyuskan expanded capabilities through appropriation and control of the exotic, but their magical machinery finally throws men back on their own resources. In contrast, women's magic involves men in intimacies, expresses the ambiguous pleasure and danger of those intimacies, and tends to have occulted origins.

As the most immediate expression of the unknown in romance, woman instigates and is allied with adventure. Chapter 5 considers how adventure figures and critiques gender constructions. Adventure is first of all a masculine pursuit, a self-risking solitary endeavor. But adventure does not represent escape from the feminine. Diana's uncanny foreknowledge together with Emelye's un- explained resistance in the *Knight's Tale* identify the feminine with the very terrain of adventure. Victories won in combat, land taken by conquest, and marvels appropriated or overcome replay metonymically the lover's ultimate conquest of his lady. At the same time, the adventurer's vulnerable submissiveness to errancy and accident recalls feminine pliancy. Particularly when they are subject to love, men experience a crossgendering that puts them at risk of resembling women. For their part, women have adven- tures that may involve crossgendering but that more importantly contrast with and reinterpret men's adventures.

Masculinity in Romance

ASCULINITY is a persistent concern in Chaucer's tales deriving from romance, although it often
seems a subtext to more evidently political and social issues. The *Knight's Tale*, for example, begins
with a briefly sketched contrast between Theseus's
conquest of the Amazons and his pity on the widows of the siege
of Thebes. Why does he subdue one group of women and aid the
next? A plausible reading of the difference in terms of social issues
might center on the wise Athenian's concern to redress disorders,
in the first case the unnatural rule of women and in the second
case the desecration of bodies and the reversals of Fortune suffered by the widows. Amazonia and Thebes have perpetrated disorder; there is a significant parallel between Theseus's responses
to the two foreign encounters. From the perspective of gender it
could be added that there is as well a significant contrast between
his responses to the two encounters with women. Conquering
and marrying the Amazon queen is a sexual as well as a political
action, one that eroticizes masculine dominance and feminine
submission. In contrast, taking pity on the widows of Thebes reveals in Theseus a compassion that may seem feminine, complicating his masculinity. Similarly, Palamon and Arcite are most
evidently political adversaries to Theseus. Their Theban blood
carries the destructive rivalry of Polynices and Eteocles from
Thebes into Athens, and their desire for Emelye challenges Theseus's authority. Yet the Thebans' rivalries have implications as
well for their masculinity, as the young men measure their desire
for Emelye against Theseus's ability to constrain it and as their
desire becomes both a component of their chivalric relation with
one another and a constitutive feature of their sexual identities.
This chapter's three divisions look for the gendered subtext to
such interactions.

My first concern is to suggest how romances use gender difference to establish masculine identity. Not only does heterosexual courtship become an important arena for self-definition, romances elaborate a range of distinctions between men's and women's social comportment, duties, and rights that gender the concept of identity so important to the early development of the genre. Masculine and feminine identity differ in that the centrality and complexity assigned to masculinity in romance makes it more than simply the reverse of femininity. Difference from woman does not, paradoxically, exile from man all traits associated with the feminine.

After a brief look at the function of difference in elaborating masculinity, this chapter turns to two complications in that paradigm. The tendency to identify masculine with universal experience meets a countertendency in romance in the constraints the community places on heroic autonomy. These are not merely external; the hero of romance is constituted so fundamentally by his culture that he resembles the postmodern subject more closely than the Lockean individual. Self-definition involves recognizing and accepting the social composition of personal identity.

Courtship in romance expands masculine interactions in that it is secondary to them and reproduces them in crossgendered and eroticized form. Courtship clarifies the ambivalently adversarial and desiring relations between men in the genre's version of chivalric culture. Where courtship and chivalry intersect, they may appear to be in competition; but finally courtship extends masculine identity by providing a new arena of interaction for men.

As the leading form for long fictions in the later Middle Ages, romance was so pervasive an influence that Chaucer's awareness of the genre can hardly be in question. The place of romance in Chaucer's conceptions of gender alone is so prominent and nuanced that I cannot touch on many of its aspects. Those I have chosen are so normative in the genre that they might be illustrated from numerous texts. In this first chapter I treat a few illustrations in some detail; in later chapters the references are usually briefer. Throughout, my aim is not to imply Chaucer's knowledge of particular texts but to assume his awareness of the genre's shape and history, rather as we might assume a twentieth-century writer's awareness of the novel, and to choose illustrations that are reasonably familiar to twentieth-century readers or particularly apposite to the Chaucerian tales under discussion.

MASCULINITY AS A FUNCTION OF DIFFERENCE

From the perspective of gender difference, masculinity is a composite of traits that contrast to feminine ones, such as bravery in contrast to timidity, and traits that are identified as feminine but are absorbed into masculinity, such as pity. This first aspect of masculine identity is not specific to romance. Examples can be drawn from numerous genres and historical behaviors to illustrate the double definition of masculinity by opposition and by relation to femininity, but the two episodes that open the *Knight's Tale*, in which Theseus defeats the Amazons and takes pity on the women bereaved by the siege of Thebes, illustrate the process in miniature.

A salient feature of romance is its figuring of women as the desired opposites of men. In a study of *Eneas* in relation to its precedents, Stephen Nichols argues that the representation of courtship crucially distinguishes romance, marking the point at which the isolation of love lyric and the univocality of earlier narrative writing yield to a dialogue between the lover and the resisting, unknowable woman who "subjects love to interpretations other than those flattering constructions placed on it by the bemused lover in his solitary lyric reverie. . . . The voice of the beloved may be the first intimation of alterity intruding into the monologism of the lover" (49–50). Feminine difference is also the focus of Jean-Charles Huchet's account of *Eneas*: Lavine "incarne l'altérité dont le héros et le roman ont besoin, qui pour voyager, qui pour s'écrire" (incarnates the alterity needed by the hero and the romance, the former in order to journey, the latter in order to be written) (*Roman médiéval*, 218). For both critics the assertion of woman's difference from man informs the genre's poetics as well as its configurations of gender.

Romance plots often extend the strangeness of woman's sexual difference into an ethnic, religious, or political identity that opposes that of the hero. Eneas's Trojan lineage, Bevis of Hampton's Christianity, and Theseus's Athenian wisdom gain clarity in oppositional (and then accommodating) relationships to the Latin Lavine, pagan Josian, and Amazonian Hippolyta. Eneas's self-definition takes place through his adversarial yet desiring relation to the woman whose land he is seeking to colonize. The initial opposition to Eneas's desire is strongly feminine: Lavine's mother stands against her husband's wish and the gods' decree in resisting Eneas's suit, asserting that Trojans are sodomitical and treacherous.[1] Eneas refutes the maternal accusation in his heterosexual devotion to Lavine, fusing the proof of his masculinity with a demonstration of Trojan trustworthiness.

Before the specifics of plot, a recurring set of differences between men and women in romance constructs masculine identity by alienating from it the traits assigned to femininity. The tower chamber from which Lavine watches and reacts to events is the center of a feminine sphere that marks the fields and the fighting below as a masculine space. Womanly timidity, passivity, and pity confirm the masculinity of bravery, initiative, and severity. Amazons reverse the process by rejecting feminine traits for their masculine counterparts; the defeat of the Amazons dramatizes masculinity establishing its claim to difference and ascendancy over the feminine. The briefly told episode that begins the *Knight's Tale* barely recalls this significance, developed at length in Boccaccio's *Teseida* and the *romans antiques*.[2] The following chapter traces the disappearance of Amazonian prowess from romance as the Amazons regain their beauty and enter into courtship. In the *Knight's Tale* the two qualities assigned to Hippolyta, that she is "faire" and "hardy" (I 882), refer as briefly as possible to the contradictory feminine attractiveness native to her and the masculine courage she adopts; and the notation that Theseus

[1] For a discussion of the episode, which together with Eneas's and Lavine's thoughts of love constitutes the romance poet's major departure from Virgil's *Aeneid*, see the third section of the present chapter.

Translations in all chapters are mine unless otherwise noted.

[2] See chapter 2 and Boccaccio, *Teseida*: Hippolyta leads the Amazons "although a woman" and in order to do so exiles from herself all "feminine fear": "La quale, ancora che femina fosse / e di bellezze piena oltre misura, / prese la signoria, e sì rimosse / da sé ciascuna feminil paura . . ." (bk. 1, st. 9). Noting that her followers practice "uomini fatti, non femine," she attributes their rejection of Cupid to their desire to show manly courage ("per voler virile animo mostrare," bk. 1, st. 24). Courage in these formulations remains so firmly a masculine trait that its adoption does not enlarge but rather suppresses and distorts the Amazons' femininity. Timidity, beauty, and love are the traits natural to the women, who are restored to themselves by contact with Theseus and his men (bk. 1, sts. 132–33).

conquered Scythia "with his wysdom and his chivalrie" (I 865)
chooses traits specific to masculinity in the binary paradigm that
exiles irrationality and timidity to an idea of the feminine. Although brief, the *Knight's Tale*'s first episode invokes a familiar
instance of defining gender by differentiation.

The assertion of difference between man and woman is fundamental to romance not only as a means of defining the masculine
self by contrast with the feminine other but as a precondition for
expanding identity beyond the limitations difference imposes.
Conceiving genders by binary opposition has a diminishing as
well as a defining effect, restricting masculinity in the process of
clarifying it. A counterprocess recuperates for masculinity some
traits associated with women. The womanly intercessions that
inspire Theseus's pity in the *Knight's Tale* illustrate this expansive process. The widows of the siege of Thebes introduce a conventional role for women as inspirers of masculine pity or mercy,
a role more fully evoked when Theseus comes upon Palamon and
Arcite in combat, condemns them to death, but instead shows
mercy on them when the queen and all her women intercede for
the lovers. In the earlier scene, Theseus's anger turns to pity less
evidently as a man's response to the pleas of women than as a
ruler's response to injustice, or a thoughtful person's response to
the vagaries of Fortune. He inquires "What folk been ye," apparently without regard to their sex, yet they identify themselves in
gendered terms as "us wrecched wommen" and as widows of the
siege of Thebes (I 905, 921, 936). Their closing plea to "Have on us
wrecched wommen som mercy, / And lat oure sorwe synken in
thyn herte" (I 950–51) and the causal connection between Theseus's perception of "hem so pitous and so maat" and his own
"herte pitous" (I 953, 955) begin to make the association between
femininity and masculine pity that the scene in the grove works
out more fully.

Both scenes partake of a cultural topos reaching beyond romance to the biblical model of Esther and the historical inter-
ventions ascribed to Queen Philippa on behalf of the burghers of
Calais and to Queen Anne on behalf of various malefactors including Simon Burley and participants in the Rising of 1381.[3] The

---

[3] Specific historical allusions in the *Knight's Tale* to actions of Anne and Philippa have long since been proposed (see note to ll. 1742–60 in the *Riverside*

topos tempers a ruler's severity by inspiring pity in him through the pleas of women who are moved specifically by their gendered identity: the ladies weep over Palamon and Arcite "for verray wommanhede," and Theseus's response begins in "compassioun / Of wommen" rather than of the young men (I 1748, 1770–71).

One way of understanding Theseus's response in terms of gender is to posit a limitation in masculinity that contact with the feminine redresses. Jill Mann has recently analyzed pity and patience in the *Canterbury Tales*, particularly the Knight's and Franklin's tales, in these terms. Her model of the "feminised hero" takes passive qualities such as pity to be so firmly linked to womanliness that they remain gender-marked even when adopted into male behavior: "The 'compassioun' Theseus feels for women is itself a womanly quality implanted in him. It feminises him without rendering him effeminate," she argues (*Geoffrey Chaucer*, 174; see also 87–127, 165–85). An attractive implication of this analysis, Mann points out, is the escape it offers from reading genders as implicit hierarchies in which tenderer emotions are inferior because exclusively feminine. Indeed, Mann claims for Chaucer an escape from gender divisions themselves: "A feminist reading of Chaucer needs, not to perpetuate the sterile antitheses between active and passive, to stigmatise female passivity only to find that the obverse of this is approval of male activity, but rather to recuperate Chaucer's careful integration of activity and passivity into a fully human ideal that erases male/female role-divisions" (185). Mann's approach is a welcome departure from the critical simplification and consequent impasse to which she refers, but the handling of gender-marked traits in romance suggests to me that the "fully human ideal" is finally masculine. Traits marked feminine can indeed be integrated into masculine behavior, but the current does not run in reverse from masculine into feminine identity; and the complications of masculine behavior that femininity figures contribute to enlarging and universalizing rather than feminizing the masculine experience.

Chaucer). Paul Strohm's chapter "Queens as Intercessors" undertakes a wider investigation of interceding queens in relation to the *Knight's Tale* that has the advantage of providing a cultural context for intercession without requiring Chaucer's reference to a specific instance: *Hochon's Arrow*, 95–119.

When Theseus sees the Theban widows "so pitous and so maat" and leaps off his horse "with herte pitous" (I 953, 955), it does indeed appear that the pitiful position of women has generated Theseus's pity, has invited in the ruler a tender behavior that masculinity prohibits. The cultural convention of interceding queens and the longer scene of intercession for Palamon and Arcite clarify, however, that a ruler may use intercession as the occasion for showing pity while considering it nonetheless part of his own repertoire of adjudicating impulses. Indeed, the very conventionality of feminine intercession suggests a scripted role assigned to queens within the larger scene of rulers' justice. Queen Anne had not even arrived in England when Richard II began pardoning rebels in her name (*Peasants' Revolt*, 313–14, 332). Whether or not the historical Richard tended to severity and the historical Anne to mercy, a standing cultural pattern made it appropriate for rulers to attribute pardon and leniency to women's inspiration.

The intercession of Hippolyta and her ladies connects their plea for mercy to their "verray wommanhede" through their submissive gestures of kneeling and striving to kiss Theseus's feet and their attempt to divert his attention from the young men to themselves, transforming anger into pity: "Have mercy, lord, upon us wommen alle!" (I 1748, 1757) As women they express pity and they are fit occasions for pity. However, in the dynamic of the scene (as in historical instances) their gender is not mercy's ultimate repository. The interceding women come to resemble not agents of mercy but allegorical figures in a psychomachy of the ruler's decision making. Rather than expressing an exclusively feminine impulse, the scene locates pity in women as a way of describing the subordinate place it holds in the all-encompassing masculine deliberation. Theseus does not designate mercy a feminine but rather a lordly response:

> And softe unto hymself he seyde, "Fy
> Upon a lord that wol have no mercy,
> But been a leon, bothe in word and dede,
> To hem that been in repentaunce and drede,
> As wel as to a proud despitous man
> That wol mayntene that he first began.
> That lord hath litel of discrecioun,

> That in swich cas kan no divisioun
> But weyeth pride and humblesse after oon." (I 1773–81)

Theseus's version of the unmerciful man is the lion, the less than human; the lord is rightly merciful although he is first of all just. His identification of mercy with masculinity despite the kneeling women before him reinforces the narration of the tale, signaling the narrator's masculine perspective whether we identify him as the Knight or Chaucer or a less embodied voice. Before Theseus speaks, the narrator has first degendered pity in the aphorism for Theseus's change of mood, "pitee renneth soone in gentil herte," and then glossed pity as a function of reason: "althogh that his ire hir gilt accused, / Yet in his resoun he hem bothe excused" (I 1761, 1765–66). Already pity is associated not with women but with the masculine faculty of reason. The progression from anger to mercy through women's intercession indicates that the ruler's impulse to mercy is subordinate to his impulse to justice, but both are masculine—that is, "fully human" in the traditional gendering that conflates maleness and humanity as the universal experience. The women's plea dramatizes an opposition not from but within man, a facet of his lordship.[4] Identifying pity, patience, and tenderness with women, even as it defines masculinity by opposition, prepares for an idea of masculinity that itself encompasses oppositional traits in subordinate relation to severity and decisiveness.

Romances do not provide parallel depictions of women who successfully integrate masculine traits into femininity, reinforcing the gender inequivalence figured when traits identified with femininity are absorbed into masculine complexity. Women can imitate masculine behavior, but the imitation remains just that; ruling and fighting do not become feminine behaviors when they are practiced by women. For example, the Theban women who inspire Theseus's pity at the beginning of the *Knight's Tale* join his attack on Creon in the *Roman de Thèbes*:

[4] Strohm, treating historical instances of intercession, makes the valuable point that "female intercession is gratifying to men and answers the dictates of male desire, but it remains less than completely subsumed so long as it continues actively to specify the coordinates of actual female behavior in the world" (*Hochon's Arrow*, 105).

> Li dus assaut mout vassaument
> La cité o tote sa gent;
> Il meïsmes o un mouton
> Les murs quassot tot environ:
> Donc veïssez femnes ramper,
> O mauz d'acier les murs fausser;
> Le mortier gratent trop fortment,
> Pertus i firent plus de cent;
> Ne lor chaleit quis oceïst,
> Ne qui onques mal lor feïst:
> Mout se combateient fortment.
> Grant pitié en aveient gent:
> Por les femnes fortment ploroent,
> De l'assaillir mout se penoent.[5]

[The duke boldly attacked the city with all his men; he himself broke the walls all around with a battering ram. Then you could have seen the women climbing and cracking the walls with steel hammers; they scratched at the mortar ferociously and made more than a hundred holes in it. They didn't care about being killed or injured but fought very stoutly. The men took great pity of it; they wept much on account of the women and threw themselves into the assault.]

The women play a significant role not militarily, their tapping and scratching only a faint echo of Theseus's battering ram, but by inspiring pity among the men who then undertake the significant work of the assault. That "gent," people, designates the men who weep for "les femnes" contributes to universalizing the masculine experience and subordinating the feminine to it. Even the women's fearlessness derives from their devotion to their dead husbands and lovers. It is a shadow of lost masculine courage rather than a new feminine trait, a distant echo as is the tapping of their hammers to Theseus's battering ram.

In women rulers and warriors as well, leadership and chivalry

---

[5] *Thèbes*, ed. Constans, 10073–86 (edition based on MS Brit. Lib. Add. 34114). Compare Bib. Nat. f. fr. 784, *Thèbes*, ed. Raynaud de Lage, ll. 10443–63, for which a similar argument could be made. Wise, 127–37, argues for Chaucer's use of *Thèbes* in the *Knight's Tale*'s account of the end of the siege of Thebes. See also Nolan.

remain masculine and coexist uneasily with these characters'
identity as women. The Dido of *Eneas* loses her ability to rule
when she begins to love Eneas:

> Molt soloit bien terre tenir
> et bien soloit guerre baillir,
> or a tot mis an nonchaloir
> et an obli par non savoir.
> Amors li a fait oblïer
> terre a tenir et a garder. . . .
> Cele qui maintenoit l'onor
> a tot guerpi por soe amor.   (1409–14, 1431–32)

[She had known well how to govern the land and make war but now
she let everything slide and be forgotten in her heedlessness. Love
has made her forget to govern and keep her land. . . . She who had
maintained her land has given up everything for love.]

In failing to integrate love with rule Dido fulfills her sister Anna's
aphorism that "Ne puet estre longue par fenne / bien maintenu
enor ne regne" (a land or realm cannot be governed well for long
by a woman) (1349–50). Dido's surrender to love contrasts with
Eneas's success at simultaneously conquering Italy and courting
Lavine, gendering the integration of love and rule as a masculine
capacity by contrast with Dido's womanly failure to do so. The
warrior Camille resembles Dido in that she successfully pursues
chivalry by isolating herself from men; she responds to the sexual
taunting of an adversary, "mialz sai abatre un chevalier / que
acoler ne dosnoier; / ne me sai pas combatre anverse" (I know
better how to defeat a knight than to kiss or make love; I do not
know how to do battle on my back) (7123–25). Chivalry and rule
remain masculine behaviors that divide the women who practice
them from their gendered identity as lovers of men.

   For Dido's and Camille's isolation from men when they rule
and fight signals not only the masculine gendering of those practices but also the feminine gendering of love. One of the major
expansions masculinity achieves in romance transforms the feminine suffering and submission of love into a formative masculine
experience. Waiting, longing, and victimization in love may
sound oddly feminine in an early romance hero such as Eneas,

whose lament directly echoes Lavine's and recalls the women's
laments in Ovid's *Heroides*.[6] In later plots, particularly in the line
of influence through the *Romance of the Rose* to Chaucer, love-
suffering becomes more characteristically masculine than feminine. Later chapters examine the play of genders around love in
romances. Here my focus is on the wider cultural process by
which traits relegated to femininity in binary gender distinctions
can be reabsorbed into masculine identity.

Theseus's defeat of the Amazons and marriage to Hippolyta locate the feminine outside the realm of chivalry and rule, thereby
associating that realm with the masculine. The tale's second episode, in which weeping women beg for his pity, makes a subordinate place in masculine behavior for softer emotions that have
been relegated to womanhood. These narrative realities—that
masculinity is expanded rather than feminized by the practice of
pity and that masculine behaviors do not become feminine when
practiced by women—contribute to centering romance on the
masculine subject, and to identifying masculine experience with
human experience in general.

HERO OR SUBJECT?

That romance treats masculine experience as if it were universal
does not free masculinity from constraints and contradictions. Although the genre's heroes strive to establish an identity distinct
from all others, their identity is not only contingent on public
recognition but deeply implicated in that of the community. Critical studies have investigated how the heroes of romance must
negotiate tensions between private desires on the one hand and

[6] According to Yunck, Lavine's sufferings suit the Ovidian treatment "since
Ovid was largely concerned with feminine love psychology," but the similar treatment does not suit Eneas: "most modern readers will find this Eneas, groaning,
self-pitying, and bed-ridden in the throes of his love agony, something of a grotesque" (*Eneas: A Twelfth-Century French Romance*, 36–37). The groaning and
self-pity that seem right in a feminine voice seem "grotesque" in a masculine one
precisely because they are gendered feminine in the sources and are just under-
going absorption into masculinity. The explanation cited by Yunck from Adler,
that Eneas's middle age and experience are what render his love-suffering grotesque, evades the significance of the *Eneas* poet's crossgendering of Ovid's "feminine love psychology."

social constraints on the other (e.g., Hanning, *Individual*; Ferrante, *Conflict*; Bloch, *Etymologies*). My emphasis is slightly different. Despite the dramatized tension, romances depict chivalric society actively producing its members such that the self is significantly an aspect of the community. As important to romances' version of masculine identity as the tension between self and society is the process of internalization by which men incorporate the constraints of community into their own identities.

No feature of romances is more evident than their focus on a hero, a central character with whose destiny the plot is concerned. Heroes of romance may need assistance in youth and correction in maturity, but their achievements invite admiration even when narrators take a certain ironic distance from them (see D. H. Green; Haidu; Jauss, "Negativität"). In contemporary descriptions romance is definitively "of" the hero, concerning him and pertaining to him: "Off Hauelok, Horne, and of Wade; / In Romaunces that of hem ben made," as the *Laud Troy Book* puts it, or as in *Richard Coer de Lyon*,

> Ffele romaunses men maken newe,
> Off goode knyȝtes, stronge and trewe;
> Off here dedys men rede romaunce,
> Boþe in Engeland and in Ffraunce. . . .
> (see *Sources and Analogues*, 556–59)

The *Tale of Sir Thopas* similarly designates the genre by naming its heroes, and imitates the conventional strategy of claiming superiority to previous works by comparing one hero to another:

> Men speken of romances of prys,
> Of Horn child and of Ypotys,
>   Of Beves and sir Gy,
> Of sir Lybeux and Pleyndamour—
> But sir Thopas, he bereth the flour
>   Of roial chivalry.   (VII 897–902)

Yet to be the flower of chivalry and the focus of plot does not fully describe the hero of romance. The contingency of heroic merit on a range of social relations qualifies the impression of autonomy conferred by the dominant place assigned to titular characters in generic descriptions. The solitary adventures on which "Lybeux" (the Handsome) departs to establish his identity do so because he sends all his defeated adversaries back to Arthur, who gave him his temporary name, and submits his bride to Arthur's approval. Lybeaus's identity consists in the recognition he wins from the court, from Arthur as much as from his lost father Gawain. The relation of heroic figures to their lords, followers, and lovers varies so widely in romance that it evades formulation as a generic motif, yet that relation is integral to the notion of the romance hero.

At one extreme of the genre's possibilities, the hero's will subsumes the community's need, so that his self-interested actions guarantee his society's well-being. Many Anglo-Norman and Middle English romances such as the Bevis and Horn stories cited in *Sir Thopas* follow this model. In striving to regain their patrimonies, Bevis and Horn defeat pagan armies and oppose tyrannical kings to the benefit of all their countrymen. Alternatively, in *Guy of Warwick*, the Tristan and Lancelot romances, and many romances about young love, the hero's will tends to be at odds with the public order, creating crises of identity that are difficult or impossible to resolve. Guy's beloved Felice demands that he leave court until he has become the best knight in the world, but his parents and his lord oppose Felice's command on the ground that he owes them superior allegiance. Guy himself, once married, repents of his adventures for love and undertakes compensatory feats for good causes in defense of Christian, feudal, and national rights. Although Guy's efforts like Horn's build his reputation, his efforts and his reputation are deeply involved in familial and institutional relations.

Indeed, the term *hero*, with its implications of isolating uniqueness and autonomy, is not fully appropriate to these characters' strongly interdependent identities.[7] The adventuring knight constructs a distinct identity through his choices and actions, but his

[7] Noting not only the naïveté and need for assistance that make romance heroes' progress educative but also the genre's focus on "events which are closer to states of being than to acts," Jameson argues that "the very category of the 'hero' as such belongs more properly to a dramatic literature, and that we therefore need to mark the contemplative nature of romance as narrative by the choice of some other term for the human figuration of which its pattern is in part woven": "Magical Narratives," 139; corresponding to *Political Unconscious*, 112–13.

trajectory toward distinction must be made known to others because identity is finally in the gift of the community.

The Canterbury tales that draw heavily on romance show a particular interest in the relation between identity and community. *Sir Thopas* takes the dominance of titular heroes so literally that the problem of interrelations vanishes, and with it the meaning of heroic gestures. Thopas has a father, but filial duty, patrimony, and family honor receive no challenge; Thopas is in love, but his devotion to an elf-queen is neither in conflict with his dynastic and feudal obligations nor an occasion for self-transformation. Middle English romance is not an imposing referent for *Sir Thopas*, but its exemplars do make sense of their heroes' actions by relating them to demands of family, nation, and secular self-redemption. The *Tale of Sir Thopas* parodies romance in part by isolating the central character, stranding him on an empty stage where his rushing about looks absurdly autonomous.

Other tales decenter the position of hero by doubling characters in that position. Palamon and Arcite occupy together a primary role that could also be claimed by Theseus; the *Squire's Tale* promises to have two equivalent protagonists, at least, in Algarsyf and Cambalo; and Aurelius tries to double the absent Arveragus in the *Franklin's Tale*. So persistent is Chaucer's doubling that an explanation for it on the level of genre should be sought.[8] It could be seen as an intensification or a revision of the tendency to provide titular characters with close companions. A few romances such as *Amis and Amiloun* have two protagonists, and many feature close friends such as Guy's Terri and Horn's Athulf; often friendship gets involved in courtship with interesting implications for gender that I discuss in the last section of this chapter.[9] Friendship is an important issue for the *Knight's Tale*, but more

---

[8] Mann's chapter "The Feminised Hero" (*Geoffrey Chaucer*, 165–85) argues that the lack of a single hero in various tales is a way of emphasizing a model of sufferance and patience over a model of the active and aggressive hero. I agree that doubling characters in the position of hero questions the possibility of autonomous action, but I argue that rather than feminizing men, the doubling examines (as the romance genre examines) certain constraints on masculine identity in relation to community.

[9] Leicester, 221–42, understands the *Knight's Tale*'s plot shift from Theseus to Palamon and Arcite as an instance of shifting from an epic to a romantic vision, from the attack on Creon in which "the image of the hero tends to overpower the

generally Chaucer's dispersal of the romance hero's role into two or more protagonists encourages us to consider their relatedness as an aspect of their identity.

The *Franklin's Tale* explores interrelation as a characteristic of identity by nudging its apparent hero Arveragus to the edge of the action, doubling him in the suitor Aurelius, and revealing each man's identity to be contingent on public norms and perceptions. Aurelius first distinguishes himself in conventional courtliness as he "syngeth, daunceth passynge any man / That is, or was, sith that the world bigan" (V 929–30). His behavior is so paradigmatic that Dorigen does not interpret his "general compleynyng" (V 945) as expressing a particular desire for her. The array of formal expressions he has chosen—"layes, / Songes, compleintes, roundels, virelayes" (V 947–48)—finally yields to his more pointed declaration:

> I wolde that day that youre Arveragus
> Wente over the see, that I, Aurelius,
> Hadde went ther nevere I sholde have come agayn.
> For wel I woot my servyce is in vayn. . . .   (V 969–72)

Even in his expression of personal desire, the lover aligns himself with the husband to express his longing. The effect is inextricably comparative and competitive; identity turns as much on similarity as on distinction.

Honor, the most important of masculine virtues in romance, is likewise both personal and public (Brewer, "Honour"; Blamires). The account of Arveragus's return from seeking worship in arms makes his achievement a function of its recognition: "Arveragus, with heele and greet honour, / As he that was of chivalrie the flour, / Is comen hoom, and othere worthy men" (V 1087–89). The subtly effective construction "as he that was," in contrast to "who was," communicates the achievement in terms of similarity. Arveragus is the flower of chivalry above all others, but still in comparison to some ideal or set of similars. The "othere worthy men" accompanying him are both his fellows in arms and the ground of contrast for his achievement. Like Aurelius in his love for Dorigen, Arveragus must define himself by excelling at recog-

---

larger forces in whose name he putatively acts" (227) to the complications of relatedness in friendship and love.

nized behaviors, in relation to other men who similarly define themselves.

Indeed, to say that romance heroes signify through their confrontations with the world may still be to imagine heroes too autonomously and their confrontations too unilaterally. Aurelius does confront forces external to him, but he is also generated by them. His excellence at singing and dancing, like Arveragus's worship in arms, instantiates not only the paradigms of chivalric culture as it is represented in romance, but that culture's claim to produce individuals who are meritorious precisely in their paradigmatic behavior. Lee Patterson's illuminating discussion of subjectivity in the *Knight's Tale* begins from the premise that "chivalry entailed a form of selfhood insistently, even exclusively, public. It stressed a collective or corporate self-definition and so ignored the merely personal or individual." For Patterson the Knight's formulaic *General Prologue* portrait reflects a chivalric validation of public over individual identity, and it is the Knight's entry into tale-telling that releases him "into the problematic of self-definition that motivates the *Canterbury Tales*" (*Chaucer*, 168–69). This problematic motivates romances as well, although differently from the *Canterbury Tales* as a whole. The very range of subjectivities the pilgrims come to represent, as well as the transgressiveness of a Pardoner or a Wife of Bath, contrast with romance's relatively positive vision of identity's contingency on shared chivalric principles. Romances specify that the collectivity does not simply recognize but generates masculine identity and that the social constitution of individuals is a positive cultural pattern, one that sustains community by bringing men into its law and ultimately by reproducing its law within masculine consciousness.

Thus the modern resonances of the term *individual* and of the critical dyad *individual/society* can be misleading in discussions of romance. The postmedieval conception of the individual, as developed in relation to the Enlightenment and the rise of the novel, is that persons are self-determining agents who exist independently of their competitive environment.[10] As a counterbalance

[10] The classic study on the relation between the novel and Enlightenment ideas of the individual is Watt; McKeon reassesses Watt and emphasizes the persistence of romance in the novel.

to that atomistic Lockean version of the "individual," it is helpful to measure identity in romance against the postmodern version of the "subject." Both "individual" and "subject" are concepts developed in and for postmedieval periods, but identity as romance imagines it may have more in common with the postmodern than the Lockean model.

Theories of the subject are diverse in many respects but concur in rejecting the idea that the individual is a self-determining being whose essential identity persists beneath its reformation by culture and ideology. In contrast, postmodernists urge that the human subject is the site of many intersecting social discourses and practices that have in the subject a constitutive rather than a reforming or educative power. Subjects are constructed by their cultures rather than confronted with them. Michel Foucault's work, because its orientation is historical and its focus is on how societies regulate their subjects, invites comparison to romance's version of the relation between self and community. Foucault's subject is pervasively formed and controlled by a universe of forces but most crucially by the modern state. For Foucault the objectifications that produce the subject are modern phenomena from which the medieval period is in contrast relatively free; the forces at work on the subject are so powerful, and in Foucault's rhetoric so sinister, that the subject's tendency to internalize control in self-regulation is but the final instance of the compelling power exerted upon it.[11]

Medieval romance, importantly informed by chivalric ideology, pictures a less coercive process in which the subject both instantiates the collectivity and responds to it by shaping the requirements of collective identity. Postmodern theory, at least in its earlier stages, sees the subject so completely a product of large social forces that meaningful resistance and indeed agency of any kind become virtually unimaginable.[12] Still, the postmodern con-

[11] Foucault, *Discipline and Punish*, *History of Sexuality*, and "The Subject and Power"; on other postmodern theories of the subject see Smith.

[12] Recent theorists have worked to enlarge the subject's agency while preserving the framing perception that social discourses and practices produce their subjects. Alcoff argues that postmodern insights can be taken to define "positionality," the subject's "external situation" rather than "internal characteristics," so that the subject can take action either within or against that situation (433). Agency is also

ception that social practices generate the consciousness of historical subjects answers well to depictions of men in romance, and it
is a valuable counterbalance to the conception of the essential,
transhistorical individual who exists in confrontation with the
world. As an example, one aspect of Foucault's ideas about self-
regulation clarifies the place of judicial procedures in romance. In
several works but predominantly in *Discipline and Punish*, Foucault argues that institutional regulation can induce in the subject a self-regulation that perpetuates institutional power from
within. The seventeenth century saw the origins of a "disciplinary society" which sought to exercise a thorough and detailed
control that contrasted to the intermittent discipline of earlier
societies; one instrument of the pervasive control exerted by the
new disciplinary society was a "panoptical" surveillance of its
prisoner/soldier/student subjects so implacable and minute as
to finally induce self-surveillance in them (195–228). Although
many specifics distinguish Foucault's modern cases from any
medieval ones, the place of judicial procedures in romance offers
a parallel to Foucault's observation that self-surveillance follows
from institutional regulation.

   In Chaucer's use of romance, judicial encounters follow a trajectory from subjecting men to institutional judgment toward
producing in them an internalized standard of self-judgment. The
trajectory is of long standing in the genre; from the twelfth century onward romances frequently feature judicial trials, duels, and
ordeals and extend the adversarial and deliberative character of
judicial procedure into the wider plot of courtship and chivalric
adventure. Specific judicial encounters may set protagonists in
opposition to malicious accusers, political and amorous rivals,
and even their own feudal lords, but by placing these encounters
in the wider scene of events, romances transfer deliberation from
the judicial to the personal in knights' self-testing on adventure
and in lovers' interrogating monologues. For Bloch the inquest,
with its verbal depositions and counterarguments, is an "implicit
legal model underlying romance" (*Medieval French*, 199; see 189–
214); in Haidu's terms "the essential conflict is not between the

---

a major concern for Smith (on Foucault see esp. 168n) and for the contributors to
Feminism and Foucault.

individual and the world, but in what the individual himself desires" (106). I concur in rejecting the dichotomy between individual and world and further reject the concept of the autonomous
individual. Identity in romance partakes of the collectivity and
resistance to social forces gives way to self-regulation not as a
concession to power through which power reproduces itself but as
an enlightened recognition of the interdependence of subject and
society. The *Knight's Tale* illustrates the earlier stages of the process and the *Franklin's Tale* its further development.

Theseus interrupts the two lovers fighting in the grove "withouten juge or oother officere" (I 1712) in his capacity as the ruler
under whose eye all disputes should be adjudicated. Theseus
echoes Arcite's phrase in transforming the private duel over Emelye into a public tournament that will "darreyne hire by bataille"
(I 1609, 1853). The *Squire's Tale* obscurely forecasts a similar adjudication for "Cambalo, / That faught in lystes with the bretheren two / For Canacee er that he myghte hire wynne" (V 667–
69). The spectacle with which Theseus replaces the duel brings
Palamon and Arcite under the control of Theseus and the collective gaze of the chivalric community, whose judgmental relation
to the spectacle reinforces and prepares for Theseus's final judgment. The seating in the lists is so arranged "That whan a man
was set on o degree, / He letted nat his felawe for to see" (I 1891–
92); before the fighting, groups of people attempt to predict who
will fight well based on their arms and physiques (I 2513–20,
2590–93); as the fighting begins, "Ther seen men who kan juste
and who kan ryde" (I 2604). The contestants' visibility makes
them available to judgment.

Theseus's round lists might be considered a precursor of Jeremy
Bentham's Panopticon, the circular prison observed from a central
point which for Foucault epitomizes the modern state's method
of controlling groups in architectural spaces that provide for unidirectional surveillance. The lists are panoptical in bringing the
lovers' willful resistance to Theseus's law under institutional visibility and regulation.[13] The obscured actions of the gods provide

[13] The lists are, however, a structure for one occasion and Theseus's role is not
transferable, in contrast to Foucault's panoptical surveillance, which is perpetual
and can be carried out by any (or no) functionary since the observer is hidden from
the observed.

an analogue to the unidirectional surveillance that characterizes the modern Panopticon. But the lists do not objectify and isolate their subjects to the same extent. Observers interact productively with combatants in the gift of Emelye, in the look she and Arcite exchange at his victory, and in the adulation of the crowd for all the participants. Further, the purpose of containment in the lists is not to control the rivalry between Palamon and Arcite by isolating it, but to incorporate the rivalry they have considered private into the chivalric community in the broadest terms:

> For every wight that lovede chivalrye
> And wolde, his thankes, han a passant name,
> Hath preyed that he myghte been of that game;
> And wel was hym that therto chosen was,
> For if ther fille tomorwe swich a cas,
> Ye knowen wel that every lusty knyght
> That loveth paramours and hath his myght,
> Were it in Engelond or elleswhere,
> They wolde, hir thankes, wilnen to be there—
> To fighte for a lady, benedicitee!
> It were a lusty sighte for to see.   (I 2106–16)

The hundred knights each man brings to the tournament are not merely supporters of the lovers' separate claims but men themselves moved by chivalry and love, and men typical of others "in Engelond or elleswhere." The particularity of desire that Palamon and Arcite claimed each for himself dissolves into the common experience of their estate. The episode pictures subjects constituted similarly by chivalric culture, subjects whose similarities arise from willed subscription to that culture's values. Although the subject of postmodern theories is shaped more passively, even unilaterally, by the modern world, the conception that identity arises from social context illuminates the judicial combat better than the conception that autonomous individuals struggle against society. Palamon and Arcite's submission to judicial combat expresses the communal component in their own identities that makes the tournament an appropriate way to work out their fate.

The final effect of panoptical surveillance according to Foucault is that those subjected to it reproduce it within themselves. The panoptical experience is so irresistible that it becomes internalized in self-reform. For Foucault, earlier centuries in which control operated intermittently and repressively did not know this circularity by which control extends itself, recruiting its very objects into its processes. But romances do dramatize an analogous internalization of legal constraint, and declare it to be a positive and enabling process, as a few examples of characters' articulated relations to judicial procedure may show.

Palamon and Arcite's eager submission to judicial combat implies a perceived consonance between its adjudication and their own desires. The *Wife of Bath's Tale* acts out a fuller internalization by which the imposition of public judgment moves the subject toward self-reform. The knight condemned for rape in Arthur's court wins pardon from the court of ladies and the queen "sittynge as a justise" (III 1028) through his (merely rote) acknowledgment that women desire sovereignty—an acknowledgment that would (if internalized) render rape impossible. The question posed to him by his old wife repeats the judicial situation in requiring an answer of the knight that again recognizes women's desire for sovereignty. Here the rule of the court fades into self-rule, first in the wife's mocking metaphor for the knight's behavior to her:

> . . . O deere housbonde, benedicitee!
> Fareth every knyght thus with his wyf as ye?
> Is this the lawe of kyng Arthures hous?
> Is every knyght of his so dangerous?   (III 1087–90)

Linking the normative behavior of "every knyght" to the "lawe of kyng Arthures hous" recalls the court's condemnation of the knight's aberrant behavior, in part by positing for Arthur's knights an internalized code of constraint at the opposite extreme from rape. The imagined knights' "lawe," however comic, forecasts the wife's arguments for living by internalized standards. In her curtain lecture birth is unimportant without "gentil dedes" and "vertuous lyvyng"; wealth obscures merit but poverty can instruct a man "his God and eek hymself to knowe" (III 1115, 1122, 1202). The old wife urges the knight to conduct himself (and to judge her) according to principles shared by the truly gentle— the plural "we," "us," and "oure" that speak through the wife—in a move parallel to incorporating Palamon and Arcite's "fighte for a lady" into the paradigm of chivalric culture at large. The Wife of Bath's knight chooses to make himself doubly subject to his culture in answering his wife's question "as yow liketh, it suffiseth me" (III 1235). Only by accepting that the knight has listened to his wife and been changed by her words can we explain the difference between "My love? . . . nay, my dampnacioun!" and "My lady and my love, and wyf so deere, / I put me in youre wise governance" (III 1067, 1230–31). Unless he is "glosing" her like Jankyn, which is unlikely in view of his thoughtful sigh (III 1228), the old wife has talked him into loving and respecting her. In conceding sovereignty to his wife he accepts her culturally authoritative arguments concerning the regulated behavior of true gentility; more specifically he surrenders the fiction of autonomy that alone could have justified his crime.

The *Franklin's Tale* completes the internalization of judicial procedure by submitting characters who are concerned with governing themselves to the judgment of the audience. Arveragus and Dorigen make private vows that parallel those of their marriage, occasioning the narrator's long comment on self-governance ("After the tyme most be temperaunce / To every wight that kan on governaunce" [V 785–86]). Legal terminology infiltrates the characters' language concerning their personal pledges:

> I yow relesse, madame, into youre hond
> Quyt every serement and every bond
> That ye han maad to me as heerbiforn,
> Sith thilke tyme which that ye were born.   (V 1533–36)
>
> . . . I wole of hym assaye,
> At certeyn dayes, yeer by yeer, to paye. . . .   (V 1567–68)
>
> . . . wolde ye vouche sauf, upon seuretee,
> Two yeer or thre for to respiten me. . . .   (V 1581–82)
>
> Have I nat holden covenant unto thee?   (V 1587)
>
> Sire, I relesse thee thy thousand pound. . . .   (V 1613)

Speaking in legal terms of bond and covenant, release and acquittal, surety and oath incorporates a public standard of reliability into personal behavior, particularly in combination with the characters' tendency to generalize themselves in statements such as

Trouthe is the hyeste thyng that man may kepe.   (V 1479)

Thus kan a squier doon a gentil dede
As wel as kan a knyght, withouten drede.   (V 1543–44)

Thou art a squier, and he is a knyght;
But God forbede, for his blisful myght,
But if a clerk koude doon a gentil dede
As wel as any of yow, it is no drede!   (V 1609–12)

Each man speaks at decisive moments in terms of social groups to
which his particular actions should measure up.[14] Self-regulation
leads to behavior the characters agree is gentle and generous; the
closing invitation to the audience to judge "whiche was the
mooste fre" (III 1622) perpetuates the idea of shared standards of
behavior that can underlie judgments in courts as in courts of law.
To be gentle is to "kan on governance," to regulate one's behavior
more subtly and thoroughly than feudal law itself.

Scenes of judgment and self-judgment provide one of many indications that, however independently capable a romance hero may
appear, his identity derives from the chivalric community and
constantly refers him to the community's standards. Another illustration could be developed from the discourse of love, aptly
termed a "class dialect" in Larry Benson's wide-ranging historical and literary studies ("Courtly Love," 243; *Malory's "Morte
Darthur"*). When Arcite declares that "Love is a gretter lawe, by
my pan, / Than may be yeve to any erthely man" (I 1165–66), he
intends the metaphor to license his freedom to love as he chooses.
But love also has the force of "lawe" in that it brings all lovers
under the sway of elaborated poetic conventions that figure their
experience and shape their behavior. All lovers are said to feel
particular, symptomatic pains and pleasures; love (figured as a
feudal lord and a god) constrains his subjects even as he creates
them: "he kan maken, at his owene gyse, / Of everich herte as that
hym list divyse" (I 1789–90). The intimate experiences of the
heart are shared social experiences that constrain as well as enlarge masculine identity.

[14] Knapp, 126–28, discusses in similar terms how law is internalized in the *Wife
of Bath's Tale*.

   The third section of this chapter treats one such constraint, placed on masculinity at the very origin of courtship when male friendship may seem to challenge heterosexuality's claim to ascendancy.

"FOR LOVE AND
FOR ENCREES OF CHIVALRYE"

The scene in which Lavine reveals to her mother that she loves Eneas, with its full-blown physical symptoms of love and its breathless stammering of Eneas's name syllable by syllable, has long been recognized as paradigmatic for romancers who follow (e.g., Dressler; Fourrier, 334–35; *Ipomedon*, ed. Holden, 55–56).[15] A less discussed aspect of that scene, the mother's response that Eneas is a sodomite, also resonates through ensuing romances in their tendency to mark courtship's origin on the site of relations among men, whether erotic or social. Here I will trace three ways in which courtship superimposes itself on male relations. The accusation that Eneas "priseroit mialz un garçon / que toi ne altre acoler" (would prefer to embrace a boy rather than you or any woman) (8572–73), the alignment of love and chivalry as parallel paths to self-realization, and the challenge love poses to chivalric companionship make an issue of the ways in which two orientations, toward heterosexual courtship on the one hand and masculine relations on the other, occupy overlapping terrain in men's allegiances. Here critics have noted the element of conflict, but I would like to explore instead the analogies that connect rather than simply opposing the demands of courtship and male friendship.[16] So viewed, courtship appears a secondary formation, a palimpsest text that overwrites masculine relations without fully obscuring them. Supplementing and deriving from them, courtship reveals ambivalently combative and desiring bonds among men as well as between men and women.

[15] A short version of the following discussion was published as "Brotherhood and the Construction of Courtship."

[16] Scaglione exemplifies most recently the perception of conflict in romances between chivalric and sexual relations: "the ideal noble knight must be a great fighter to be a worthy lover, but can hardly be both at the same time. . . . We must fight to qualify for love, yet we cannot love while we fight" (11–12).

Lavine's mother's reaction against her daughter's declaration of love associates sodomy with treachery:

> Que as tu dit, fole desvee?
> Sez tu vers cui tu t'es donee?
> Cil cuiverz est de tel nature
> qu'il n'a gaires de femmes cure. . . .
> o feme ne set il joër,
> ne parlerast pas a guichet;
> molt aime fraise de vallet;
> an ce sont Troïen norri.
> Molt par as foiblemant choisi.
> N'as tu oï comfaitemant
> il mena Dido malemant?
> Unques feme n'ot bien de lui,
> n'en avras tu, si com ge cui,
> d'un traïtor, d'un sodomite.   (8565–68, 8574–83)

[What have you said, insane fool? Do you know to whom you've given yourself? This wretch is of the sort who hardly care for women. . . . He doesn't know how to play with a woman, nor would he speak at that little barred gate, but he likes very much the meat of a young man. The Trojans are raised on this. You've chosen very poorly. Haven't you heard how badly he treated Dido? Never has a woman had any good from him, nor will you as I believe, from a traitor and a sodomite.]

Political enmity between the Latin queen and the invading Trojans can explain the queen's hostility to Eneas and, more specifically, her condemnation of his earlier treacheries such as abandoning Dido. Ethnic hostility could further motivate the charge, as the queen's assertion that Trojans are raised in sodomy illustrates, but that hostility does not account so well for Lavine's expression of the same fears later in the courtship or for the charges of homoerotic orientation that reappear in other works such as *Lanval*, *Gylle de Chyn*, and *Perceval* when men turn down the advances of demanding women.[17]

---

[17] Marie de France, *Lanval*, ll. 277–92; Gautier de Tournay, *Gille de Chyn*, ll. 3535–62; Gerbert de Montreuil, *Continuation de Perceval* 1.1554–1601; see also Heldris de Cornuälle, *Silence*, ll. 3935–49.

In all these cases the charge of sodomy arises when heterosexuality is striving to establish a claim on men. The discourse of courtship between men and women that develops in later medieval lyric and romance does not have an exact homoerotic counterpart. Medievalists (albeit with less categorical assurance than modernists) presently concur that "homosexual" identity is a modern development and that in medieval periods homoerotic behavior was understood as a habit or perversion that did not challenge the binary gender distinction.[18] In contrast, male-female eroticism was becoming, in medieval literature and culture generally, a richly elaborated focus of identity. The contrast helps explain why Lavine's mother does not accuse Eneas simply of misogyny with regard to Dido, but instead with a passion for boys that the affair with Dido might seem to refute. Even an inveterate sodomite is to be imagined as a deviant heterosexual.[19] Masculine intimacy is seen as a threat to courtship, and not simply as its exclusive opposite. Lavine's mother warns that male-male eroticism will dominate and determine male-female eroticism:

> s'il lo pooit par toi atraire,
> nel troveroit ja si estrange
> qu'il ne feïst asez tel change,
> que il feïst son bon de toi
> por ce qu'il lo sofrist de soi;
> bien lo lairoit sor toi monter,
> s'il repueit sor lui troter. . . . (8588–94)

[If he could attract (a boy) by means of you, he wouldn't find it strange to make a trade such that the other one could do as he liked

[18] Cormier and Kuster, responding to John Boswell's argument for homosexual subcultures in *Christianity, Social Tolerance*; see also the essays by Boswell, David M. Halperin, and Robert Padgug in *Hidden from History*. Greenberg titles his chapters on ancient and medieval periods "Before Homosexuality." Brundage also questions a number of Boswell's arguments on the status of homoerotic behavior in the Middle Ages.

[19] Although the term *heterosexual* could be said to have no meaning before the term *homosexual*, I use the former in order to acknowledge the identity-generating complex of meanings that surround male-female courtship in the late Middle Ages, and I eschew the latter in favor of more limited descriptive terms such as *homoerotic* and *homosocial* for sexual and social relations among men in the Middle Ages.

with you because he permitted it himself; he would gladly let the
other mount you if he could in turn mount him.]

This scenario departs from the clerical argument that informs
some of the queen's remarks, the argument that contrasts unpro-
ductive sodomy to fruitful heterosexuality (on that argument see
Cormier, 216–28; Boswell, 137–66; Bullough). Here sodomy subsumes heterosexuality into its own economy rather than exclud-
ing it. Lavine's sexuality will be merely the instrument of the primary relation between men.

Although attributed to the exotic Trojans, the relations in the
queen's scenario provide an unsympathetic version of the contemporary historical pattern of passage from the condition of chivalric "youth" to courtship and marriage. *Eneas* can be read as a
literary transformation of the historical situation of *juvenes*,
younger sons who were excluded from inheritance and who made
their fortunes in bands of fellow knights, marrying late if they
were sufficiently bold and fortunate to win an heiress. Jean-
Charles Huchet has analyzed Eneas's career in terms of Georges
Duby's research on the *juvenes* of twelfth-century France (Huchet, *Roman médiéval*, 27–38; Duby, "Jeunes"). Huchet, however, does not note Duby's later implications that erotic relations
of some kind united these bands of youths, such that courtship
"may have masked the essential—or rather, projected into the
realm of sport the inverted image of the essential: amorous ex-
changes between warriors" (*William Marshal*, 47). Across many
cultures, homoerotic behavior is not unusual in groups of young
men, if only as a stage preceding heterosexual adulthood. Gervase
of Canterbury, Henry of Huntingdon, Guillaume de Nangis, and
John of Salisbury note sodomy among other noble depravities in
contemporary courts; Orderic Vitalis typifies the chroniclers'
views in considering sodomy a male weakness among many,
rather than a defining sexual orientation: he regrets that in the
time of William Rufus young men, in contrast to their forebears,
"shamelessly gave themselves up to the filth of sodomy. . . . Our
wanton youth is sunk in effeminacy, and courtiers, fawning, seek
the favours of women with every kind of lewdness" (4:188–89; see
also Goodich, 4–6; Cormier and Kuster, 593–94; *History of Private Life*, 591–92; Jacquart and Thomasset, 88–89, 105–7). For Or-

deric and other chroniclers sodomy corrupts sexuality and blurs sexual orientation, but for romances the accusation of sodomy has a clarifying function, that of validating heterosexuality by claiming its only alternative is disgraceful.[20]

The medieval discourse of chivalric relations avoids the overtly sexual in its terms of allegiance, loyalty, and brotherhood, just as the text of *Eneas* does not sustain feminine suspicions in the relations among warriors depicted beyond the women's monologues. Yet the work's suppressed invocation of erotic bonds among knights recalls the possibility of such bonds in contemporary knighthood. In broader terms of gendered allegiance, the competition between opposite- and same-sex orientations that the women's monologues imagine throws particular emphasis on Eneas's later hesitancy to communicate with Lavine when he is with his men:

> Tot a veü quant que manda,
> molt s'en fist liez, bien lo cela:
> ne volt que sa gent lo saüst
> ne que nus d'aus l'apercüst. . . .
> Il l'esgardot molt dolcement,
> s'il ne s'atarjast por la gent;
> ne regardot pas de droit oil.   (8871–74, 8887–89)

[He saw everything she had sent him (in her letter) and was very glad of it, but he hid it well: he didn't wish his men to know it or for any of them to notice the letter. . . . He looked at her very sweetly but didn't linger on account of his men; he didn't look at her directly.]

Even when his men notice Lavine's interest in Eneas and point her out on the battlements with jocular warnings, Eneas avoids interaction with Lavine:

> Un po s'an sozrist Eneas,
> qui antandi tres bien lor gas,
> et nequedant si s'an gardot
> que voiant aus l'oil n'i tornot,

[20] For discussions of the *Eneas* plot as a whole in terms of erotic and social allegiances see Gaunt, Burgwinkle. Gaunt, 20–21, usefully invokes Rubin's "obligatory heterosexuality" to explain the strategy of sodomy accusations.

> mais al trespas li refaisoit
> alcun sanblant que il l'amoit,
> quant n'antandoient pas a lui.   (9253–59)

[Eneas, who well understood their jokes, smiled a little; he nonetheless refrained from looking toward her in their sight, but in passing
he made some sign that he loved her when his men weren't paying
attention to him.]

Eneas's behavior sustains the feminine suspicion that masculine
relations compete in some sense with heterosexual relations.[21]
The one kind of relation hides from the other: among men Eneas's
courtship is the object of smiles, even of his own smile, despite
the devotion he simultaneously feels for Lavine. The group of
male companions mocking the isolated Lavine provides a context
for her fear that Eneas's masculine circle excludes her:

> Molt me prisast mialz Eneas,
> se j'aüsse fanduz les dras
> et qu'eüsse braies chalcies
> et lasnieres estroit liees.
> Il a asez garçons o soi,
> lo peor aime mialz de moi. . . .   (9155–60)

[Eneas would have liked me much better if I had split my robes and
worn breeches and tightly tied thongs. He has many boys with him;
he loves the worst of them more than me.]

Lavine's fantasy of crossdressing assumes neither that male-male
eroticism is exclusive of male-female eroticism (as in the modern
notion of "homosexual" identity) nor that male-male eroticism is
simply interchangeable with male-female eroticism (as the clerical diatribes claim). That is, Lavine imagines competing with
those Eneas loves better than her, not instead of her, by dressing
like a boy, not becoming a boy. Lavine's sexual rivalry with boys
is only one, perhaps delusory expression of a substantial social

---

[21] Gaunt attributes this competition to a generic shift in process in *Eneas* from
epic, which values bonds among men, to romance, which makes a hero's heterosexual bond primary. The position has merit, but the persistence of such competition in later romances argues that the genre typically engages heroes in balancing
chivalric and romantic allegiances.

competition in *Eneas* between masculine loyalties and heterosexual love. The discourse of courtship in this and similar romances both constrains masculine loyalties by suggesting they
are sexually transgressive and glorifies heterosexuality as sodomy's alternative, a culturally sanctioned and elaborated source
of identity in contrast to sodomy's illicit irregularity.

By founding courtship on banishing homoeroticism, *Eneas* begins
to imagine the difficulties masculine identity must negotiate to
establish a heterosexual union within a society that strongly values bonds among men.[22] Many later romances associate chivalric
bonds and courtship without invoking the limit case of sodomy.
Aligning success in heterosexual love with chivalric accomplish-
ments generates well-recognized tensions and oppositions in romance between private fulfillment and public renown. The alignment also involves a consonance between love and chivalry that
contributes to defining masculine identity by bringing to light an
ambivalence in each relation. It might seem that a knight of romance like those of epic would love his companions and compete
with his adversaries, but particularly in relation to courtships,
chivalric interactions in romance reveal themselves to be both
combative and desiring, while love takes on the language and dy-
namics of combat.

Chrétien de Troyes's *Erec et Enide* provides familiar examples
of a peculiar intimacy between knights that appears when women
come into the calculus of prowess. In his adventures with Enide,
Erec is defining his relation to her through entering into active
and complex relations with adversaries. Although Erec does defeat adversaries who are simply hostile, his major encounters with
Yder son of Nuht, Guivret li Petiz, and Maboagrain pit him
against men who become through combat his companions and
friends. Their gestures in combat mirror one another and their
hostilities end in mutual recognition:

> Asanblé sont au chief del pont;
> la s'antre vienent et desfient,

---

[22] Sedgwick's discussion, although specifically focused on heterosexual and homosocial components in nineteenth-century masculinity, is useful also for earlier
periods.

as fers des lances s'antre anvïent
anbedui de totes lor forces.
Ne lor valurent deus escorces
li escu qui as cos lor pandent:
li cuir ronpent et les es fandent
et des haubers ronpent les mailles,
si qu'anbedui jusqu'as antrailles
sont anglaivé et anferré. . . .
"Andui avons mestier de mire,
et j'ai ci pres un mien recet,
n'i a pas sis liues ne set;
la vos voel avoec moi mener,
si ferons noz plaies sener."   (3758–67, 3878–82)

[They come together at the head of the bridge; there they face and
challenge each other. With all their strength they attack each other
with their iron-tipped lances. Their shields hanging from their necks
were no more good to them than husks; they tear the straps and
break the boards and split the links of each others' hauberks so that
both of them are pierced through to the entrails. . . . "We both need
a doctor, and I have a refuge nearby, not six or seven leagues from
here; I want to take you there with me, and we'll have our wounds
dressed."]

The mutuality of Erec's and Guivret's blows is the basis of their
mutual respect and desire for each other's friendship. This kind of
encounter is not characteristic of epic and chronicle. Fredric
Jameson attributes the friendly resolution of such combats to an
emerging sense of class identity among knights in the twelfth century that made the older notion of an evil adversary less expres-
sive of chivalric consciousness than the romance version of an
adversary who proves to be akin to the hero.[23] Guivret and Erec
wrap one another's wounds in strips of cloth torn from their cloth-

---

[23] Citing Yder's case from *Yvain*, Jameson argues that "romance in its original
strong form may then be understood as . . . a symbolic answer to the perplexing
question of how my enemy can be thought of as being *evil* (that is, as other than
myself and marked by some absolute difference), when what is responsible for his
being so characterized is quite simply the *identity* of his own conduct with mine,
the which—points of honor, challenges, tests of strength—he reflects as in a mirror
image": *Political Unconscious*, 118 (his italics).

ing; repentant Yder joins the court of King Arthur; defeated Maboagrain reveals that he spent his youth in Erec's own household
and that all his family will rejoice at Erec's victory over him. In a
less military register, the *Franklin's Tale* still invites the Jame-
sonian reading, its competition among men illustrating in their
own interpretation not so much their differences as their shared
merit and values. The emergent class identity that Jameson notes
overlaps significantly with gender identity in that women are so
often the occasion for conflict and interaction among men in romance. Erec overcomes Yder in defending Enide's beauty, Guivret
in a series of adventures for which Enide is a kind of bait, and
Maboagrain in response to his challenge that Erec is not worthy to
approach his lady. In each case we can read the woman as "la
métonymie du seigneur," in Christiane Marchello-Nizia's formulation, the projected embodiment of chivalric honor over which
the contestants dispute (980). I suggest further that the heterosexual relation imitates the chivalric one, expanding and complicating knightly identity.

The analogy between love and combat reaches back to troubadour lyric for its rhetorical formulations and to chronicles for the
topos that women are the audience for chivalric behavior and
their favors its reward.[24] Courtship in romance, configured as
combat's metaphoric recasting as well as its motivation, follows
the logic of chivalric encounters in which adversarial struggle
gives way to accord. Although the proud lady whose resistance at
last melts is the most familiar figure to cite, romance can discover
the same dynamic in a variety of cases, even that of the helpful
wife Enide. Erec has forbidden her to speak as a way of testing her
motives for speaking: is she concerned for her own standing and
safety or for Erec's? When she warns Erec of Guivret's approach,

> Ele li dit; il la menace;
> mes n'a talant que mal li face,
> qu'il aparçoit et conuist bien
> qu'ele l'ainme sor tote rien,
> et il li tant que plus ne puet.   (3751–55)

[24] On lyric and metaphoric violence see Bloch, *Medieval French*, 153–61; two
familiar instances from chronicle are Geoffrey of Monmouth, 164, and Wace,
10511–42.

[She speaks to him and he threatens her, but he has no desire to hurt
her because he perceives and knows well that she loves him above
everything, and so does he love her completely.]

Open threats that yield eventually to love and alliance characterize as well the relations between Erec and his important challengers. During the combat with Guivret, Enide shows her love by
tearing at herself, mimicking the wounds Erec is giving and receiving as if to himself in mirrored combat.[25] She is the object of
his threat but experiences his pain; she is his opponent and (like
his opponent) his double as well. What do these equivalences
imply? They might encourage an erotic reading of combat: its mutuality and contact might suggest displaced passion, and the destruction of armor a displaced representation of undressing. But
such erotics, as in *Eneas*, are so suppressed as to appear mere false
constructions aroused by courtship's intrusion into a previously
masculine space. The parallels between combat and courtship
work more strongly in the opposite direction, such that courtship
appears a development from chivalric relations, an overt sexual-
izing and regendering of chivalry's combative and fraternal components. Enide in an earlier scene echoes the adversarial challenge
of groups of men, "de chevaliers et de sergenz" (of the knights and
the men-at-arms), who doubt Erec's valor after marriage; she herself provides a relation both adversarial and desiring for Erec.[26]
During their adventures the inner conflict she feels between fear
of Erec's injunction to silence and desire for his safety casts her
love in the terms of combat (e.g., ll. 2962–78, 3708–50). Tearing at
herself and weeping as she watches Erec fight Guivret, Enide is
not only metonymically restaging their conflict but also revealing
its affective complexity. Lavine's jealous sense of competition
with boys similarly points to affectivity among men even as Eneas
is consolidating his heterosexuality. But unlike Lavine, who feels
threatened by courtship's analogies to bonds among men, Enide

[25] Christine Darrohn has worked out this analysis in her conference paper
"'They reach for each other': Violent Bonding in *Erec et Enide*" (Fordham
Medieval Conference, 1994).

[26] The masculine opinion Enide respeaks to Erec is that of "si conpaignon,"
"trestoz li barnages," and "de chevaliers et de sergenz" according to the narration
(2439, 2455, 2459).

respeaks and refigures masculine interactions such that her relation to Erec feeds back into his chivalric activity.

A third way of building courtship into men's relations is the triangulated erotic rivalry of two men for one woman. Chaucer's Canacee, Dorigen, and Emelye take part in this structure, although the final lines of the *Squire's Tale* only begin to introduce Canacee's case. Those of Dorigen and Emeleye illustrate that the relation between men in specifically erotic triangles is strong and complex, and is more the focus of development for the tale than is the relation of either man to the woman in question. Aurelius refers to Arveragus in his first declaration to Dorigen, as we have seen, comparing himself to his rival. On comparative grounds Dorigen's status as "another mannes wyf" makes her desirable (V 1004). Aurelius does note her sorrow when Arveragus sends her to him, but his mercy on her depends on his acquiescence to Arveragus, who inspires him and to whom the squire addresses his decision: "Madame, seyth to youre lord Arveragus / That sith I se his grete gentillesse / To yow, and eek I se wel youre distresse. . . ." (V 1526–28) By conceding Dorigen to Arveragus but framing his concession as a "gentil dede" (V 1543) equivalent to that of his rival, Aurelius emphasizes the comparative over the competitive aspect of his relation to Arveragus. Their rivalry, working itself out in courtship and gentle deeds rather than chivalric encounters, resolves like Erec's rivalries through emulation into accord.

In the *Knight's Tale* masculine allegiance precedes a love that appears to invert and destroy friendship. Arcite, as we have seen, denies any integration of the love experience with masculine allegiances ("Love is a gretter lawe, by my pan, / Than may be yeve to any erthely man"), and the narrator's proverb concurs that "love ne lordshipe / Wol noght, his thankes, have no felaweshipe" (I 1625–26). In such a plot it may seem implausible to argue that love is overwritten on fellowship, that love is a secondary formation that clarifies and develops masculine relations. However, by combining the romance paradigms that the origin of courtship refuses fellowship (here illustrated from *Eneas*) and that courtship develops within chivalric relations (here illustrated from *Erec et Enide*), the *Knight's Tale* positions love as a productive expansion of Palamon and Arcite's experience of brotherhood.

As in *Eneas*, masculine relations in the *Knight's Tale* become problematic at the point of courtship's origin. Supplementing the queen's accusation of sodomy is Eneas's complaint against his brother Cupid:

> Amor me fet molt grant oltrage,
> qui me moine an tel maniere:
> sos ciel n'a si vil chanberiere
> que il menast plus a desroi
> ne plus vilment que il fait moi,
> qui sui ses frere et il est miens.
> De lui me deüst venir biens,
> tot mal me fait et tot me mate,
> voirs est que prïé mal achate.   (8940–48)

[Love, who is treating me thus, is doing me a very great wrong: there is no chambermaid so base under heaven whom he would mistreat more vilely than he is mistreating me, who am his brother as he is mine. Good things should come to me from him, but he is doing me every wrong and utterly defeating me. Truly my friendship gets little reward.]

As love transforms brotherhood into opposition, Eneas imagines even his gender misapprehended by this brother who treats him worse than he would a chambermaid. Palamon expresses a similar sense of wrong, of the proper order reversed, in his claim that Arcite's oath of brotherhood should prevail over his competitive love for Emelye.

Eneas's complaint has the privilege over subsequent romantic complaints that Cupid, a son of Venus, is indeed his own brother, such that the onslaught of love is evidently and even comically at odds with brotherhood in the most immediate sense. Other lovers consistently reimagine falling in love as an encounter between the lover and the God of Love rather than the woman herself. When Arcite complains in the grove that "Love hath his firy dart so brennyngly / Ystiked thurgh my trewe, careful herte," he too reformulates the adversarial aspect of love as a masculine contest (I 1564–65). Arcite expresses love in terms of combat to clarify the heterosexual experience in terms of familiar masculine experience: love is a new species of combat. The rhetorical device perpetuates the association between Palamon and Arcite's beleaguered fraternity and their love for Emelye, and not only by expressing the onslaught of love as a masculine struggle between lover and Love. Arcite's image of love's arrow piercing his heart presages the rivalry Palamon feels on hearing his cousin's confession: "[he] thoughte that thurgh his herte / He felte a coold swerd sodeynliche glyde" (I 1574–75). The wounded heart aligns Arcite's unrequited love and Palamon's betrayed brotherhood as analogous cases, locating masculine rivalry on the site of courtship by translating the latter into the language of the former.

A second rhetorical parallel perpetuates courtship's involvement in brotherhood. From the earliest romances the monologues and complaints of lovers draw on lyric for a rhetoric of isolation and suffering. Among the most familiar lyric devices taken into romance is the address to an absent and uncaring object of love. Lavine indulges in lyric apostrophe when she addresses Eneas as she first realizes she is in love, "Amis, ne retorneroiz mie? / Molt vos est po de vostre amie" (Beloved, will you never return? You care very little for your friend) (8355–56).[27] Such apostrophes, far from implying a listening presence, are predicated on the addressee's absence. When apostrophe enters romance plots, it can produce an ambiguous tension between the lover's self-isolating lyricism and the beloved's accessibility to speech. Arcite illustrates the ambiguity in passing years of service to Emelye without addressing to her the kind of complaint he delivers (therefore can still deliver) in the grove: "Ye sleen me with youre eyen, Emelye! / Ye been the cause wherfore that I dye" (I 1567–68). This rhetorical topos of willed isolation also marks the friends' apostrophes to one another on Arcite's release from prison. Although Arcite's lament addresses "O deere cosyn Palamon" and Palamon's addresses "Arcita, cosyn myn," each speaks inconsolably to himself rather than to his brother, as the closing lines of each monologue indicate: Arcite ends his lament with a second apostrophe not to Palamon but to the similarly absent beloved ("Syn that I may nat seen you, Emelye, / I nam but deed, ther nys no remedye"), and Palamon ends his lament with the third-person notation that he is dying "For jalousie and fere of hym Arcite"

[27] On the emergence of romance in relation to lyric and other genres see Nichols; Kay, 171–211; Kelly, 306–20; Ferrante, "Conflict of Lyric Conventions and Romance Form."

(I 1234, 1273–74, 1281, 1333). Romantic love has set each young man in lyric isolation from his brother as well as from his beloved. The event of Arcite's release concretizes a separation already recognized in the rhetoric of complaint and apostrophe.

That love and friendship share a rhetoric and compete for allegiance in the *Knight's Tale* raises the possibility, as in *Eneas*, of an erotic component in friendship that is analogous but hostile to romantic love.[28] The young men's reconciliation on Arcite's deathbed tallies with David Halperin's argument that in classical texts "death is the climax of [male] friendship, the occasion of the most extreme expressions of tenderness. . . . Indeed, it is not too much to say that death is to friendship what marriage is to romance" (79).[29] More overtly, heterosexual desire introduces open hostility into brotherhood, complicating and heightening Palamon and Arcite's affective relation far beyond the neonatal simplicity of the image first introducing them as "Two yonge knyghtes liggynge by and by, / Bothe in oon armes" (I 1011–12) on the battlefield at Thebes. The trouble within their brotherhood will be resolved when they leave complaint to become engaged in events. The friendship of Theseus and Perotheus—in its productive mutuality an ironic contrast to that of Palamon and Arcite—sets events in motion with Arcite's release. The resolution to the young friends' interrelated alienation and desire is chivalric, the duel and tournament affirming the capacity of masculine relations to further and resolve courtships.

Palamon and Arcite's duel in the grove begins to recall Erec's major encounters in commingling hostility with allegiance. Arm-

[28] According to Dellamora, 152–53, Pater, 7, understood Palamon and Arcite's friendship to be erotic. Colin Morris, 96–120, has examined the many parallels between terms of male friendship and heterosexual courtship. He emphasizes contrasts, whereas Boswell, e.g., 188–200, believes expressions of male friendship to be directly erotic.

[29] Halperin proposes that as depicted in the texts he considers, male friendship borrows imagery from sexual and political vocabularies "to identify and define itself" (84), whereas I propose the reverse, that heterosexual interaction patterns itself on male relations. Jaeger argues that the vocabulary of friendship in monastic and clerical writing is the basis of the vernacular vocabulary of secular courtesy and heterosexual love developed in the eleventh and twelfth centuries (*Origins of Courtliness*, 127–75; "Amour des rois"). From this rhetorical perspective, courtship is again a secondary formation on masculine relations.

ing, that ritual of masculine dressing so important to romance that it occupies all of the second fit of *Sir Thopas*, reintroduces a simulacrum of brotherly behavior:

> Ther nas no good day, ne so saluyng,
> But streight, withouten word or rehersyng,
> Everich of hem heelp for to armen oother
> As freendly as he were his owene brother.... (I 1649–52)

Dispensing with words and salutations seems to be the precondition for the gestures of arming that reintroduce brotherhood even in the context of enmity. The duel is, paradoxically, the point of reentry into brotherhood, as the shared chivalric code of fair play dictates the rivals' mutual aid in preparing for battle. Their enmity continues to evoke their earlier fellowship in Palamon's expressions of mutuality as he denounces the two of them to Theseus: "We have the deeth disserved bothe two. / Two woful wrecches been we, two caytyves" (I 1716–17). The language of enmity and courtship's metaphoric language of despair are indistinguishable when Palamon begs Theseus to "sle me first, for seinte charitee! / But sle my felawe eek as wel as me" (I 1721–22). Theseus, however, resists the young men's alienation both in noting that love is a common ground of experience uniting all three men to other lovers and in arranging a tournament that gives expression to Palamon and Arcite's rivalry within the wider frame of shared chivalric values.

The tournament restores the positive valence of masculine companionship, first by mitigating each lover's isolation through the company of fellows he assembles. Arcite implies that his prayer to Mars speaks for the men with whom he will fight, in promising that for victory "in thy temple I wol my baner honge / And alle the armes of my compaignye" (I 2410–11). The narration emphasizes that knights there and elsewhere would strive "to fighte for a lady," or more precisely, to join such an occasion "for love and for encrees of chivalrye" (I 2115, 2184). The motive is common to participants on both sides, and the whole undertaking is implicated in the sustenance of the state, their own estate, and the law. In the tournament, a public spectacle that serves social purposes such as displaying Theseus's power, enacting the aristocracy's common purposes, and submitting a private dispute to judicial authority, the adversaries can indeed be admonished that fighting is their duty: "Tho were the gates shet, and cried was loude: / 'Do now youre devoir, yonge knyghtes proude!'" (I 2597–98)

The greatest success of the tournament, as for Erec's encounters with his most important adversaries, is that it furthers courtship by perpetuating and deepening the relations among knights. Like the mutual blows that express shared merits in Erec's combats, the shared purpose of the knights on both sides of Theseus's tournament leads to their easy reconciliation at its end. The occasion itself was honorable, so that even those who fell or were captured share in honor:

> Ne ther was holden no disconfitynge
> But as a justes or a tourneiynge;
> For soothly ther was no disconfiture. . . .
> For which anon duc Theseus leet crye,
> To stynten alle rancour and envye,
> The gree as wel of o syde as of oother,
> And eyther syde ylik as ootheres brother. . . .
>
>   (I 2719–21, 2731–34)

The adversaries who become "ylik as ootheres brother" adumbrate Arcite's reconciliation with Palamon, providing a wider context than the deathbed for Arcite's account of their enmity as a thing of the past ("I have heer with my cosyn Palamon / Had strif and rancour many a day agon" [I 2783–84]). Love has opposed brotherhood in this plot, but in conceding Emelye to Palamon, in inviting their union as he dies, Arcite subsumes Emelye into a restored economy of brotherhood. The tournament has set the brothers on opposite sides, apparently reversing the condition in which they were found "liggynge by and by, / Bothe in oon armes," but in effect the tournament has expanded the brothers' chivalric experience by incorporating love as an occasion for their rivalry and reconciliation. Here as in many romances, men negotiate the difficult demand that they establish a heterosexual bond but maintain strong homosocial bonds by building the former into the latter, redoubling and extending masculine relations through courtship.

Feminine Mimicry and Masquerade

OMANCES, in contrast to much medieval literature, abound in representations of women. This chapter argues that in their female characters romances work out both a version of femininity generated by masculine courtship and a critique of that version of femininity. Female characters, moreover, themselves stage this critique within the terms of their social construction. Dorigen confronted with Aurelius's suit, the abandoned falcon of the *Squire's Tale*, the Amazons of the *Knight's Tale*, and the Wife of Bath's shape-shifting fairy deploy the language and paradigms of conventional femininity to press against their positioning within it. Placing Chaucer's characters in the company of others from a variety of romances clarifies the strategies each woman uses to articulate and question her lot. In each case, respeaking and remanipulating familiar gender paradigms offers ways around them.

The representation of women is a central problem of feminist criticism. In what sense are women visible or absent in literary language? What is the relation of a discourse such as that of courtship in romance to the historical identities of medieval (or modern) women? An early paradigm of impressive explanatory force was Simone de Beauvoir's conception of woman as the Other of masculine identity, the category of strangeness that by opposition founds a coherent meaning for masculinity. "Once the subject seeks to assert himself, the Other, who limits and denies him, is none the less a necessity to him: he attains himself only through that reality which he is not, which is something other than himself" (139). This conception of woman as a "second" sex that consolidates the identity of men is modified by recent French feminists for whom the representation of woman in the realm of masculine discourse is altogether impossible; the feminine cannot be constituted even as an "other" but is instead the "sex which is not one," in Luce Irigaray's phrase, the negative or absence within conceptions that are already fully masculine.[1] Conceiving woman as negativity revises and critiques De Beauvoir's concept of the Other, but each analysis explains how a difference might exist between literary invocations of masculine and feminine, such that the latter becomes a function of the former and further that a different sort of gap divides literary representation from historical situation in the case of each gender.

In many respects medieval romance does conceive gender as a binary but unreciprocal division that constrains femininity to masculine terms. One consequence of the conception is that historians and critics recognize complex transformations at work between the historical situation of women and literary representations of, for example, an adulterous and authoritative Queen Guinevere. In contrast, romances represent the practical and ideological situation of men with sufficient directness that John Stevens's transgeneric definition may ring true to critics of several persuasions: "the concerns of medieval romance are the concerns of all narrative fiction: man loving; man fighting; man with his lover, his leader or his friends; man alone; man facing mystery, or death; man seeking for God" (9). Romance, that is, insistently exemplifies De Beauvoir's argument that the masculine stands for the universal experience. The prominence of courtship in romance is compatible with this version of masculinity. Barbara Johnson begins *The Critical Difference* with the assertion, even more encompassing than Stevens's and apparently incompatible with it, that "if human beings were not divided into two biological sexes, there would probably be no need for literature" (13). Yet her analysis of love from Guillaume de Lorris's *Roman de la Rose* to Honoré de Balzac's *Sarrasine* traces the process of deferral by which romantic love becomes indistinguishable from masculine narcissistic love. "What is at stake is not the union between two

---

[1] *This Sex*; see also Irigaray, *Speculum*, 133–46. De Beauvoir does suggest that masculine and feminine are not a true binary, e.g., "In actuality the relation of the two sexes is not quite like that of two electrical poles, for man represents both the positive and the neutral, as is indicated by the common use of *man* to designate human beings in general; whereas woman represents only the negative, defined by limiting criteria, without reciprocity" (xv, her italics).

people, but the narcissistic awakening of one. Seeing La Zambi-
nella is Sarrasine's first experience of *himself* as an object of love"
(9). Henri Rey-Flaud's *Névrose courtoise* and Jean-Charles Huchet's *Roman médiéval* argue as well that *fine amor* is an evasion
rather than an elaboration of intimacy between the sexes and that
the place of women in the paradigms of literary courtship, far
from figuring an amelioration in the historical position of women,
reinforces the cultural distance between the sexes by expressing
in the literary image of woman the disorientation and strangeness
of emotional experience: "La femme est l'Autre du récit qui en
parle" (Woman is the Other of the tale that narrates her) (Huchet,
Roman médiéval, 218; see also Huchet, "Psychanalyse"). Such
recent work on medieval literature tends to mesh the ideas of
masculine self-definition through the feminine and of a consequent absenting of woman from discourse.[2] That is, such work
tends to resist the claim in French feminist theory that the feminine is altogether beyond representation—the claim, in Julia Kris-
teva's famous assertion, that "a woman cannot 'be'; it is something which does not even belong in the order of being" (in *New
French Feminisms*, 137). In medieval literary studies, by contrast,
the process of negation is textual; the literary work records cultural conceptions of gender including the trace of woman's absenting from representation. These studies estimate highly the
capacity of language to articulate and comment on the problematic status of the feminine. Literature can consequently represent
not only the dominant cultural versions of gender but also what
those versions suppress and what might resist them.

The paradox by which romance figures women yet negates
them is important to several chapters of this book. This chapter
investigates how romance also invites readings that move beyond
its own dominant gender paradigms. Here some theoretical work
on social construction is valuable and deserves a brief review. In
the work of Irigaray the feminine sex is "not one" in part because,
as the indeterminate negativity in a masculine signifying system,

[2] Outstanding examples that are of importance to this study are Dinshaw;
Hansen; the essays by Fisher, Halley, and Roberta L. Krueger in *Seeking the
Woman*; and Heng, "Feminine Knots" and "A Woman Wants." An early and
ground-breaking essay on the masculine perspective and the roles of female characters is Ferrante, "Male Fantasy and Female Reality."

the feminine is multiple, unstable, and diffused. Although Irigaray remains committed to a conception of woman that is at least
metaphorically based in biological sex, the deconstruction of binary difference from which her argument derives initiates a theoretical shift away from the binary paradigm toward questioning
the bond it implies between biological sex and gendered identity.[3]
The deconstructionist critique of the merely apparent separateness and stability of binary oppositions together with its focus on
the semiotic composition of consciousness sustain feminist efforts to reconceive biological sex as partaking not of a natural
ground for identity but of a shifting discursive network that constitutes historical subjects in particular places and times.[4] The
concept that identities are constructed by numberless intersecting pressures that have no single cause or origin calls into question whether biological sex is "prior" to gender: is that version of
sex not merely a further discursive construction through which
we interpret the relations between body and identity? Judith Butler concludes that "the tacit constraints that produce culturally
intelligible 'sex' ought to be understood as generative political
structures rather than naturalized foundations" (147). However
enforced and constraining, sex and gender are arbitrary in the
sense that they are culturally elaborated, and differently in different times and places.

   The position that identity is socially constituted connects the
literary representation of gender to historical women and men.
Insofar as construction is a discursive process, it can take place in
poetic language as in legal codes, moral instruction, school texts,
and a wide range of further articulations. For those who, with
Michel Foucault, view construction more as a matter of repeated
practices than of ideological influences, literature partakes of social practice—as an aspect of the relationship between author and
patron, a site of interaction for individuals of a particular audi-

---

   [3] Fuss, 55–72, argues compellingly that Irigaray's "strategic" essentialism serves
a larger constructionist project and that her bodily metaphors should be taken
metonymically.
   [4] Davidson provides a fine discussion of feminism in relation to Jacques Der-
rida's concept of the subject and agency; valuable feminist analyses of the implications of Michel Foucault's work for gender studies are Fraser and *Feminism and
Foucault*.

ence, and a reiterable expression of belief that solicits admiration, imitation, or identification. As a literary historian I am convinced that the registers of belief and of practice inform one another and need not be sharply distinguished. Through both registers literature participates in the social construction of its authors and consumers. In consequence we need not think of literary representation and historical identity as opposed conditions, since identity is itself a representation. The work of literature and the historical person are both enmeshed in culturally elaborated ideas and practices that constitute gender simultaneously for art and life. In these terms genres are analogous to the social rankings called "degrees" or "estates," ranks that express like so many genres a set of possibilities for the social performance of masculinity and femininity.

It has seemed that the concept of constructed identity is constraining to the point of determinism, substituting for the potentially essentialist bonds linking sex to gender a nexus of historical forces that determine subjects so ineluctably as to deny or severely restrict any possibility that they might act with self-critical awareness to analyze and change the conditions of their construction—that they might act, that is, as agents of their own destinies. But gender theorists have argued within the context of work on the constructed character of gender and sex that multiple sites of agency invite responses to construction.

Butler asks, "If there is no recourse to a 'person,' a 'sex,' or a 'sexuality' that escapes the matrix of power and discursive relations that effectively produce and regulate the intelligibility of those concepts for us, what constitutes the possibility of effective inversion, subversion, or displacement within the terms of a constructed identity?" (32) Irigaray's earlier proposal, based in the contrasting relation to language of women and men in a gender system that assigns men the power to signify and women the position of image, was that resistance to the feminine position is possible through mimicry, that is, through the deliberate acting out of prescribed femininity in an effort to thwart its limitations and reveal its hidden mechanisms: "if women are such good mimics, it is because they are not simply resorbed in this function" (*This Sex*, 76). Teresa de Lauretis, while recognizing the power of the dichotomous association of language and image with men and women respectively, opens the heterosexual binary to a more complex range of gendered identities by recognizing constraints on all subject positions and by finding a richer potential for response in the temporal space of identity formation. Because the constitution of subjects is a historical process, ongoing as well as specific to time and place, its unfolding may be visible in the experience of the reflecting subject who can then intervene and comment using the terms of the discourse at work: "the only way to position oneself outside of that [dominant, constitutive] discourse is to displace oneself within it—to refuse the question as formulated, or to answer deviously (though in its words), even to quote (but against the grain)."[5] Butler argues similarly that the multiplicity of intersecting and contradictory forces constituting identities betrays the unnaturalness of gender and "holds out the possibility of a disruption of their univocal posturing." For Butler as for De Lauretis, the process of construction in time provides the invitation to deconstruct its appearance of naturalness. As "the repeated stylization of the body," gender and sex both form the subject and allow for "parodic proliferation and subversive play" (Butler, 32–33). Each writer argues that agency occurs through strategic repetition in the course of developing wider social theories that reach far beyond the limits of my brief summary. My purpose in this chapter is to establish two vantage points for considering the representation of women in romance; I draw these from the constellation of ways in which gender theorists describe agency as reacting to cultural construction by drawing on its own terms to critique it.

This chapter examines two kinds of distortion that female characters work on gender roles, each of which could be described as answering deviously, quoting against the grain, or parodying the imperatives of gender. In the first case, vocal mimicry uses courtly topoi against themselves in characters' attempts to resist

---

[5] *Alice Doesn't*, 7. In "Eccentric Subjects" De Lauretis pushes the possibilities for resistance to the process of construction by proposing that since the process is multiple and even contradictory (involving many intersecting forces such as social class, religion, and race in conjunction with gender), it may invite a thinking beyond binary gender, a "dis-identification" by which each subject may perceive several self-identities that, in their disunities, invite "a redefinition of the terms of both feminist theory and social reality from a standpoint at once inside and outside their determinations" (126, 139).

the scripted roles of courtship. In the second, physical distortions question the consonance between feminine identity and bodily appearance.

QUOTING AGAINST THE GRAIN

Framed by her protestation "ne shal I nevere been untrewe wyf" and her instruction to "lat swiche folies out of youre herte slyde" (V 984, 1002), Dorigen's promise to love Aurelius if he can remove the rocks along the coast of Brittany is suspect:

> But after that in pley thus seyde she:
> "Aurelie," quod she, "by heighe God above,
> Yet wolde I graunte yow to been youre love,
> Syn I yow se so pitously complayne.
> Looke what day that endelong Britayne
> Ye remoeve alle the rokkes, stoon by stoon. . . ."
>
> (V 988–93)

How are we to understand the contradiction between the promise of love and the assertions of wifely loyalty? In Giovanni Boccaccio's *Filocolo*, apparently Chaucer's source for the plot of the *Franklin's Tale*, the wife's private thoughts illuminate her demand: "She said to herself, 'It is an impossible thing to do, and that is how I shall get free of him.'" Her suitor understands that she has found a "cunning stratagem" to get rid of him.[6] Meaning is more elusive in Chaucer's tale both for readers, who are privy only to Dorigen's desire that the rocks not threaten her husband's return, and for Aurelius, who laments the task's difficulty but apparently does not consider its assignment equivalent to a rejection.

The last chapter of this study argues that such alterations to Chaucer's sources have to do with the concept of adventure that develops in medieval romance, a concept that configures women as a ground of adventure through their contradictions and unknowability. Aurelius responds as if Dorigen's words were an enigmatic encouragement, a mystery to be explored and suffered.

---

[6] "Fra sé dicendo: 'Questa è cosa impossibile: io mi leverò costui da dosso per questa maniera,'" she conceives "una sottile malizia": Boccaccio, *Filocolo*, 396–97; trans. Havely, *Chaucer's Boccaccio*, 155; cf. Boccaccio, *Decameron*, 877–82 (fifth story, tenth day).

This chapter attends not to how lovers perceive women in romance but to how women articulate and respond to their positioning by lovers. The project might seem an impossible archaeology since, as outlined above, the feminine in romance can accurately be described as the place where masculinity is not—the space of adventure, in the present case. According to the *Franklin's Tale*, however, that very condition of femininity can be pointed out and pressed upon by a character so constructed. Dorigen's reply to Aurelius resists the conventional feminine role in courtship by scrambling and exaggerating it.

Most readers concur that Dorigen reiterates her framing words of refusal through the impossibility of the assigned task; that she speaks "in pley" (V 988) signals the task's unthinkable difficulty and undermines its similarity to "many a labour, many a greet emprise" through which Arveragus won her (V 732). Readers generally agree that not only the overt refusal that frames the task but also Dorigen's astonishment when the task is performed—"she wende nevere han come in swich a trappe" (V 1341)—and the analogies she strikes between the prospect of acquiescence and historical instances of maidens "defouled with mannes foul delit" (V 1396) indicate that she is attempting throughout to discourage Aurelius.[7] The problem, then, is not whether she means to encourage Aurelius but why she chooses a tactic to discourage him that does not work.

Dorigen's ultimate failure to deflect Aurelius's courtship has led Robert Kaske to condemn her for "feminine flightiness": although she means the task to be "a graceful way of saying no," the effort fails because "in an area of endeavor where 'no' often enough means 'perhaps,' and 'perhaps' almost inevitably means 'yes,' it will not do" (61–62). This interpretation draws on the overwhelming presumption in courtly literature that a woman worthy of courtship will eventually accede to a worthy suitor. Given that Dorigen has already conformed to this pattern with Arveragus, it might be argued that the impossible task she invents is a further instance of participation in courtship's dynamic of resistance and submission, as Aurelius seems determined to hope,

---

[7] E.g., Ferster, 154–57; Mann, *Geoffrey Chaucer*, 115; Morgan, 295; Lee, 173. Charnes, in contrast, argues for complications in Dorigen's feelings rather than in her rhetorical situation.

or that her submission to Arveragus exempts her from further participation, as Dorigen's references to Arveragus seem to insist. Rather than assessing blame for the parties' misconstruals, I would like to read the difference between Dorigen's desire to refuse Aurelius and his focus on the assigned task as an illustration of the difficulty of expressing resistance to courtship in romance.

The literature of courtship does not suggest that a plain "no" would have persuaded Aurelius to stop importuning Dorigen; indeed, as Kaske recognizes, refusal is itself scripted into courtship as a first stage of feminine responsiveness. The *Book of the Duchess*, in which fair White "sayde 'Nay' / Al outerly" (1243–44) when first approached by the black knight, looks back to romance tradition as codified in the anger of Bel Aceuil and the sudden appearance of Dangier when the lover first speaks of love in the *Romance of the Rose*:

> Thanne Bialacoil, affrayed all,
> Seyde, "Sir, it may not fall;
> That ye desire, it may not arise. . . ."
> With that sterte oute anoon Daunger,
> Out of the place were he was hid.
> His malice in his chere was kid.
>
> (in *Riverside Chaucer*, 3113–15, 3130–32)

In early romances women are with some frequency the aggressors in love or at least suffer its pangs as quickly and acutely as their suitors. Josian comes to Bevis's bed in the various versions of *Bevis of Hamtoun*, and *Tristan* as well as Chrétien de Troyes's *Cligés*, which has been called in other respects an "anti-Tristan," portray women falling as quickly and uncontrollably in love as their men.[8] Later romances, particularly under the influence of the *Romance of the Rose*, develop a strongly narrative impulse within courtship by relocating the difficulties that divide the knight and his beloved from external circumstances to the lady's own resistance. With this development, refusal becomes an integral part of courtship, an expected first response that the lover's efforts can overcome.

---

[8] E.g., *Boeve*, ll. 670–772; *Beues*, ll. 1093–1199 (A-text). Fénice contrasts the events of the Tristan story to the conduct she and Cligés should follow: Chrétien de Troyes, *Cligés*, ll. 3105–24, 5199–5203, 5249–58; see also Van Hamel, Weiss.

Dorigen's task of removing the rocks, like her direct refusal, has a place in paradigms of courtship: it parallels the resistant lady's demand that her suitor perform extraordinary deeds in order to win her love. In the romances of Guy of Warwick, Felice requires that the young Guy become the best knight in the world before she will marry him (*Gui*, ll. 1055–82; *Guy*, Auchinleck MS, ll. 1131–60); in the romances of Ipomedon the heroine's courtiers have nicknamed her La Fière in recognition of her proud vow to marry only the world's best knight (Hue de Rotelande, *Ipomedon*, ll. 119–42; *Ipomadon*, ll. 98–132). Guy and Ipomedon do meet these demands, but criticism of the demands' prescriptive control is implicit in Guy's rejection of his past life of empty conquests for exploits in God's service after marriage, and in Ipomedon's teasing evasiveness once La Fière is anxious to accept him.[9] In Jean Froissart's *Méliador* the lady Hermondine intends her conditions to be discouraging: she resists her suitor Camel, who is afflicted with the undesirable habit of sleepwalking, by announcing that she will marry the knight who proves himself best in five years of tests and adventures. The vow generates an enormously complex plot in which Méliador's success displaces Camel's suit (ll. 1836–2147). Jean de Condé's *Dit dou Levrier* further exemplifies the imposition of great tasks as a way of deflecting love. Here the lady demands seven years of unstinting generosity and participation in tournaments and wars "pour los à querre" (to win renown) (460). The narrator comments, "Ensement parla la pucielle / A l'escuyer si comme celle / Qui de lui se voet descombrer" (the maiden spoke to the squire as if she wanted to get rid of him) (477–79), and indeed she refuses his love even after he has fulfilled all her conditions, driving him into insanity. His faithful dog's ministrations preserve him from death until, after much suffering, he is cured by a fairy in pity for his story.[10] These plots illustrate that extraordinary demands, even when motivated by distaste, no more deflect courtship than do outright refusals; in-

[9] See my *Insular Romance*, 109–15, 164–70, 198–211. The proud vow and Ipomedon's resistance are both played down in the Middle English version; in the *Book of the Duchess*, White avoids placing such demands on suitors (ll. 1019–33).

[10] Ribard notes Jean's use of the term *lai* to describe this work at ll. 63, 1577, 1613, 1620 and argues that the work does fit the genre. On the *Franklin's Tale* and Breton lays see Donovan, 173–89.

stead, both feminine strategies are productive of plots centered on the striving lover. The dubious merit ascribed to women's specific demands sharpens the image of courtship as a process of masculine self-improvement rather than mutuality and intimacy.

Dorigen's words to Aurelius comment on the constrained situation of women in the literature of courtship. First, that Dorigen finds herself ventriloquizing encouragement as she attempts resistance reveals that there is no vocabulary of refusal in this generic context. Both the lady's resistance to a first declaration of love and her extravagant demands might well be signs of acquiescence. Even Dorigen's references to her husband, as we have seen in the first chapter, are consonant with Aurelius's version of his courtship as a competitive confrontation with Arveragus, a relation between men. The only way for Dorigen to communicate refusal to Aurelius would be to relocate herself altogether outside of sexual circulation, and the many stories she later recalls can only imagine that outside as death (V 1367–1456).

Considering Dorigen's reply to Aurelius as a literary problem revises the estimation we might draw from the "rash promise" motif and the ensuing critical judgments that Dorigen is "foolish" and "flighty" (see Wurtele). Chaucer's particular version of the rash promise suggests that Dorigen is neither rash nor flirtatious but rather that her desire to refuse is at odds with courtly discourses that do not admit a language of refusal. Located in and constrained by the literary conventions of courtship, Dorigen's reply illustrates the wider situation of gender construction. Like men and women of history, Dorigen experiences the limitations that discursive forms and encoded practices (here genres rather than lived behaviors and beliefs) impose on the expression of desire. As social standing, common law, superstitions, and so on can constrain historical persons' gendered identity and behavior, in similar terms the literature of courtship constrains Dorigen to a particular feminine identity and range of response.

Dorigen's reply further illustrates, however, that it is possible to move beyond simply reiterating established forms. By juxtaposing two conventional responses that characterize different stages of courtship, by proposing a task that refers specifically to her husband's safety, and by proposing an impossibly difficult task, she clarifies for readers, if not for Aurelius, a dislocation between her intention and the language in which she can express it. Dorigen's failure to convince Aurelius of her disinterest reveals the difficulty of being heard to speak against courtship. Scanning the rhetorical horizon for a way to describe her position, she settles on a strategy of distorting and exaggerating the scripted role for feminine negations in masculine courtships. This peculiar kind of mimicry, this quoting against the grain, both clarifies the restrictions under which she speaks and articulates a resistance to them.

The deceived falcon who recounts her plight to Canacee in the *Squire's Tale* resists her literary gendering differently from Dorigen, by reversing male and female roles from Jean de Meun's exemplum of the caged bird in the *Romance of the Rose*. The *Squire's Tale* as a whole prepares for the condemnation of men's "newefangelnesse" by asserting an essential "wommanly" virtue (V 610, 486): Canacee is "ful mesurable, as wommen be" (V 362); the falcon attributes Canacee's gentle pity to her sex:

> That pitee renneth soone in gentil herte,
> Feelynge his similitude in peynes smerte,
> Is preved alday, as men may it see,
> As wel by werk as by auctoritee;
> For gentil herte kitheth gentillesse.
> I se wel that ye han of my distresse
> Compassion, my faire Canacee,
> Of verray wommanly benignytee
> That Nature in youre principles hath set.   (V 479–87)

Although she begins, in that line Chaucer uses more often than any other, with the claim that "pitee" is common to all of "gentil herte," the falcon specifies that Canacee's arises from her "wommanly benignytee."[11] The falcon's shift from locating human compassion in gentility to locating womanly compassion in feminine nature exemplifies a wider effort in the tale to formulate a conjoined beneficence and alienness in women that differentiates them from men. This uncanny combination, most evident in women's magical functions in romance, here finds its explanation

---

[11] For other occurrences of the line and for comprehensive notes on the tale's critical history, see the *Squire's Tale* in the *Variorum Edition*.

in Nature's allotment of particular attributes to women that contrast, in the binary model that arguments from nature always invoke, with masculine attributes.[12] The sympathy that unites "Canacee and alle hir wommen" (V 633) with the wronged falcon illustrates both a special feminine capacity for compassion and a certain exoticism that connects women more closely than men to the animal world—so closely, indeed, that a bird can voice feminine positions more vividly than Canacee herself.

The tale's positing of a distinctively feminine sensibility prepares for the falcon's analysis of her lover's inconstancy:

> I trowe he hadde thilke text in mynde
> That "alle thyng, repeirynge to his kynde,
> Gladeth hymself"; thus seyn men, as I gesse.
> Men loven of propre kynde newefangelnesse,
> As briddes doon that men in cages fede.
> For though thou nyght and day take of hem hede,
> And strawe hir cage faire and softe as silk,
> And yeve hem sugre, hony, breed and milk,
> Yet right anon as that his dore is uppe
> He with his feet wol spurne adoun his cuppe,
> And to the wode he wole and wormes ete;
> So newefangel been they of hire mete,
> And loven novelries of propre kynde,
> No gentillesse of blood ne may hem bynde.   (V 607–20)

Although the passage begins by using "men" to signify humanity in general, it is men in the gender-specific sense whose behavior resembles that of caged birds. The tercelet's puzzling inconstancy is explained in the axiom that "men loven of propre kynde newefangelnesse." The falcon has already gendered an axiom concerning her own behavior: "bihoveth hire a ful long spoon / That shal ete with a feend" (V 602–3). Recalling as well the gentle heart's glide from human to feminine in the falcon's first words to Canacee, the caged-bird passage more visibly splits the universal "man" into men and women. The falcon's persistent divisions draw on the creative energy that romances as well as lyrics and

---

[12] On women and magic see chapter 4; two informative overviews of arguments from nature are Allen and Maclean.

dits amoureux find in gender difference. Yet even as the falcon's complaint recalls this familiar dynamic, it works some striking revisions on masculine and feminine categories.

The falcon revoices a topos that Chaucer knew from Boethius's *Consolation of Philosophy*, which he translated with the aid of Jean de Meun's French version. In both sources the bird's gender is a function of grammatical gender: the feminine *ales garrula* of Boethius becomes a masculine *oiseaus* in Jean's translation.[13] Chaucer chooses in *Boece* the feminine "sche," presumably in deference to the Latin substantive over Jean's translation since the argument concerns a behavior universal not only to men and women but to all creation. The tamed lion, the caged bird, the bent tree, and the sun all strive to revert to their good and natural paths: "Alle thynges seken ayen to hir propre cours, and alle thynges rejoysen hem of hir retornynge ayen to hir nature."[14] Chaucer's shift from the feminine bird in his translation of the *Consolation* to the masculine bird in the *Squire's Tale*'s adaptation of the passage corresponds to a shift from illustrating laudable universal order through the caged bird to illustrating harmful masculine inconstancy.

From the perspective of gender and romance, the revision of *Boece* in the *Squire's Tale* responds most directly to Jean de Meun's revision of the same Boethian passage in La Vieille's teachings on how to manipulate lovers. The old woman whose job it is to guard the chastity of the dreamer's beloved in the *Romance of the Rose* urges instead that women should profit from taking as many lovers as they can entice; in this they are only following their feminine nature like the bird who strives to escape the cage:

> Ausinc sachiez que toutes fames,
> saient damoiseles ou dames,
> de quelconques procession,

[13] Boethius, bk. 3, meter 2, ll. 17–26; Jean de Meun, bk. 3, meter 2, ll. 13–18. That grammatical gender is not innocent of sexual connotation is illustrated throughout medieval allegory, e.g., in Jean's crossgendering of Bel Aceuil: see Zink. On the universal versus the gendered sense of "man" in Chaucer's works see Fyler, "Man, Men, and Women."

[14] *Boece*, bk. 3, meter 2, ll. 39–42. Chaucer uses "sche" and "hir" to refer to the bird at ll. 27, 28, 29, and 31, calling into question the editors' correction "[hym]"

ont naturele entencion
qu'el cercheroient volentiers
par quex chemins, par quex sentiers
a franchise venir porroient,
car torjorz avoir la vorroient. (13929–36)[15]

[Know that in the same way all women, whether maids or ladies of
whatever station, have a natural inclination to seek gladly by what
roads and paths they may get their liberty, for they constantly desire
it.]

The caged bird represents the woman constrained by law but pro-
miscuous by nature who sells her favors dearly to avenge herself
on men's duplicity. "Briefment tuit les bolent et trichent, / tuit
sunt ribaut, par tout se fichent, / si les doit l'en ausinc trichier"
(all men, in short, trick and cheat women, all are ribalds and always try to get their way, so women should cheat them right
back) (13235–37). Women should indulge their natural promiscuity to defend themselves against men's depredations by exchang-
ing sex for gifts with as many men as possible. La Vieille's application of the Boethian example illustrates just what Philosophy is
warning against in the caged-bird passage, that false goals such
as wealth can distract humans from the truly good: "naturel en-
tencioun ledeth yow to thilke verray good, but many maner er-
rours mystorneth yow therfro" (*Boece*, bk. 3, prose 3, ll. 6–8). La
Vieille's distortion of Boethius's example marks her with the im-
morality and illogic that Jean draws into her character primarily
from clerical antifeminist writing.

La Vieille invokes the caged bird to comment, as in the *Squire's
Tale*, on specifically courtly deceptions. La Vieille's teachings on
love echo between women the conversation between the God of
Love and the lover in Guillaume de Lorris's commencement to
the *Romance of the Rose*. Her teachings are part of the *Rose*'s
immensely complex response to romance—a response that involves both Guillaume's codifying transformation of romance's

---

for "hem" (singular for plural) at l. 25 (see textual note, 1155). *Ales* as a substantive
is sometimes given masculine modifiers but is usually feminine as in the present
case.

[15] On the relations of this passage to the *Squire's Tale*, see David, 112–13.

events into an emotional drama and Jean's multifaceted critique
of Guillaume.[16] With reference to the *Squire's Tale*, the most suggestive relation between La Vieille and the wronged falcon is that
they both argue from personal experience that all men are inconstant. They do so from radically different perspectives, however.
La Vieille speaks as a disabused pragmatist; her revisions to the
God of Love's instructions seem to invert his ideals for lovers'
conduct. The God of Love's ten commandments to the lover en-
join generosity and faithfulness; La Vieille counters with the instruction "ja larges ne saiez; / en pluseurs leus le queur aiez"
(never be generous; give your heart in several places) (13007–8).[17]
Yet her discourse of manipulation clarifies retrospectively the
manipulative subtext in the God of Love's instructions. Love's
overt incitements to deception, for example by bribing servants
and feigning impatience when separated from the beloved, are for
La Vieille contiguous and compatible with his commands that
men should dress and behave in such a way as to incite love.[18] La
Vieille's focus on deception analyzes romantic courtship as in-
completely mystified self-interest. Women scheme and manipulate, in her view, in response to the courtly manipulations practiced on them by men. Her discourse suggests that the misogyny
Jean builds into her voice is not so much distinct from courtship,
a clerical antifeminism that takes a dim view of desire for women,
as it is latent within courtship itself. In reinterpreting the God of
Love's overt formulation of courtship as a mystified desire that
honors all women, La Vieille resists the codification of the feminine as it has developed in romance.[19] More problematically, she
attempts to make a place for feminine agency in courtship (albeit
an amoral and heavily contested place) by urging women to parody masculine deceptiveness, studying and exaggerating it in
order to take control of courtship.

[16] A recent discussion of Guillaume's debt to romance is Hult, 186–208, 257–62;
the locus classicus on the *Romance of the Rose*, courtly literature including romance, and Chaucer is Muscatine, *Chaucer and the French Tradition*.

[17] La Vieille instructs Bel Aceuil to disobey the God of Love's ninth and tenth
commandments at ll. 12981–13006; contrast the God of Love's instructions according to Guillaume, ll. 2199–2252.

[18] Guillaume, ll. 2121–98, 2543–62; compare *Romaunt of the Rose*, ll. 2247–88,
2695–2716.

[19] Guillaume, l. 2103 ("Toutes fames ser et honore"); *Romaunt of the Rose*, l.
2229.

The similarity between La Vieille's and the falcon's experience of masculine inconstancy, their sense that all men are inconstant, and their invocation of Boethius's caged bird to exemplify gendered behavior suggest in concert that Chaucer speaks to the precedent of the *Romance of the Rose* in this passage from the *Squire's Tale*. Whereas La Vieille signals her amorality by extracting Boethius's exemplum from his argument for rejecting worldly desires and reusing it to license women's promiscuity, the falcon illustrates with the same exemplum a rehabilitation of women's merit that runs throughout the *pars secunda* of the *Squire's Tale*. Both La Vieille and the falcon give the Boethian bird a gender-specific meaning, but by reversing that meaning from feminine to masculine flightiness, the *Squire's Tale* resists the complicity between courtly and misogynist constructions of the feminine that Jean de Meun's text illustrates.[20] La Vieille reveals that complicity but works within its terms, and consequently speaks less directly against the grain of gender constraints than does the wronged falcon.

Indeed, the falcon works a series of inversions on masculinity in her account of the tercelet's behavior. Her analysis splits men's "gentillesse of blood" from their "kynde," attributing the doubleness she has experienced from her tercelet to a contradiction in men's nature:

> So newefangel been they of hire mete,
> And loven novelries of propre kynde,
> No gentillesse of blood ne may hem bynde.
> So ferde this tercelet, allas the day!
> Though he were gentil born. . . .   (V 618–22)

By setting the faithfulness that "gentillesse of blood" would guarantee against the inconstancy that "propre kynde" inspires, the falcon ascribes to men a paradoxical, disunified nature reminiscent of that ascribed to women in romance. Her metaphors of veiling and preening also reverse the culturally pervasive associations

---

[20] By the fifteenth century the association of men with courtly deceptions and *novelerie* has become a topos (see Benson, "Courtly Love"). In *Partonope* Melior complains that ". . . well by me / Eche woman may ensampell take. / For fayre wordes men can make / I-nowe, tyll they haue here luste. / Here loue wolde they neuer after truste, / Butte besy hem tyll they haue a newe. . . . / Ye loue so well Nouelrye" (6015–20, 6024).

between women and deceptively alluring appearance: her suitor's falseness is "wrapped under humble cheere / And under hewe of trouthe" in colors dyed "depe in greyn" (V 507–8, 511); his falseness is imperceptible because "So peynted he and kembde at point-devys / As wel his wordes as his contenaunce" (V 560–61). His preening, like that conventionally attributed to women, is inextricably self-enhancing and self-concealing. Further reversing the positions of feminine and masculine in the falcon's account are the several animal metaphors for her suitor's conduct: "Right as a serpent hit hym under floures" (V 512); "Anon this tigre, ful of doublenesse, / Fil on his knees" (V 543–44); and of course the caged bird who is so oddly analogous to both a man and a tercelet. These metaphors revise the tale's first and framing association between Canacee's sympathetic femininity and the natural world of the birds. Within that initially exoticized feminine space, the falcon articulates masculinity as a still more animal, unstable, and elusively metamorphosing duplicity. By so figuring men's nature, the falcon establishes her own claim to a contrasting and distinctively feminine reliability: Canacee hangs her cage in "veluettes blewe / In signe of trouthe that is in wommen sene" (V 644–45).

The falcon's radical inversions take place, as do Dorigen's distortions and exaggerations, in a playful context that might counter their effort to speak against the grain of gender construction. That Dorigen speaks "in pley" may not only express her alienation from courtship but also restrict the impact of her words, setting her critique of courtship off the record. The detached narratorial comments on Dorigen's two laments in the *Franklin's Tale*—she mourns "As doon thise noble wyves whan hem liketh" and plans for "a day or tweye" to kill herself—further lighten the weight accorded to her words (V 818, 1457). The *Squire's Tale* so insists on feminine *trouthe* and yet in so fantastic a mode that its claims too may be suspect. The Wife of Bath, whose resistance to social rank as well as gender constructions will figure in the third chapter of this study, recalls Dorigen in declaring that "myn entente nys but for to pleye" (III 192). Her powerfully illogical "fantasye" may implicitly cancel her gender inversions even before they are articulated—as in Chaunticleer's "*Mulier est hominis confusio:* /

Madame, the sentence of this Latyn is, / 'Womman is mannes joye and al his blis'" (III 190, 516; VII 3164–66). The latent masculine retort seems to be the necessary context for the feminine articulations that oppose it.

Calling these articulations "feminine" is not to deny the cultural authority of male writers such as Chaucer or the masculine perspectives of dominant literary conventions. What is "feminine" about Dorigen, Canacee, and the falcon works itself out in terms of those conventions. For Chaucer, treating women's voices lightly places them in a register where playing with gender becomes possible. Within the limitations of his literary situation, Chaucer's playfulness illustrates the theoretical concept that mimicry and misquotation can reconfigure the cultural constraints placed on gender. Dorigen's parodic exaggerations of a feminine voice, like the falcon's inversions of gendered attributes, do not so much escape the categories they critique as they mime and estrange them, placing a distance between the conventional categories and the speaker who is asked to instantiate them.

EMBODIED VOICES

The falcon's cries and self-wounding in the *Squire's Tale* introduce a strategy of expression that is based not in speech but in the close association between femininity and the body. Striking herself with wings and beak "til the rede blood / Ran endelong the tree ther-as she stood," the falcon communicates the loss she has suffered through her physical suffering (V 415–16). Critics have noted a cultural referent for this scene in Christian sacrifice: the dry tree in which the falcon sits suggests the cross, and the falcon herself recalls the self-wounding pelican that represents Christ in bestiaries.[21] Romances provide a referent more apposite to the tale's generic affiliations and the falcon's predicament. The courted lady, seen and understood first of all as an alluring and adorned body, may find that manipulating her body communicates more effectively than does voicing her positions.

---

[21] See Meindl and the summary of further work in the *Variorum Edition* of the *Squire's Tale*, 204–5n. The variorum editors do not approve specifically Christian references, but I would defend a less focused invocation of martyrdom for love in the passage.

The identification of the feminine with the corporeal is of course not specific to romance: as De Lauretis summarizes, "the representation of woman as image . . . is so pervasive in our culture, well before and beyond the institution of cinema, that it necessarily constitutes a starting point for any understanding of sexual difference and its ideological effects in the construction of social subjects" (*Alice Doesn't*, 37–38; see also Ferrante, *Woman as Image*). Medieval romance is a notable and, for later literature, a foundational site for elaborating and refining the connection between femininity and the observed body. The origin of love in looking on a woman's beauty, a lyric topos soon allegorized in the God of Love's arrows shot to the lover's eyes in the *Romance of the Rose*, dictates in romance the precedence of physical description (rhetorical *effictio*) in introducing female characters and *effictio*'s place in adumbrating traits of character.[22] The masculine gaze, as we have seen in the first chapter, both establishes feminine beauty as its object of desire and sees masculinity reflected back to itself in the difference between the ideal feminine and masculine identity. Moreover, when the courted lady looks back at her suitor, her look affirms the primacy of his deeds over his appearance. The paradigmatic exchange of looks takes place at a tournament or a siege where the knight takes inspiration for his deeds from looking on his lady, while the lady's gaze witnesses to deeds of prowess among knights (see Fradenberg, *City, Marriage, Tournament*). Romances persistently conceive the female body in terms of its desirability for courtship, licensing a certain inertness in the worthy woman that contrasts with her suitor's active demonstration of merit.

The destruction of beauty draws meaning from this grounding of the courted lady's identity in her appearance. For example, when Herodis learns in *Sir Orfeo* that a fairy king will steal her away from Orfeo, her wordless lament communicates to Orfeo by reversing her complaisant beauty. Orfeo observes her bodily anguish and asks,

> O lef liif, what is te,
> Þat euer ȝete hast ben so stille,

[22] An early instance of a feminine portrait in which great beauty promises good character is that of Enide (Chrétien de Troyes, *Erec et Enide*, ll. 401–41, 509–46); see Sargent-Bauer.

& now gredest wonder schille?
Þi bodi, þat was so white y-core,
Wiþ þine nailes is al to-tore!
Allas! þi rode, þat was so red,
Is al wan, as þou were ded;
& al-so þine fingres smale
Beþ al blodi & al pale.
Allas! þi louesom eyȝen to
Lokeþ so man doþ on his fo!

(Auchinleck MS, 102–12)

Although Herodis's cries and self-wounding await a verbal explanation, they already have meaning for Orfeo as shocking reversals
of her feminine attractiveness. Herodis's quietness and her rosy
and fair complexion are identifying traits for Orfeo that she reverses through her cries, pallor, and bleeding. She seems to be undoing her relation to Orfeo, most evidently in that her "louesum
eyȝen to / Lokeþ so man doþ on his fo," but more generally in
destroying her beauty. When she speaks, her narrative of abduction by the fairy king confirms her body's visible message of division from her lover. By communicating her loss first of all through
a bodily spectacle rather than speech, Herodis recognizes as does
Orfeo that her body is crucial to her identity in the relationship
she is losing.

The abandoned falcon of the *Squire's Tale* similarly laments
first of all in cries and self-mutilation that she later glosses in her
narrative of loss. Exceptional beauty is again the context for
beauty's destruction:

Ther sat a faucon over hire heed ful hye,
That with a pitous voys so gan to crye
That all the wode resouned of hire cry.
Ybeten hadde she hirself so pitously
With bothe hir wynges til the rede blood
Ran endelong the tree ther-as she stood.
. . . ther nas nevere yet no man on lyve,
If that I koude a faucon wel discryve,
That herde of swich another of fairnesse,
As wel of plumage as of gentillesse
Of shap, of al that myghte yrekened be.

(V 411–16, 423–27)

As in *Sir Orfeo*, the spectacle of self-wounding communicates before speech. Indeed, Canacee in some sense "hath understonde what this faucon seyde" before she asks the falcon to explain why "evere in oon she cryde alwey and shrighte" (V 437, 417). The falcon's cries and blood, manifesting her grief on the scene of her beautiful body, signify either "sorwe of deeth or los of love" (V 450). In the syntax of courtly sentiment her self-destruction has sufficiently determinate meaning to amount to a kind of speech.

The falcon's self-wounding communicates bereavement to Canacee, but it also expresses a profound helplessness in the face of events. Herodis and the falcon represent their incapacity to act effectively through their acquiescence to courtship's conflation of the body with identity. Their violence might protest the conflation, but their violence is nonetheless directed against themselves. Canacee so describes the falcon's action in the telling reflexives of "ye youreself upon yourself yow wreke" (V 454). In attacking their bodies Herodis and the falcon suggest that externally directed action is impossible for them; instead they turn on their bodies both to signal and to yield to the equivalence struck within courtship between their external appearance and their identity.

A bodily distortion that could resist that relation is the Amazonian practice, widely attested in classical and medieval sources, of removing one breast. This practice represents the Amazons' war-making identity (in that it facilitates the use of bow or shield), their refusal to nurture sons (whom they kill, maim, or turn over to their fathers), and their resistance to amorous relations generally in favor of virginity and chastity. The very etymology of the name *Amazon* is said to derive from the practice: in the version from the prose *Roman de Troie*, "maintenant que elle est nee, li copent elle[s] sa senestre mamelle por estre plus delivre a l'escu porter, et por ce ont elles a non Amazoines, c'est a dire: sans l'une des mameles" (as soon as she [a daughter] is born, they cut off her left breast so she will be more able to carry a shield, and because of this they are called Amazons, that is to say, lacking a breast).[23] The one bare breast the Amazons show in battle further empha-

[23] Quoted from MS Bib. Nat. f. fr. 1612, in Benoit de Sainte-Maure, *Roman de Troie*, 6:304.

sizes their rejection of passivity and sexuality together. The Amazon queen Penthesilee of Benoit de Sainte-Maure's *Roman de Troie* associates her companions' war making with chastity:

> Tu cuides que nos seions taus
> Come autres femmes comunaus,
> Que les cors ont vains e legiers:
> Ço n'est mie nostre mestiers.
> Puceles somes: n'avons cure
> De mauvaistié ne de luxure;
> Le regne qui nous apartient
> Defendons si que rien ne crient:
> N'est peceiez, arz ne maumis. (24091–99)[24]

[You think we are like ordinary women who have fragile, weak bodies: that is not at all our way. We are virgins; we have no care for wickedness or lust; we defend the realm that belongs to us such that it fears nothing; it is not ravaged, burned, or ruined.]

Yet this Penthesilee has come to aid the Trojans out of love for Hector, a motivation Benoit adds to his source as he omits mastectomy from his description of Amazonian ways (ll. 23302–56; Petit, "Traitement courtois," 68). In the *Roman d'Alexandre*'s Amazonian episode the queen's emissaries fall in love with followers of Alexander and the Amazons' practices do not include mastectomy (ll. 7237–70, 7395–7643). The women of Scythia in Thomas of Kent's *Alexander*, in contrast, do not fall in love with Alexander or his men, and "De la destre part n'ont cressant mameles; / Hom les ard de fer quant sunt jovenes puceles" (on the right side their breasts do not grow; they are seared with iron when they are little girls) (6177–78). Other *romans antiques*, in the above episodes from *Troie* and the *Roman d'Alexandre* and in *Eneas*'s depiction of the woman warrior Camille, show a preoccupation very early in the history of romance with Amazonian prowess and chastity as a potential model for femininity.

The *romans antiques* suppress the Amazonian gesture of re-

---

[24] Virgil (and classical sources) have the Amazons uncover a breast in battle (*Aeneid* 1.491–93, 11.648–49. On the significance of baring a breast in relation to chastity in the Christian tradition, see Miles; Fradenberg's chapter "The Black Lady" discusses cultural associations between winning an exotic woman and conquering land (*City, Marriage, Tournament*, 244–64).

moving a breast, so telling in classical and many medieval works, as part of a process that relocates the dynamic of women's resistance and subordination from Amazonian militancy to the metaphorical combat of courtship. For classical writers the Amazons were not positive figures but challengers to Athenian civilization, outsiders aligned with animals and barbarians whose "topsy-turvy world," in W. B. Tyrrell's phrase, must be destroyed in order for Greekness and masculinity to attain their proper ascendancy.[25] As mythic adversary to all that is Greek, the Amazon is to be subdued by the superiority of Greek men, whether in battle or by rape or marriage. The *romans antiques* present Amazons and woman warriors more positively, and not only in evading classical references to their practices of killing or crippling their sons and removing one of their daughters' breasts. The romances' revisions amount in the favorable interpretation of Aimé Petit to "une féminisation des Amazones," culminating in their "normalisation" when they fall in love and marry in the *Roman d'Alexandre*.[26] Now they are exemplary in both prowess and beauty, they are chaste but available to courtship, and they have recovered susceptibility to tenderness with their previously lacking breasts. As I see it, however, the gestures of subordination that accompany the Amazons' reintegration with masculine culture qualify Petit's argument for a completeness or amplitude in women that is predicated on the restored breast.

When Alexander hears of the Amazons' prowess in the *Roman d'Alexandre*, he first conceives their independence as a military issue: "Se je icele terre nen ai en ma baillie, / Et je ne puis avoir sor eles segnorie, / Dont porrai je bien dire ma proësce est faillie" (If I cannot take control of that country and have lordship over the women, then truly I can say my prowess has failed) (7251–53). But

[25] Tyrrell, 63; on monomastia see Tyrrell, 47, 49; on the meanings of Amazons in classical literature see also duBois.

[26] Petit, "Traitement courtois," 75; see also Petit, "La Reine Camille." Petit quotes Honoré de Balzac's association between the breast and feminine qualities (versus the masculine connotations of riding) from *La Comédie Humaine*: "J'ai remarqué que la plupart des femmes qui montent bien à cheval ont peu de tendresse. Comme aux Amazones, il leur manque une mamelle, et leurs coeurs sont endurcis en un certain endroit" (I have noticed that most women who ride horses well have little tenderness. Like Amazons, they are lacking a breast, and a place in their hearts has hardened) ("Thème des Amazones," 74).

the Amazon queen's warning dream of a peahen and her chicks taking refuge from an eagle by running into the kitchen transposes the conflict to the domestic sphere, preparing for her emissaries' amatory bonds with Alexander's men as they deliver her message of fealty to Alexander. Even in her message the language of love and fealty are indistinguishable: "La roïne vos mande que ele est vostre amie, / Son anel vos envoie par molt grant drüerie" (the queen wants you to know that she is your friend [or sweetheart]; she sends you her ring out of great devotion [or passionate love]).[27] Penthesilee of the *Roman de Troie* is similarly drawn to the cause of Troy by her love for Hector, although his death preserves her status as a chaste queen (ll. 23357–416). Consensual surrender, amatory and political, overcomes the Amazons' militant opposition from within their own consciousness: rather than suffering defeat by men, they suffer susceptibility to men's desires for love and rule. Deleting the practice of removing a breast at birth from their accounts of Amazon society, the *romans antiques* prepare to transform the Amazon from an opponent of masculine culture into an admirable figure of beauty and prowess, a worthy participant in courtship.

The *Knight's Tale* traces this shift from classical to romance versions of the Amazon in its presentation of Hippolyta's and Emelye's contrasting fates. Boccaccio records the shift in the *Teseida*, curiously, by noting the practice of mastectomy when he narrates Teseo's conquest of the Amazons, but praising Emilia's beautiful breasts at the time of her marriage to Palemone (bk. 1, st. 5n; bk. 12, st. 61). Boccaccio pictures the defeated Amazons transforming themselves as they set down their arms and look on Teseo's men, becoming modest, beautiful, and well-dressed, taking smaller steps and singing sweetly (bk. 1, sts. 132–34). Are we to imagine that love even swells the seared breast? The opening episode of the *Knight's Tale* draws instead on the classical sensibility of Statius's *Thebaid*, where the only context for Hippolyta's marriage is the military conquest of the Amazons; marriage is not so much a consequence as an aspect of the queen's defeat. The women of Athens observe the spectacle of Hippolyta's subjected and altered body, marveling that she has broken with Amazon

---

[27] Ll. 7597–98; compare "La roïne vos mande que vos estes ses drus" (l. 7585); the warning dream is at ll. 7305–34.

custom, "quod pectora palla / tota latent, magnis quod barbara semet Athenis / misceat atque hosti ueniat paritura marito" (that all her breast is hidden beneath her robe, that although a barbarian she has intercourse with the mighty Athenian, that she comes to bear children to her enemy and husband) (bk. 12, ll. 537–39). Although "patiens ... mariti foederis" (accepting patiently the marriage contract), Hippolyta is still identifiably barbarian, an outsider brought under Athenian control by force (bk. 12, ll. 534–35).[28] In the *Knight's Tale* as well, marriage is consequent on military defeat with no intervening movement of consensual subordination or self-transformation on the part of the Amazons. Parallel clauses recount that Theseus has "conquered al the regne of Femenye ... And weddede the queene Ypolita" (I 866, 868); that it would be too long to tell "of the grete bataille for the nones" and "of the feste that was at hir weddynge" (I 879, 883). No reference to courtship mediates between Hippolyta's defeat and her marriage. The classicism of this opening episode will, however, be tempered in the case of Hippolyta's "yonge suster Emelye" (I 871).

Young Emelye and the scions of Thebes, Palamon and Arcite, echo the combat and alliance of Hippolyta and Theseus in the new register of courtship. The shift from warfare to courtship plays out a generic shift from epic to romance. The *Roman d'Alexandre* dramatizes this shift by juxtaposing the Amazon queen who swears fealty because of Alexander's military superiority and her very young emissaries Floré and Biauté who fall in love with two of Alexander's followers. To be sure, military confrontations remain important in romances subsequent to the *romans antiques*, but I have argued in the first chapter that one generic distinction of romance is to figure women as objects of heterosexual courtship, courtship as metaphorical combat, and the experience of love as integral to knightly identity.[29] Palamon and Arcite, the younger generation's version of the Theban brothers Eteocles and Polynices who make war with each other over their

---

[28] Chaucer's opening scene draws on Statius, bk. 12, ll. 519–610.

[29] Theseus gains this aspect of knightly identity retrospectively through his speech on love claiming that "in my tyme a servant was I oon" (I 1814). That he has passed beyond the time of service to love reinforces the connection between love and youth, while also suggesting a hierarchy of commitments, drawn from philosophical literature, in which romantic love has a relatively low standing.

rights to rule, transfer that rivalry to the affective conflict over Emelye.[30] Palamon and Arcite's persistently combative metaphors for Emelye's effect on them accomplish in turn her displacement from warrior to courted lady: Palamon is "hurt right now thurghout myn eye" by "the fairnesse of that lady that I see" and Arcite agrees that Emelye's "fresshe beautee sleeth me sodeynly" (I 1096, 1098, 1118).

Palamon and Arcite's experience of love, as argued in the preceding chapter, expands and complicates their chivalric relation to one another, but the experience of their courtship does not similarly enlarge Emelye's Amazonian identity. Her lethal beauty replaces Amazonian prowess in battle rather than doubling it; Emelye is conspicuously inactive throughout the tale except for unknowingly wounding her lovers with her beauty. In contrast to the more aware and resourceful Emilia of Boccaccio's *Teseida*, for Emelye beauty is so consonant with passivity that her status as Palamon and Arcite's beloved diametrically reverses her status as Amazon. Here the conjoined beauty and prowess of Penthesilee, Floré, and Biauté in the *romans antiques* yields to the later romances' fully demilitarized women. Even as early as *Eneas*, the death of Camille, a virgin warrior though not an Amazon, foregrounds a contradiction between prowess and beauty in women. All Turnus's followers marvel at Camille, "qui tant ert proz et tant ert bele" (who was so brave and beautiful), and on her tomb they note again the consonance of prowess and beauty in her: "Ci gist Camile la pucelle, / qui molt fu proz et molt fu belle" (here lies the maiden Camille who was very brave and very beautiful) (4094, 7663–64). But Eneas's follower Tarcon taunts her, just before she is killed, that her chivalry is incompatible with femininity:

> Feme ne se doit pas combatre,
> se par nuit non tot an gisant;

[30] On the relation between Palamon and Arcite and Eteocles and Polynices of the *Roman de Thèbes* and the *Thebaid* see Patterson, *Chaucer*, 198–202; Anderson. Anderson argues strongly for the epic associations of the *Knight's Tale*, particularly for its imitation of Statius across its use of Boccaccio, but his argument (212–19) that Palamon and Arcite's private and affective rivalry revises the military and political rivalry of Eteocles and Polynices in my view sustains a generic shift toward romance rather than an allegiance to epic.

la puet fere home recreant . . .
. . . ne mostrez vostre proësce.
Ce ne est pas vostre mestier,
mes filer, coldre et taillier;
en bele chanbre soz cortine
fet bon esbatre o tel meschine.

(7076–78, 7084–88)[31]

[A woman should not enter into combat, except at night lying down;
there she can defeat a man. . . . Do not show your prowess. That is
not your business, but rather spinning, sewing, and clipping. In a
pretty room behind the bedcurtains it's good to fight with a maiden
like you.]

Tarcon's comment on femininity, which the *Eneas* poet adds to
Virgil's episode, charges that for women there is no reciprocity of
literal and metaphorical combat. Identifying women so fully with
sexuality and domesticity allows Tarcon to claim that Camille's
presence on the battlefield is a gauche attempt at seduction:
"Venistes ça por vos mostrer? / Ge ne vos voil pas acheter; / por-
tant blanche vos voi et bloie" (Do you come here to show yourself? I do not want to buy you, though I see you are fair and blonde)
(7089–91). Assigned to an authoritative Trojan voice, this critique reinforces the plot's wider contrasts between Dido and Camille and the superior Lavine, preparing for Camille's death not
only on the battlefield but in the genre as a model of femininity
that combines prowess with beauty. The woman warrior revives
in Renaissance versions of romance, but for later medieval romances, as Edmond Faral has noted, it is Camille's *effictio*, the
static portrait of her beauty, that becomes paradigmatic rather
than her prowess.[32]

---

[31] *Eneas* adds the comments on femininity to the corresponding speech in Virgil's *Aeneid* 11.732–40. Compare Thomas of Kent's similar conclusion to his account of Scythian women allied with Alexander: "Mult vienent bel en l'ost; donc
dient li purvers: / 'Cy freit bon combatre en un bois a envers!'" (They looked so
fine in the army that lecherous men said, "These would be good to fight in a woods
on their backs") (6190–91).
[32] Concerning Camille's portrait (ll. 3959–4046), Faral comments, "sans doute
les contemporains ont-ils apprécié cette singulière production, puisque, doréna-
vant, dans tous les romans postérieurs, elle sera prise comme modèle et fournira la
formule de tous les portraits à venir" (contemporaries no doubt approved of this

The history of women warriors in the *romans antiques*, tracing how courtship's metaphorical combat comes to supplant military confrontation, prepares for Emelye's ascendancy over the "faire, hardy queene of Scythia" (I 882) in the plot of the *Knight's Tale*. In Emelye hardiness is divorced from fairness, which alone defines her desirability for her lovers. I will argue in chapter 5 that her lovers' radical detachment from her productively complicates her identity for them, invoking a sense of adventure around her. In considering here the feminine body's potential for communication, it is the lovers' apprehension of her beauty that deserves mention. Only her beauty speaks to them, and so compellingly as to transform their lives. On the one hand, their susceptibility to beauty and Emelye's to a responsive affection—in the "freendlich ye" she casts on victorious Arcite and the tender love that follows on her marriage to Palamon—contrast her status as courted lady to Hippolyta's as defeated Amazon (I 2680, 3103). Yet Emelye's susceptibility to love appears in these post-facto notations so muted as to interrogate its substantiality. Moreover, Emelye's body communicates to her lovers independently of her will, knowledge, and desire, calling as much attention to the disconsonance of her body and her faculties as to their final harmony. In the end, Emelye's fate seems more to repeat Hippolyta's than to contrast with it. The matches arranged for her first with Arcite and later with Palamon resemble Hippolyta's with Theseus in that all are under the control of Theseus and instantiate his victory over the Amazons. Palamon and Arcite's sense that Emelye is fiercely resistant rather than merely ignorant of their suit is consonant with her Amazonian origins and her expressed resistance in the temple of Diana. The virtually spurious mutuality of Emelye's two matches invites readers to reconsider whether courtship's metaphoric combat has transformed or only mystified the combative hostility enacted in Amazon culture and its conquest. That Emelye's fairness is the sole referent for Palamon and

---

remarkable passage since from then on, in all subsequent romances, it was used as a model and furnished the formula for all the portraits to come) (413). Huchet analyzes in detail the gendered implications of Camille's portrait: *Roman médiéval*, 68–74. On Renaissance significances for Amazons in relation to gender, see the essays by Margaret Sullivan, Alison Taufer, and Susanne Woods in *Playing with Gender*.

Arcite's love further invites us to recall that severing a breast sig-
nified for the Amazons severing the bond between feminine
beauty and involvement in heterosexual courtship. Mastectomy
vanishes as the romance genre returns Amazons to the domestic
scene of courtship and marriage. Emelye's experience of undesired
love illustrates the loss of feminine agency entailed in that return
to the unmutilated body.

In the context of courtship, then, Amazons represent a disappearing rather than a potential site of assertion through bodily distortion. A third kind of distortion, more characteristic of the genre
than either self-wounding or Amazonian mastectomy, provides a
language for female characters that comments more fully on the
relation between body and identity. By their own magic or under
enchantment, female characters in romance may take more than
one bodily form. Shape-shifting can be read in two directions, one
tending toward reinforcing an image of feminine alienness and
contradiction. This is the more accessible reading of shape-shifting, linked to wider literary contexts such as the theological, medical, and legal disputations on "Is woman a monster?" and "Is
woman inhuman?" Ian Maclean in his useful survey notes that
medieval writers treat these questions facetiously and finally af-
firm woman's humanity (12–13, 30–33, 70–72). The questions
nonetheless voice possibilities that are not fully contained by
their negation. Shape-shifting in romance offers a striking con-
cretization of feminine uncanniness, whether by mixing human
with animal forms as in the serpent-woman Melusine, by juxtaposing contradictory images of woman as in the loathly-lovely
Ragnell, or by simply deceiving the masculine gaze. The uncanniness of women's shape-shifting is the starting point for my reading in chapter 4 of magical powers ascribed to women in romance.
Here I will pursue a different and perhaps less evident reading that
finds in shape-shifting an attempt to break the bond that ties feminine identity to bodily appearance.

The loathly lady of the *Wife of Bath's Tale* has close literary
affiliations with those of the *Marriage of Sir Gawaine* and the
Weddynge of Sir Gawen and Dame Ragnell who transform themselves for Gawain when he marries them in exchange for their aid
and surrenders sovereignty to them. John Gower's tale of Florent

in the *Confessio Amantis* uses a similar plot to a more neatly didactic end than do the Arthurian versions. Melusine, who meets a desperate Raymondin in the woods and aids him in return for marriage, is a rather distant analogue to Chaucer's loathly lady in that Melusine's transformations take place every week and constitute an ongoing test of submission for Raymondin, until he breaks his promise not to seek her out on Saturdays and so brings about her permanent transformation into a serpent. A still more distant analogue is the enchanted lady of *Le Bel Inconnu* and *Lybeaus Desconus* who requires only a kiss from one of Gawain's kin to transform her from serpent to woman.[33]

Beyond the masculine experience of contradiction lies the further implication in shape-shifting that feminine identity is not inherent in bodily appearance. Shifting from superlative repulsiveness to attractiveness redoubles the emphasis on appearance that characterizes the feminine position in courtship, but undermines the derivation of stable meaning from appearance. Shapeshifting offers, if not a way out of the body, a way to indict its tyranny over the feminine by dramatizing its arbitrariness. Further, by countering their repulsive manifestations with hyperbolically appealing ones, shapeshifters raise the possibility that beauty is not native to woman but is an artificially produced masquerade. The concept of womanliness as masquerade has a long history in psychoanalytic theory, where it has seemed to represent not a strategy for confronting gender construction but either a given of woman's construction or a compulsive exaggeration of the given. So fully does the identity formation of women associate them with the body, the image, and the desired over against masculine thought and signification that, in Joan Riviere's influential study, for a woman to locate her meaning in the gestures and behaviors of stereotypical femininity is inescapable. Citing the case of a successful professional who felt driven to flirt and act subservient to her male colleagues, to "put on a mask of womanliness" in compensation for her competence, Riviere comments, "The

---

[33] On the occurrence of the shape-shifting woman in a wider literary context see Sumner, ed., *Weddynge of Sir Gawen*, xiii–xxvii. My quotations from the *Marriage of Sir Gawaine* and *Weddynge of Sir Gawen* are from *Sources and Analogues*, 235–64 (Whiting reproduces earlier editions with a few corrections); the tale of Florent is quoted from Gower, *Confessio Amantis*.

reader may now ask how I define womanliness or where I draw
the line between genuine womanliness and the 'masquerade.' My
suggestion is not, however, that there is any such difference;
whether radical or superficial, they are the same thing" (210, 213).
For Riviere, womanliness is itself a mask, a fabrication that answers masculine desire by meeting that desire's specifications.

The classic version of masquerade sees no escape from
woman's identification with her body, but recently a few related
suggestions have opened the idea of masquerade to the possibility
of resisting that identification. Mary Ann Doane proposes that
Riviere's account in fact attributes to masquerading women "the
distance, alienation, and divisiveness of self" which is denied to
women conceived as coterminous with their image but which is
accorded to men in the model of development that relates men's
awareness of difference between body and identity to the capacity
to signify in language ("Masquerade Reconsidered," 47; see also
Doane, "Film and the Masquerade"). Masquerade demonstrates a
self-consciousness that belies the cultural association of femininity with the imagistic, unreflective object of desire. The woman
reads her own image and reproduces herself, perhaps in a playful
exaggeration that pushes at the limits of her construction. Irigaray, who uses "masquerade" only negatively, with Riviere, to describe women experiencing desire by experiencing themselves as
the objects of masculine desire, develops also an idea of mimicry
or "playing with mimesis" that resembles Doane's revised masquerade. To mimic is to "assume the feminine role deliberately.
Which means already to convert a form of subordination into an
affirmation, and thus begin to thwart it. . . . To play with mimesis
is thus, for a woman, to try to recover the place of her exploitation
by discourse, without allowing herself to be simply reduced to it"
(This Sex, 76). We have seen that Dorigen and the falcon attempt
such mimicry in their responses to courtship. Taking "discourse"
in its wider sense of any system of signification that encodes a
specific endeavor would apply Irigaray's mimicry to gendered behavior as well as to language. Judith Butler sees a similar potential
for bodily significations, in that they challenge the association of
the body with "mute facticity," with an innate sexuality that precedes the constructions of gender. Under the rubric of "performa-
tive subversions" she argues that a range of bodily exaggerations

and distortions, such as glamour, crossdressing, and drag, can in their deliberateness shift entrenched dichotomies between body and intellect, and between female and male (128–29).[34] This constellation of approaches to bodily manipulations, arising from a variety of theoretical projects whose differences I do not mean to elide, provides a context for considering how shape-shifting comments on feminine identity in romance.

Shape-shifting women put on beauty like a costume, rewarding a kiss, marriage, or obedience with a superlative body. Their assumed and hyperbolic beauty amounts to a masquerade that marks a distinction between their identities and their played-up bodies. The "olde wyf" of the *Wife of Bath's Tale* introduces her transformation with offhanded confidence and tailors her new shape to her audience's taste: "But natheless, syn I knowe youre delit, / I shal fulfille youre worldly appetit" (III 1046, 1217–18). Further, the shape-shifting masquerade deploys the grotesque as well as the glamorous to exaggerate and question femininity. Here two problems complicate the effort to find agency and self-definition in masquerade: most of the plots in question identify the shapeshifter with her beautiful rather than her grotesque body, and most shapeshifters finally claim that they were not responsible for their grotesque forms.

It might be argued that the works under consideration make the beautiful woman the only true form of the shapeshifter since the misshapen body is associated with a spell or a test of faith, and the shapely body rewards the man who breaks the spell and passes the test. Dame Ragnell describes the spell she was under as a bodily deformation ("thus was I disformyd") and the narration concurs that breaking the spell restores the lost truth of her body: "she was recouered of that she was defoylyd" (*Weddynge of Sir Gawen*, 699, 710). In *Lybeaus Desconus* the enchanted serpent body falls off to reveal the naked beauty that the spell merely concealed: "þe warmys tayle and wynge / Anon hyt fall fro hyre" (Cotton MS, 2009–10). But the persistence of recognizably female qualities in the deformed bodies questions the equivalence the plots seem to strike between beauty and the natural identity of

---

[34] For a fine discussion of aspects of female disguise in medieval literature see Fradenberg, *City, Marriage, Tournament*, 244–64 ("The Black Lady").

woman. Dame Ragnell's "hangyng pappys to be an hors lode," the "lothly wommannysch figure" of the tale of Florent, the lady "witched" in the *Marriage of Sir Gawaine* to "walke in womans liknesse, / Most like a feend of hell," and the vermilion lips of the serpent that kisses Giglain against his will instantiate a repulsive, aggressive womanhood that supplements the desirable femininity these women can also manifest.[35] The loathly lady's unsolicited lustfulness contributes to her association with wildness and bestiality, as Richard Bernheimer has shown, but it also contributes to her intimate threat to men: "Whosoeuer kisses this lady," Sir Kay remarks, "of his kisse he stands in feare" (Bernheimer, 33–38; *Marriage of Sir Gawaine*, 239). The shapeshifter masquerades in both the beautiful and the deformed bodies, then, because both are exaggerated versions of womanhood that solicit a sexual reaction from men. This doubling of the masquerade complicates its challenge to gender categories. If both bodies are female, what are the defining characteristics of femaleness? In every case the transformed body recalls its other form by the perfect opposition of its qualities: Chaucer's hag "so loothly, and so oold also" now "so fair was, and so yong therto" (III 1100, 1251). The destabilizations that shape-shifting accomplishes are substantial and significant despite the plots' concluding promise that the shapeshifter has achieved a stable body.

In those conclusions, Melusine, Dame Ragnell, and other transformed wives claim that a stepmother or an angry mother was responsible for both the monstrous body and the monstrous demand for masculine submission; the wife, for her part, wants only to serve and obey.[36] Belatedly attributing the grotesque body to absent women does not cancel the masquerade performed by unfolding femininity into repulsiveness versus attractiveness; to the extent that the masquerade was the mother's, it is still feminine and still disrupts the bond between identity and body. Moreover, the closing abdication of agency does not fully encompass the ex-

---

[35] *Weddynge of Sir Gawen*, l. 241; Gower, *Confessio Amantis*, bk. 1, l. 1530; *Marriage of Sir Gawaine*, 240; Renaut de Beaujeu, *Le Bel Inconnu*, ll. 3181–3211 ("Li diables m'a encanté, / Que j'ai baissié otre mon gré," ll. 3209–10).

[36] The tale of Florent, *Weddynge of Sir Gawen*, *Marriage of Sir Gawaine*, and *Melusine* attribute the transformation to a mother or stepmother; male enchanters are responsible for the serpent form in *Le Bel Inconnu*.

uberant spectacle that the enchanted woman can make of herself. Melusine does shut herself up on Saturdays, but when Raymondin can no longer resist peeping in at her, she could not have displayed herself more provocatively: she reclines naked in a raised marble bath combing her hair; her enormous tail "so long it was that she made it to touche oftymes, whyle that raymondyn beheld her, the rouf of the chambre that was ryght hye."[37] Ragnell's demand for a public wedding and her gross display of gluttony at the wedding feast are presumably her own flourishes on the stepmother's transformation of her shape, flourishes that make her grotesque body memorable and meaningful even after her return to beauty. These works accomplish obliquely a masquerade that the *Wife of Bath's Tale* takes on directly by refusing even the attempt to explain away the shapeshifter's double body and the perplexing residue each form leaves in its opposite.

Far from experiencing shame or displeasure at her foulness, Chaucer's old wife deploys it, "smylynge everemo," to explore the limits of masculine desire (III 1086). The knight's miserable conviction that "it wol nat been amended nevere mo" (III 1099) contrasts with the old wife's superior control both in her masterly verbal demonstration that nothing is amiss and in her physical self-transformation. The body that answers to the knight's worldly desire is a second case of the superlative spectacle she offers to his gaze. In her ugly form, "a fouler wight ther may no man devyse"; after transforming herself, she presents herself theatrically in a second visual spectacle: "Cast up the curtyn, looke how that it is" (III 999, 1249). This emphasis on the visual seems to provide reliable information—the knight "saugh verraily al this" and is joyful (III 1250–52)—but the very representation of two female bodies denies the complete veracity of either and contributes to constituting both as masquerades of womanliness, exaggerated facades reflecting back to the knight his own standards of repulsion and desire.

The old wife's playful mimicry of ugliness and beauty opens the question of whether her words might partake of her masquerade.

---

[37] English *Melusine*, 297; cf. the French *Mélusine*, 242: "du nombril en aval estoit en forme de la queue d'un serpent, aussi grosse comme une tonne ou on met harenc, et longue durement, et debatoit de sa coue l'eaue tellement qu'elle la faisoit saillir jusques a la voulte de la chambre."

The superlative submission of "dooth with my lyf and deth right as yow lest" suits masquerading beauty just as the earlier reproach "ye faren lyk a man had lost his wit" matches the aggressiveness of the ugly body (III 1248, 1095). Dame Ragnell in her ugly form similarly charges Gawain to "shewe me your cortesy in bed" and switches her attitude with her body in the first words out of her pretty new mouth: "She sayd, 'What is youre wylle?'" (630, 643). Changes so extreme, particularly the timing of Ragnell's submissive words, which come before the testing question has even been put to Gawain, reinforce the possibility that these husbands may be winning access not to the lady's true identity but to a performance playfully calibrated to their "worldly appetit."

Where then is identity in masquerade? To the extent that the shapeshifter establishes a detachment from her two superlative bodies, acting out their parts to win her chosen man, she experiences the double alienation from and social configuration of the body that we have seen in the process of masculine self-definition. Melusine illustrates this experience after Raymondin's betrayal, lamenting that "al they that myght come into my presence had grete Joye to behold me / and fro this tyme foorth they shal dysdayne me & be ferefull of myn abhomynable figure."[38] She speaks of herself both from without, as the object of responses from those who see her, and from within as a "me" who exists beyond and beside the two bodies she inhabits. She experiences herself independently of her public effects, but she remains socially identified by those effects. The Wife of Bath expresses a similar sense of a self that persists unchanged in her young and her old body, although age changes her status with men:

> Unto this day it dooth myn herte boote
> That I have had my world as in my tyme.
> But age, allas, that al wole envenyme,
> Hath me biraft my beautee and my pith.
> Lat go. Farewel! The devel go therwith!
> The flour is goon; ther is namoore to telle;
> The bren, as I best kan, now moste I selle.   (III 472–78)

---

[38] *Melusine*, 319; the passage in the French *Mélusine* is "ceulx qui me souloient faire grant joye quant ilz me veoient, se deffuiront de moy, et auront paour et grant hidour de moy quant ilz me verront" (259).

The stability of feeling in "myn herte" divides Alison's consciousness from the depredations of age, and the resulting sense that her
body is a resource to be manipulated adumbrates the tale's representation of a fully mobile body that can even reverse temporality
as part of the move from loathly to fair.[39] The flamboyant, provocative version of femininity that Alison has enacted through five
marriages returns, as critics have long noted, in the tale's confident, manipulative, aged hag and in the sexually engaging young
wife who promises obedience. In relation to Alison's vision of herself in the prologue as a stable identity despite the diminishing
resources of her body, the tale dramatizes still more vividly that
identity is independent of appearance. The Wife's autobiography
hitches itself to the trajectory of masquerade in the tale particularly in the final moments, when the tale's romantic achievement
of a beauty matching that of "any lady, emperice, or queene, /
That is bitwixte the est and eke the west" recalls Alison's hyperbolic achievement of a faith matching that of "any wyf from Den-
mark unto Ynde" (III 1246–47, 824). The narrative and rhetorical
echoes ask the magic of shape-shifting to verify Alison's promise
to Jankyn, despite the temporal instability that affects her disenchanted body. In part, then, shape-shifting paradoxically figures
constancy rather than mobility, an integrity of the self that masquerade makes possible by alienating identity from the transitory
body.

Masquerade accomplishes the severing of identity from body
not by denying the centrality of appearance in defining womanliness, but by working within that connection. Butler describes
"subversive repetition" in similar terms: "there is no possibility
of agency or reality outside of the discursive practices that give
those terms the intelligibility that they have. The task is not
whether to repeat, but how to repeat" (148). Masquerade is a
choice within limitations so powerful that it is at least equally
interpretable in misogynist terms: the grotesque woman reacti-
vates clerical antifeminist tropes; the beautifully submissive
woman closes the potential for agency that shape-shifting figured,
if indeed it did not simply figure woman's contradictoriness. The

---

[39] Only in the *Wife of Bath's Tale* is old age a specifically named loathly trait,
linking the Wife's aging body to that of the "olde wyf" (III 1046, 1072, 1086), but
various details of other loathly bodies (sagging flesh, yellow teeth, excessive bulk)
also suggest that lost youthfulness is part of their loathliness.

constraints under which masquerading operates are similar to those under which Dorigen and the falcon quote courtship's discourse against the grain, attempting to resist its gendered configurations. Their implications countermanded, their assertions ostensibly but playful, masquerading and mimicry nonetheless provide female characters with a language in which to reconsider their place in courtship and the identity courtship assigns them in romance.

Gender and Social Hierarchy

ENDER difference is persistently hierarchical. We have seen that in romance masculinity is the "fully human" experience that femininity helps to define, that Emelye is both her lovers' exalted object of devotion and Theseus's object of exchange, and that the *Squire's Tale* imagines women to be more true and gentle than men by reversing the topos that they are less so. The Franklin suggests reciprocity in Dorigen and Arveragus's marriage by imagining it to combine two relations of unequal power:

> Heere may men seen an humble, wys accord;
> Thus hath she take hir servant and hir lord—
> Servant in love, and lord in mariage.
> Thanne was he bothe in lordshipe and servage.
> Servage? Nay, but in lordshipe above,
> Sith he hath bothe his lady and his love. . . .   (V 791–96)

The chiasmus knitting together lordship and servitude through these lines may strive toward an idea of equivalence between Dorigen and Arveragus, but that idea, if it is even latent, finds expression only by juxtaposing two conditions in which male and female have reversed hierarchical relations. Here as elsewhere in romance, gender is a system of difference that entails inequivalence.

This chapter looks at how gender inequity can intersect with, repeat, and clarify inequities of social rank and authority that might seem independent of gender. The social hierarchy, as conceived in estates literature, frames and motivates tale-telling from the *General Prologue* onward. Certain ideological contiguities between estates literature and romance invite in this chapter more consideration than in other chapters of Chaucer's diversely positioned narrators in relation to their tales. The Franklin's relatively high but precarious standing, for example, aligns him more fully with Dorigen than with the male characters in his tale. But in focusing on how Chaucer's narrators figure in his redeployments of romance, I am not proposing that Chaucer creates a fictional subjectivity for every narrator. When the Squire and the Franklin cry, "lo, my tale is this" and "my tale shul ye heere," the emphasis should, I believe, fall on the noun "tale" rather than the pronoun "my" (V 8, 728). The tale may be framed and focused by the pilgrim's traits, but need not explicate those traits. In contrast, the "roadside drama" approach, so influentially developed in G. L. Kittredge's *Chaucer and His Poetry*, can fall into a curious circularity by which the tale reveals the teller's personality, and all apparent faults of the tale become consequences of the teller's inadequacy, carefully managed by the poet who is exempt in his genius from any comment but praise.[1] Instead of the pilgrim telling the tale, the tale tells the pilgrim. In its extreme forms this critical approach owes more to Robert Browning's "My Last Duchess" than to Chaucer's literary practice. Of course the *Wife of Bath's Prologue* invents a complexly motivated voice for the tale that follows, but most of the pilgrims provide only a few contextualizing signals that prepare for the tales assigned to them. Among the most important of these signals concern genre, gender, and estate.

The Knight, Squire, and Franklin are derived in part from the romance genre that informs their tales; their ranks have a place in romance's repertoire of characters as well as in estates literature's catalog of social possibilities. These pilgrims authorize a masculine perspective characteristic of romance, yet I argue that the Franklin's perspective comes to match Dorigen's in a number of ways because his social rank is analogous to her gendered status. In contrast to Knight, Squire, and Franklin, the Wife of Bath and Chaucer's persona Geffrey speak romance from social positions that are outside its generic repertoire. Alison's womanhood and Geffrey's curiously aberrant gender contribute to establishing

---

[1] Kittredge's "rule of judgment" that *"Chaucer always knew what he was about"* (151, his italics) has been taken to mean that Chaucer's narrators did not. Lawton, 106–9, proposes that the rise of dramatic criticism in the twentieth century is responsible for the lowered reputation of the *Squire's Tale*, due to the facility with which the tale's difficulties could be referred to an inadequate teller.

that these narrators are outsiders to romance. Alison's festive resistance to her subordinate status as a woman confronts romance
with antifeminist satire and strives to imagine a social authority
for women that neither genre sanctions.

A brief overview of the literature of social estates and its place in
romance can introduce these cases. Estates literature encompasses a recurring nexus of ideas about social difference to be
found in sermons, verse satires and complaints, books of conduct
and moral instruction, and capacious fictions such as the *Romance of the Rose*, *Piers Plowman*, and John Gower's longer
works. These ideas develop a few complementary ways of imagining social difference (Duby, *Three Orders*; Dumézil; Le Goff, *Civilisation*; Mann, *Estates Satire*; Mohl). The oldest is the topos that
God has ordained complementary ways of life, usually three, the
estates or orders of those who pray, those who fight, and those
who work. The *ordines* have interdependent functions: no one
order could do without the others; each one's function sustains
the other two. Although the orders need not be conceived hierarchically, Ottavia Niccoli has shown that the concrete presenta-
tions of the three orders impose a hierarchy even when asserting
its absence, through the order of presentation, rhetorical expli-
cations of each order's importance, and iconographic representations. An instance similar to those she cites is Aelfric's description of three orders he assigns the Latin names *laboratores*,
bellatores, and *oratores*: "The laborer works for our subsistence,
the worldly warrior must fight against our foes, and the servant of
God must pray continually for us and fight spiritually against the
invisible foes" (pt. 3 [vol. 2], 122–23). The description asserts the
cleric's superiority through his climactic position in the period
and his eschatological versus merely mortal battles; the synec-
dochic "subsistence" (*bigleof*) rationalizes the laborer's heavy
contribution to the comfort of superior strata by disguising it as
mere sustenance.[2] The metaphor of the body that comes to supplement estates descriptions, for example in John of Salisbury's

---

[2] Aelfric makes overt the superiority of those who pray in continuing, "Greater
therefore is now the struggle of the monks against the invisible devils that lay
snares around us, than may be that of the worldly men that struggle against fleshly
foes" (Skeat's translation, 123).

Policraticus, similarly conveys both the interdependence of all estates and the superiority of such parts as head and arms over belly and feet.[3]

From the twelfth century the trifunctional model of estates expands to accommodate an overtly hierarchical idea of earthly distinctions in rank and profession called *conditio* or *status,* in Middle English *degree* and *estaat.*[4] The degrees subdivide the trifunctional model into narrower positions of responsibility. The shift from three broad theoretical divisions to many specific, recognizable positions such as archbishop, bishop, monk, friar, and priest invites satirical commentary on the failures and shortcomings peculiar to each worldly office. Chaucer's idealizing portraits of the Knight, Parson, and Plowman take conviction from the theoretical model of three interdependent orders, whereas the specific practices the Parson avoids and the majority of pilgrims indulge refer to the tradition of critical and satirical commentary on degrees.

A third ground for social distinction in estates literature is gentle versus churlish behavior. The topos that nobility must be deserved through virtue and that nobles who act villainously should be cast out of their estate complements satiric criticism of failure to fulfill the duties that define estates and degrees.[5] This was orig-

---

[3] E.g., the admixture of interdependence and subordination in "The feet are the name of those who exercise the humbler duties, by whose service all the members of the republic may walk along the earth. . . . [The feet] are to concentrate on the public utility in all matters. For inferiors must serve superiors, who on the other hand ought to provide all necessary protection to their inferiors" (125–26). For a strong tradition of protest against the inequities of status divisions see Owst, 210–470.

[4] *Estaat* designates both tripartite orders and smaller degrees of social difference in Middle English. For example, "A Schort Reule of Lif" attributed to Wyclif addresses the "þre statis," priests, lords, and laborers (204–8); compare Chaucer's *Manciple's Tale*: "But that the gentile, in estaat above, / She shal be cleped his lady, as in love" (IX 217–18). More often Chaucer uses *estaat* and *degree* synonymously to designate a range of relative positions: "If a man of hyer estaat or degree, or moore myghty than thou, do thee anoy or grevaunce, suffre hym" (*Melibee,* VII 1488). Paul Strohm integrates historical and literary issues of rank in *Social Chaucer,* esp. 84–109.

[5] See especially Friedman; Brewer, "Class Distinction"; Mohl, 85, 88, 119, 291–301. Brewer notes that the gentle/churl distinction may have originated in differing rights under law, but he notes that it "tends to become moral" (297).

inally a clerical topos designed to check the second estate's power by holding it to standards concerning which the Church might claim special authority. During Chaucer's lifetime the topos began to appear frequently in courtly literature, as increasing social mobility and dispersion of power from feudal hierarchies into mercantile and professional circles were challenging the gentry's traditional dominance. In this situation the concept of moral *gentillesse* offered the second estate a new ground on which to base its claims to superiority when its more fundamental economic and political superiority were being eroded.[6] The standard of moral *gentillesse*, then, might seem to undermine distinction by birth, but in effect it tends to reinforce that distinction. Those who are superior by birth should behave superlatively. A few authors including John Lydgate argue that gentle behavior could elevate a common man in God's eyes "Onto thestat off vertuous noblesse," but usually the exhortation to gentle behavior is directed to those already gentle by birth, who should strive to deserve their privileged position.[7] The exhortation to gentle behavior thus responds to both the moralizing trajectory of estates satire and the older definition of each order according to its function.

In focusing on social functions and duties, estates literature may omit women altogether, append their positions to those of male estate members, or consider them separately as a fourth estate. The irregular treatment of women springs in part from their peculiar social definition: whereas men have assigned functions to perform, women's duties derive from and relate to their sexuality. Women's statuses are typically those of virgin, nun, whore, maiden, wife, mother, and widow, replacing masculine functions on the social scene with the management of sexual status (Batany; Mohl, 20–24, 48–51; Mann, *Estates Satire*, 121–27, 203–6). Classifying women according to their sexual relations (or abstention from relations) with men has on the one hand a component of gender equality: a woman's status in this system is closer to that

---

[6] Mohl, 85, 88, 94, 119, 291–301; Vale, 14–32; Chaucer, *Minor Poems*, 67–68, in *Variorum Edition* (comments on "Gentilesse").

[7] *Lydgate's Fall of Princes*, pt. 1, bk. 2, l. 263; cf. Friedman, 221: "villany, gentility (*gentilezza*, gentilesse), and nobility denoted ambiguously birth, class, and membership in an estate on one hand, and personal viciousness or virtue on the other, an ambiguity which promoted a bias inherent in medieval society."

of her man than to that of women and men at other strata in the system (Dumont, Ortner). At the same time, as the concept of a separate "fourth estate" indicates, women are alienated from the ideal of an interdependent society in that their sexuality tends to stand in for any socioeconomic function in defining them. For example, estates literature lists among women's duties obedience, chaste behavior, care for husbands, and spinning or cloth making, but textile work in this context is a gendered trait rather than a profession. Thus the Wife of Bath is said to make cloth in her *General Prologue* portrait, but in her tale she derives wealth from her husbands and refers to spinning as a talent native to her womanhood: "Deceite, wepyng, spynnyng God hath yive / To wommen kyndely, whyl that they may lyve" (III 401–2).[8] Women's inferior position, their definition in relation to men, and the satiric penchant of much estates literature make conjunctions between antifeminist satire and the concept of estates. Jehan le Fèvre's *Lamentations de Matheolus* (bk. 1, ll. 276–89) discourse on the failings of the three estates as well as the woes of marriage, and many works on estates remobilize topoi from clerical antimatrimonial and antifeminist literature to specify the faults of wives, widows, and young women. The prominent place of misogyny in estates literature generates the already-compromised wifehood that Alison of Bath strives to justify in her prologue and tale.

Like the *General Prologue*, the tales affiliated with romance have interests in narrative and characterization that dissociate them from estates literature's traffic in types and ideals. Yet romance does overlap with estates literature in the three perspectives on social order outlined above. First, romance shares the conception that social differences order the world hierarchically. The conception is evident both in works written for aristocratic patrons such as Jean Froissart's *Méliador* and Adenet le Roi's *Cleomadés* and in works that may have popular connections such as *Havelok* and Thomas Chestre's *Sir Launfal*. *Havelok* gives social differences particularly close attention in plotting Havelok's return to kingship as a journey through the statuses of thrall, hired laborer, merchant, and knight. Although the specificity and en-

---

[8] Mann, *Estates Satire*, 121–22. Harry Bailey's wife also makes spinning the mark of womanhood in taunting her husband, "I wol have thy knyf, / And thou shalt have my distaf and go spynne!" (VII 1906–7)

ergy with which *Havelok* depicts popular life confers importance on it, Havelok's upward trajectory through social ranks demonstrates his superior merit and right to kingship. His elevation of helpful commoners to titled rank once he has regained the throne further endorses the social hierarchy in making advancement the reward for a chosen few (see my *Insular Romance*, 13–91). For Northrop Frye, medieval romances are "kidnapped" reformations in that they deny the "revolutionary quality" inherent in romance's folktale origins; true romances have a "proletarian element rejected by every cultural establishment" despite their "naive social snobbery" (163).[9] Whatever the true form of romance across the centuries may be, the conviction in medieval romances that hierarchy is natural, indeed that it derives from divine order, cannot be dismissed as snobbery or as a superficial overlay on inherently egalitarian material. It reflects a pervasive social belief that high station tends to be consonant with merit and that gentle sensibilities and values are superior to common ones.[10]

Romance plots further concur with estates literature in demanding that men deserve their estate through behavior suitable to it. A familiar way of representing the double source of identity in lineal right and personal deserving is to obscure a young man's lineage so that he is thrown back on his own capacities to demonstrate his birthright. *Lancelot do Lac*'s young protagonist, ignorant of his lineage and even of the concept of lineage, nonetheless recognizes his affinity with youths of his rank and seeks to excel in "gentillece" in order to be accorded the status in which gentle behavior is characteristic: "se li grant cuer faisoient les gentis homes, ge cuideroie encores estre des plus gentils" (if great hearts make men gentle, I believe that I will yet be one of the most gentle) (bk. 1, ll. 110–11; see Kennedy). Joachim Bumke traces the vernacular German equivalents of Latin terms for rank (*gradus, status, ordo, conditio*) and concludes that romance uses those

---

[9] Medieval romance is not Frye's focus of interest; he notes that it presents "different structural problems" from the versions with which he is concerned (4).

[10] Dumont's engaging introduction to *Homo Hierarchicus*, 1–20, illustrates that although at odds with modern Western views, the conviction that social hierarchy is both natural and valid persists today and can be an instructive contrast to egalitarian convictions.

terms to designate behavior suited to rank: "In courtly poetry, *ritters namen* is less a designation of class than a central concept of aristocratic ethics" (109; see 107–23). In these as in any number of cases, romances imagine a symbiosis between birth and deeds in which high social position both inspires and is predicated on superior behavior. The Wife of Bath's and Franklin's tales are consonant with romance, not revisionary and still less revolutionary, in asserting that *gentillesse* is a matter of virtuous conduct.

A third connection between estates literature and romance is that in both, sexuality is central to women's social identity: their status derives both from the status of men with whom they are associated and from their gendered status of inferiority to men. As the objects of courtship, female characters are assigned very high value by the men around them, a value based more surely in their sexuality than in their bloodlines since their adult status will derive from their husbands' rank. A Saracen, an orphan of uncertain parentage, an Amazon, or an enchantress can inspire love as well as a princess of unimpeachable pedigree, although typically it will turn out that a woman's lineage validates her desirability. In the preceding chapter I have argued that romance comments more richly on femininity than simply by representing it as a projection of masculine desire, but from the perspective of social rank the place of woman is constrained and subordinate. In this respect romance draws on estates systems that, whether they define men's rank in terms of function or more narrowly in occupational terms, conceive women's sexuality both as an analogously defining category and as nonoccupational, nonfunctional, a matter of self-control rather than of constructive service to society. The conception has a modern equivalent in the split between marxisms and feminisms over whether work or sexuality is the fundamental category for social analysis.[11] Variations on the marxist position that economic forces shape identity and class consciousness risk exiling the Wife of Bath, as a wife, to a radical self-in-

---

[11] In MacKinnon's well-known formulation, "sexuality is to feminism what work is to marxism: that which is most one's own, yet most taken away.... As work is to marxism, sexuality to feminism is socially constructed yet constructing, universal as activity yet historically specific, jointly comprised of matter and mind": "Feminism . . . An Agenda for Theory," 515–16. An excellent framing discussion of sexuality and social rank in literature is Kaplan, "Pandora's Box."

volvement that ignores any class interest. Yet the Wife persistently speaks as one of a group of "wise wyves" with whom she has common cause against clerics and husbands. In both the Wife's and the Franklin's tales, sexuality and social roles come to comment on one another rather than remaining analogous but distinct expressions of status.

NARRATORS DRAWN FROM ROMANCE

One way Chaucer comments on genre is by attributing tales to pilgrims whose estate, degree, or profession figures importantly in the genre's repertoire. In the case of Knight, Squire, and Franklin not only the functions each station can hold in romance but also the generational relations of the three tellers are of interest. As son and ideal son of the Knight and Franklin, the Squire embodies the importance of coming of age in romance, of courtship and marriage as movements from youth to maturity. From Charles Méla's psychoanalytic position, "tout roman est un roman nuptial où prendre femme veut dire, tel est le ressort secret de la crise, succéder au père" (every romance is a story of marriage in which to take a woman means—and this is the secret wellspring of the climax—to supplant one's father) (218). In thematic and rhetorical terms, Howard Bloch proposes that romance is "essentially *about* marriage and seems always to involve a conflict between a consensual attachment and a contractual bond, to problematize succession, and to combine structurally elements both of narrative progression and of lyric closure; and this from the very beginning" (*Etymologies*, 182). From these perspectives we might consider the marriage agreement of Arveragus and Dorigen as an attempt to stabilize the competition in romance between the contractual bonds of marriage and the consensual bonds of courtship, Dorigen's lyric complaints as expressions of resistance to narrative progression, and Aurelius's declaration of love as a generational competition with Arveragus, his senior in marital status if not in years. Palamon and Arcite similarly contrast to Theseus in status and resist his order, or so it seems, in loving Emelye against all hope of contractual union with her. The genre's narrative and lyric impulses align with maturity and youth respectively when Theseus plans an outcome declaring that "the beste game of alle" is Emelye's ignorance of Palamon and Arcite's private expressions of desire (I 1806). The Squire's romance, an up-to-date composite that by contrast relegates the Knight's epic resonances and the Franklin's ancient lay to an older generation, only predicts its courtships, projecting them forever into the future of the suspended tale. Whether or not the fragmentariness of the *Squire's Tale* figured in Chaucer's final plan, it is appropriate to the place of composite romance late in the genre's history as well as to the Squire's filial status. Late in the course of a genre, partial citations can evoke it innovatively: in Alastair Fowler's illustration, "There was a young lady of Crew / Whose limericks stopped at line two" (173).[12] The initial display of adventure-provoking gifts together with the plot outline that ends the Squire's fragment refer effectively to a kind of romance that would, if fully evoked, overwhelm the other tales with its inordinate length.

Many such questions suggest themselves under the rubric of romance and social rank. My discussion here focuses on one aspect of the *Franklin's Tale* that is prior to the generational tensions surrounding courtship and that involves gender more immediately than do the lineal relations of father and son. Critics have tended to base negative judgments of the *Franklin's Tale* in arguments that the Franklin is a social climber longing to prove that he is thoroughly gentle. Positive readings of the tale often claim that the Franklin's status is high and secure, so that he is a confident and trustworthy narrator. Resisting the dramatic tendency in both explanations, I claim that Chaucer characterizes the Franklin by the liminal status his primary designation describes— that of a rank not quite common but not securely gentle either. His insecure social rank (not a fictive personal insecurity) introduces and comes to resemble Dorigen's ambivalent social position. Dorigen may seem remote from her narrator in birth and gender, yet her precarious social standing is analogous to the Franklin's, and in consequence similar limitations and perspectives are attributed to the two characters. The resemblances between them allow Chaucer to relate estate to gender identity.

Designating the tale a Breton lay (V 709–10) forecasts its pre-

---

[12] On the *Squire's Tale* and composite romance see Goodman. Although putatively "olde" in their origins, lays were probably not out of fashion in the later fourteenth century (Donovan, 174–75).

Christian setting more surely than would the broader category of romance, but the *Franklin's Tale* and other fourteenth-century lays are not generically distinct from short romances.[13] Reading the *Franklin's Tale* in relation to romance may ask two concessions from readers for whom the tale is an expression of the Franklin's personality. I find motivations in the genre for narrative phenomena that are often referred to the Franklin's competitiveness, envy, or ignorance; and I have aligned a pilgrim narrator with a character in his tale rather than finding them so different in fictional status as to be incomparable. Readers familiar with the critical tradition of a fully dramatized Franklin whose every word is in some sense his own can nonetheless recognize that Chaucer's poetic facility constructs both the narrator and his tale. Genre and estates ideology provide perspectives on the *Franklin's Tale* that differ from, and may supplement, the mimetic aspects of composition responsible for the fictive personhood of narrator and characters. No perspective is independent of others; if I consider here the former at the expense of the latter it is in part because a long history of dramatic criticism affords me the opportunity to depart from it.

The Franklin stands Janus-like on the threshold of gentility; "with double berd" (V 1252) he warms himself at the material fire of his prosperity but looks as well to an ideal of *gentillesse* that ostensibly ignores wealth.[14] He makes explicit a relation between his status and gentle behavior as he describes his son's disinclination to "lerne gentillesse" (V 694) and tells a tale proposing that men of various degrees can deliberately imitate *gentillesse*. The tale's inspiring passages on moral worthiness can be referred to the access

---

[13] Beston argues that the lay was not conceived as a genre very different from romance; lay and romance are closely associated as well by Strohm, "Origin and Meaning"; and by Donovan, 44, 188, et passim. Hume attributes more specific meaning to Chaucer's choice of the designation.

[14] Brewer connects the Franklin's status to Chaucer's as a "new man" and finds in the anomalies of that status a "root for that recurrent symbol in his writings, to which he devotes such sympathy, the betrayed and deserted woman" ("Class Distinction," 304). See also Middleton's excellent discussion of the Franklin's social position in relation to his tale and to Chaucer's position ("Chaucer's 'New Men'"). An earlier version of the following discussion was published as "The Franklin as Dorigen."

to courtly ideals that the degree of the Franklin confers, but also to that degree's restricted claim to gentility, a claim based almost solely on behavior. Dorigen in turn expresses her limitations as she meditates that men of learning understand the universe as she cannot. Her helpless lament envisions no solution to the problem of the "grisly feendly rokkes blake," whereas Aurelius suggests a solution to Apollo in his parallel lament (V 868, 1031–79). Dorigen's passive vulnerability even to inanimate rocks—"Thise rokkes sleen myn herte for the feere"—expresses her femininity and qualifies the high standing she enjoys by birth (V 735, 893). Like the Franklin, she is doubly positioned, entitled by status but not fully enabled by it.

The precedence of womanhood over birth in defining Dorigen's position accords with the divisions in estates literature that rank men by a hierarchy of functions but that omit women or classify them according to their relation to men: Jean de Condé's "Estas dou monde," for example, subdivides the trifunctional male orders into clergy, princes, knights, justices, squires, burgesses, and so on, adding women at the end. Women should not be flirtatious, adulterous, or fickle; they should be obedient, loving, and virtuous, for, writes Etienne de Fougères, "bone fame est ornement / a son saignor" (a good wife is an adornment to her husband) (1161-62). Dorigen is drawn from and credits these ideals of womanhood when she promises to be a humble and loyal wife, defers to the superior understanding of clerics, and allows others to determine her course of action. Critics may label her "child-like" in these regards,[15] but more accurately, she is conventionally feminine in her conviction of dependence on and difference from men.

Dorigen's status derives most directly from romance, which partakes of estates ideology by dramatizing differences in kind between nobility and commons and by figuring women in terms of their roles in masculine competitions and courtships. Chapter 1 argues that *fine amor* and romance paradigms configure male self-definition in part by constructing the feminine as a purely imaginary category, a terrain on which men rival one another. Palamon and Arcite are up to their ankles in blood before Emelye is made

---

[15] E.g., Dorigen shows a "child-like inability to cope with the black rocks" (Berger, 136); her lament to Aurelius is "like nothing so much as the lament of a little girl who has just broken her doll" (Kaske, 62); she is "childish and incapable" (Luecke, 113).

aware of her role. Theseus points out the egregious imbalance between the strength of the lovers' rivalry and the merely potential bonds of love with Emelye, yet he recognizes their conduct to be typical of lovers (I 1785–1825). Aurelius, as we have seen, compares himself persistently with Arveragus as he courts Dorigen. By the tale's final scenes, Dorigen's mediate function in the masculine competition is obvious. Freely sent to Aurelius and freely sent back again, she has become a commodity whose transfer is equivalent, for the clerk at least, to a financial sacrifice (V 1604–12). On the other hand Aurelius feels pity for her, and Arveragus, though insistent that she do his will, "cherissheth hire as though she were a queene" on her return (V 1554). The admixture of honor and disregard accorded to Dorigen finally makes her less a child or a commodity than the romance image of a courtly lady, paradoxically superior and subordinated.[16]

The Franklin's situation is similarly paradoxical. Elsewhere I have argued at length that historical referents for Chaucer's Franklin clarify that his social position is gentle but only marginally so, and that his claim to gentility can base itself only in his wealth and dignity.[17] The Franklin has an equally modest claim to gentility through his literary lineage. Roy Pearcy has shown that "vavasours" in Old French romances are venerable gentlemen, settled and not militarily inclined. Their passivity distinguishes them from the knights and squires, *bellatores* in the old estates definition by military function, who make things happen in romance. Derek Brewer concludes that the Franklin has relatively high social and economic standing, but that he "can find no place in the functional triple system and is therefore lightly mocked or satirised" ("Class Distinction," 303). Insular works list franklins and vavasours along with barons and squires, but satirical writing emphasizes the difference in function. In "Sir Pride the Emperor," for example, bachelors waste their heritage on tournaments, squires aim to "contrefere les chevalers" (imitate knights) and make much of their "gentif saunk" (gentle blood), but vavasours "ke tenent houstel e meynné" (who keep households and retinues) have only their hospitality to corrupt (*Reliquae antiquae*,

---

[16] On commodification see Rubin; Irigaray, *This Sex*, 170–91 ("Women on the Market"). Commodification is important to Dorigen's situation but does not account for her mimicry of courtly discourse (see chapter 2).

[17] For more detail see my "Franklin as Dorigen," 240–43.

2:250–51).[18] The Franklin's literary heritage, like his historical affiliations, suggests that Chaucer's first audience would have perceived this pilgrim as worthy enough to be gentle, but not chivalric enough to be of the second estate in its deepest identity with
military functions. Landholding and substantial householding
distinguish gentry from bourgeoisie; within the ranks of the gentry, landholding gives the vavasour his only attribute of gentility
as opposed to the coats of arms, knighthood, or ancestral title that
other ranks enjoyed. This characteristic restriction of the claim to
status is dramatized in a number of lays and fabliaux that place
vavasours' property and family interests at odds with the adventurous depredations of knights-errant and squires (see Pearcy, 42–
49). Like the skill at jousting and singing that identify the Squire
as a squire, the Franklin's property and generous prosperity constitute his social identity.

The Franklin's attention to property and *gentillesse* have seen
much study, and my purpose here is only to indicate how both
concerns signal that his fictional status is gentle, but more peripheral than the gentility of squires, knights, and lords. The Franklin's argument that his son or his characters can "lerne gentillesse" (V 694) is a topos that aligns him with the gentry rather
than locating him outside it. In historical terms, the topos is particularly appropriate to members of the lowest and most vulnerable category of gentry in a provincial society where, as Michael
Bennett has shown, "the distinction between 'gentle' and 'common' was the crucial divide" (31). The Franklin's high but marginal station resembles that of Dorigen, whose gender severely
qualifies her birth and whose engagement in a romantic plot confers privilege but finally subordinates her to the interactions of
male characters. The Franklin's narration (that is, Chaucer's presentation of a franklin narrating) further develops the analogies
between the two characters' positions.

In romance a vavasour's marginal position importantly defines
him. The isolated, provincial, but hospitable households of gentle
vavasours are often way stations for adventuring knights. The va-

---

[18] Robert Mannyng of Brunne calls the daughters of squires and franklins "gentil
damysels" in contrast to "oþer maidens comen of þralles" (vol. 1, ll. 6545, 6549);
cf. "Li rey, le prince, e le courtur, / Cunt, barun, e vavasur / Ayment cuntes,

vasour may provide information and counsel; sometimes his daughter and the visitor fall in love, or his young sons seek to accompany the knight-errant as he continues his adventures. Chaucer's Franklin's advanced age, his renown for hospitality "in his contree" (I 340), his hope that his son will increase in merit through contact with "any gentil wight" (V 693), and his tale's affiliations with romance all suggest that Chaucer seeks to align the Franklin with the vavasours of romance (see Pearcy, Bruckner). By drawing narrators from the genres that define them, Chaucer makes his reassessments of those genres a dramatic process. Like the Wife of Bath berating antifeminist authors and the Squire forecasting adventures of noble youths, the Franklin speaks a literature by which he has been configured.

It is significant to the Franklin's narrative project that vavasours do not themselves provide the action in romance. Like beloved ladies, hospitable vavasours can urge, counsel, shelter, and comfort a striving knight, but they are essentially the witnesses and beneficiaries of heroic action rather than actors themselves. Even as providers of sons who follow the protagonist or daughters who love him, vavasours are associated with the domestic and familial, as women are, rather than with action and adventure. The genre's concerns reach beyond chivalry, but there is a structural tendency in these heavily eventful works to center attention on the characters who perform actions good or bad, and to treat peripheral characters as a kind of retinue that takes its meaning from the central figures.[19] Complementing this structure are the class and gender hierarchies discussed above, which place a franklin and a noble lady in decidedly less powerful positions than the knights whose exploits dominate the genre.

Chaucer exacerbates romance's structural and ideological subordination of the Franklin and Dorigen by showing both characters attempting to revise their status. The Franklin tries to define

---

chanceuns, et fables" (Piramus, *Vie Seint Edmund*, 49–52); "Ses barons fist mander, vavasors e terriers, / E les lonteins marchis e riches soudiers" (Thomas of Kent, *Alexander*, 537–38). For further examples see my "Franklin as Dorigen."

[19] Charnes, 303, proposes that the Franklin narrates Dorigen's waiting rather than Arveragus's adventures because "her rootedness becomes somehow linked with [the Franklin's] own—they have in common an occupation of domestic space that enables the Franklin to view things from her position."

romance action rather than resting on its periphery; Dorigen
seeks to understand her situation and to determine her own actions. Both characters are unable to manipulate the courtly traditions they confront and must consequently acquiesce to situations they sought to elude.

The Franklin begins his "gentil" story with a miniature plot
that situates him firmly in the genre of romance (V 729–60). These
first lines introduce an active chivalric lover who wins a lady of
high station and great beauty, a setting in the past of Celtic and
Arthurian tales, a plot that rises through adversities to happiness,
and a narration that is rhetorically sophisticated. Dorigen is part
of this familiar literary world: her emotional authority is the occasion for "many a greet emprise" until she is "wonne" by Avera-
gus and married to him (V 732–33).

At this point the Breton material evades the Franklin's appropriation. His long commentary on the agreement between Dorigen and Arveragus reinterprets the courtly relations typical of
romance, not in supplementing love with marriage (a development in the plot) but in commenting that the plot shows a union
of mutual freedom illustrating how "freendes everych oother
moot obeye" (V 762). The tale's events contradict the Franklin's
assertion. This union does not eliminate the problem of "maistrie" by having each spouse obey the other in all things. Rather,
Dorigen obeys Arveragus as if his will were unalterable necessity:
she complains to God about the rocks rather than to Arveragus for
going away, and she follows her husband's judgment in surrendering to Aurelius even though her exempla compare the surrender
to rape and murder. Dorigen addresses her wishes to an uncom-
prehending Aurelius and an impassive clerical tradition, but
never to Arveragus. In forecasting the mutuality of this marriage,
has the Franklin misconstrued the conventions of romance, taking literally Arveragus's promise to follow Dorigen's will rather
than reading it as a courtly topos for Arveragus's desire to improve
himself? Or is the Franklin attempting to revise the Breton lay he
has "in remembraunce" (V 714), projecting a bold departure from
courtly relations but returning to them in execution? An enormous difference separates the assertion that "Love wol nat been
constreyned by maistrye" (V 764) and Arveragus's threat to kill
his wife if she ever reveals that she followed his order to submit to

Aurelius. However we gloss that difference, and many glosses more desperate than compelling are on record, it demonstrates that the Franklin's interpretive comment on the love of Dorigen and Arveragus is not consonant with the plot of his Breton lay.

After marriage as before, Dorigen continues to occupy a role typical of courtship in that Arveragus continues to perfect himself in labors of arms, presumably looking to Dorigen as his source of inspiration but not requiring her presence or counsel to succeed. Certainly she is loved and honored, but more as a reflection of her lovers' ideals than as the agent of her own "libertee" (compare the narrator's assertion that "Wommen of kynde desiren libertee," V 768). The beautiful imagery of Aurelius's prayer to Phoebus Apollo both mythologizes and makes natural this kind of gender relation: the masculine sun guides the feminine moon, whose "desir / Is to be quyked and lighted of youre fir, / For which she folweth yow ful bisily" (V 1049–51). In this universe one might even propose that Dorigen's terror of the rocks expresses her awareness of the artful objectification that threatens to petrify her completely, like a Galatea in reverse. When her first Pygmalion leaves her for "a yeer or tweyne" on the shelf, the extended figure of stone carving expresses her friends' efforts to revive her from fixed desperation (V 809, 829–36). In the preceding chapter I have argued that the task of removing the rocks that Dorigen invents for Aurelius is an attempt to speak against his courtship by exaggerating beyond measure the role of the demanding lady and discrediting it with explicit instructions to cease and desist. When Aurelius instead fulfills her demand, again Dorigen "astoned stood; / In al hir face nas a drope of blood" (V 1339–40; see Hansen, 278–80; Shoaf, "Chaucer and Medusa"). The terms of courtly interactions constantly threaten to objectify her, despite her efforts to shape her identity.

My point is not simply that Dorigen's role is constrained by her femininity, but that the plot contradicts the Franklin's assertion that he can represent a courtly relation in which men and women enjoy the same "libertee." It is as if the Franklin begins with a desire to reinterpret or alter romance, yet soon submits to the passive role designated for him in the genre. Similarly, Dorigen's words "in pley" (V 988) attempt to parody the role of haughty lady with Aurelius, revealing that role to be no more than a sham construction from which she herself is alienated. Dorigen chooses to distance herself from convention, but Aurelius reads her mimicry unreflectively, as the kind of "emprise" by which Arveragus won her, reconstructing her words according to his own desires. Dorigen cannot determine how she is perceived, nor can the Franklin revise her role. Both vavasour and lady can inhabit romance but do not control its paradigms and plots.

In addition, Dorigen and her narrator seem not to foresee events and take a passive stance toward their unfolding. Dorigen expresses ignorance of God's ways when Arveragus departs, and does not choose a course of action when Aurelius declares, "I have do so as ye comanded me. . . . Dooth as yow list; have youre biheste in mynde" (V 1333, 1336). Even her promise to love Aurelius if he will remove the rocks along Brittany's coast is predicated on her belief in the unalterability of natural phenomena and the intransigence of events. Aghast when Aurelius declares his success, she cries, "wende I nevere by possibilitee / That swich a monstre or merveille myghte be!" (V 1343–44). After this revelation that human agency can produce change, Dorigen nonetheless begins her lament with an image more fatalistic than Fortune's conventional blindfold or ever-turning wheel: "on thee, Fortune, I pleyne, / That unwar wrapped hast me in thy cheyne" (V 1355–56). Fortune is malevolently aware and Dorigen more nearly blind than she; the "cheyne" makes axiomatic Dorigen's helplessness, not Fortune's unpredictability.

The Franklin's narrative procedure is analogous to Dorigen's sense of surprise at what happens to her. Despite having the Breton lay "in remembraunce" (V 714), the Franklin tells his tale as if events arrived unannounced to disturb the patterns his narration seems to be projecting. His ideal of mutuality does not predict Dorigen's effective lack of initiative; his account of harmonious union does not adumbrate Arveragus's long absence; Aurelius's manipulative behavior toward Dorigen cannot presage his gracious surrender to the ideal of *gentillesse*. Dorigen prepares for death but does not die, then anticipates dishonor but does not suffer it. Such experiences could well reinforce her conviction that events are unpredictable and beyond her understanding. Everything about the narration echoes her belief; as Jill Mann argues, the tale begins as if it were just concluding, with marriage, and "has to force its way onward through a whole series of blockages" until the happy ending demonstrates "the freedom of events to develop in ways other than we imagine; human beings are as powerless to forecast their development as they are to control it" ("Now Read On," 62). Such is the implication of the disparities between what seems to be predicted by the narration and what actually happens, but other characters do not find themselves so swept along in the flow of events as are Dorigen and the narrator. Arveragus's courtship and knight-errantry, Aurelius's employment of the Clerk of Orleans, and the clerk's feats of magic are willed actions that produce at least immediately the results their perpetrators desired. Dorigen and the Franklin observe in wonder the very unpredictability of *aventure* that urges the tale's men to action.

In her long meditation on suicide Dorigen does make effective use of her characteristic passivity. The comic elements in this speech (the errors, the busy multiplication of less and less appropriate exempla that buy time and postpone action) indicate that Dorigen does not want to kill herself. As in her courtly mimicry to Aurelius, her attention to "mo than a thousand stories" (V 1412) of suicidal wives emphasizes that her gender is defined in texts that precede her own. Her summary of Jerome's exempla is notoriously weak, and critics have attributed its "utter dreariness" and its "perfunctory and careless" structure to Chaucer's negligence or the Franklin's ignorance of clerical writing (Dempster, "Chaucer at Work" and "A Further Note"; Lee). Dorigen's predicament makes more immediate sense of the passage's dreariness: like Judith Fetterley's "immasculated" reader who has learned to identify with the system of values that disenfranchises her, Dorigen acknowledges and repeats Jerome's text, yet she begins to become Fetterley's "resisting" reader as the speech's rote quality and disproportionate length imply her refusal of the clerical version of her identity and duty. She resists only passively, by reciting the models long enough to elude their instruction to kill herself, but the double process of assent and postponement makes a small place for self-assertion under the sign of acquiescence. That she preserves herself precisely in order to submit to Arveragus's command reaffirms her functional dependence.

The Franklin sets himself analogously against the genre of romance in celebrating a love not "constreyned by maistrye" (V 764), but the plot's discontinuity with this model signals that indeed "thise olde gentil Britouns" (V 709) have established the tale which the Franklin remembers and repeats.[20] His stance is predominantly one of veneration for the authority of the genre. Thus it is appropriate that Arveragus, knight-errant and victorious suitor in the mold of romance, should draw Dorigen and the narrator from passivity into action. No character or event receives the narrator's editorial endorsement between the moment of pledged love-in-marriage initiated by Arveragus and the penultimate moment of Dorigen's obedient return to the garden. Having lauded Arveragus's apparent surrender of *maistrie* in the former instance, the Franklin protests in the latter not Arveragus's mastery but the imagined objections of listeners to it (V 1493–98). Dorigen and the Franklin alike are drawn to the command; Arveragus overcomes her indecisiveness and the narrator's irresolution together. So closely does the Franklin's "She may have bettre fortune than yow semeth" (V 1497) echo Arveragus's reassuring "It may be wel, paraventure, yet to day" (V 1473) that it seems the narrator is taking confidence in the plot from his protagonist rather than foreknowing it.

The precariousness of the Franklin's status, dramatized in his narration and echoed in Dorigen's role, comments on romance's literary authority and on the power of its hierarchies to disenfranchise by measures of gender and class. Insofar as the Franklin's and Dorigen's double surrender to Arveragus's command leads to a happy resolution, both characters are benefiting from the control that romance's hierarchies exert over them. But to the extent that their acquiescence takes place despite their efforts at revision and innovation, the tale dramatizes how estate and gender constrain identity as well as informing it.

The differences between Dorigen and the Franklin in fictional status (narrator versus narrated), in gender, and in social position entail that their incapacities be differently configured. The Franklin's insistence that "I ne kan no termes of astrologye" (V 1266) opposes astrological magic on Christian grounds: "hooly chirches

---

[20] The narrator's negative or ironic comments on such conventional elements of his story as Dorigen's longing for Arveragus, Aurelius's lovesickness, and the use of magic might constitute a further resistance or simply imitate the detached stance typical of romance narration (see chapter 4 on magic and my *Insular Romance*, 134–74, and references there).

feith in oure bileve / Ne suffreth noon illusioun us to greve" (V 1133–34). As a modern Christian he is ignorant of the magic that is thereby identified with his Breton tale rather than his revisionary efforts. Dorigen's parallel ignorance of magic springs from a lack of experience and learning that are importantly feminine, licensing Aurelius's pity on her: "hir trouthe she swoor thurgh innocence, / She nevere erst hadde herde speke of apparence" (V 1601–2). In this case and in general, the Franklin's inability to revise his tale aligns him with Dorigen but does not make him feminine. Rather, this and other alignments between the two characters indicate that estate and gender are interrelated social hierarchies, that they can be expressed in terms of one another, and that they mutually construct social identities.

OUTSIDERS TO ROMANCE

Two narrators, Geffrey and the Wife of Bath, have a more tenuous claim to romance than the Franklin. It is not simply that they are without the marks of gentility and relative dignity in rank that associate Knight, Squire, and Franklin with characters in their tales. Geffrey's and Alison's claims to romance are more problematic than their social standing alone would suggest. Had Geffrey recited an exemplar of tail-rhyme romance rather than a debased version, had he recited less disingenuously, had he retold rather than recited, he would have established some claim to his material. His dazed ignorance, the foil for Chaucer's complex self-presentation, gives *Sir Thopas* the sense of narratorial catastrophe that is part of its pleasure. The Wife of Bath, too, seems unauthorized to tell her tale: its affiliations to romances and Breton lays shift away from her prologue's generic bases in estates satire, biblical exegesis, and antimatrimonial tracts—a clerical mixture from which Alison draws life and departs like the Eve of amphibians leaving the sea while carrying its salt in her veins. It would seem beyond this creature's ken to speak of ladies' educative mercy, of quests and fairy knowledge. Only the Wife's idealizing nostalgia for her happily-ever-after with Jankyn anticipates the generic character of her tale.

Geffrey's and Alison's status as outsiders to romance can be explained, then, in literary and social terms, but these terms are implicated in and expressed through their gender. Here I will focus on Alison's case rather than Geffrey's, for his raises issues of authorial identity that reach beyond the framework of this study. In passing I would note that the precise status of tail-rhyme romance in the late-fourteenth-century context is not really relevant to Geffrey's failure to establish a right to his own tale. Whether tail-rhyme romances and the cited *Guy of Warwick*, *Bevis of Hamtoun*, and so on are properly to be associated with debased minstrel performance or (as seems more likely) with the lower strata of the barony,[21] Geffrey's narratorial status is inferior to that of the genre in that he delivers a burlesque of it without seeming to be aware that he is doing so. His low version of potentially more elevated material comments on the place of English influence throughout Chaucer's works.[22] At the same time, pilgrim Geffrey's rote recital of "a rym I lerned longe agoon" together with his deafness to its "drasty rymyng" assign his narration a status inferior to that of tail-rhyme romance (VII 709, 930).

Geffrey's masculinity is involved in his narratorial inferiority to romance. Memorization and repetition of a single text has just characterized the persistently "litel" boy of the *Prioress's Tale* who would neglect his schoolwork to learn *Alma redemptoris mater* "al by rote" (VII 503, 509, 516, 587, 667, 522). Geffrey's rote performance signals an analogously childish lack of authority over his text. But Geffrey's incongruous childishness is distinct from the innocent simplicity of the Prioress's martyr. In the course of exploring how Geffrey and Thopas refer to Chaucer's authorial identity, Lee Patterson notes that Geffrey and Thopas are sexualized "children with a difference" due to the "powerfully erotic valence" of "elvyssh" figures and the perpetual "prikyng" that is the physical manifestation of Thopas's love-longing ("'What Man Artow?'" 132). The incongruous conjunction of

[21] Barron, 48–62, surveys questions of audience; more focused studies are Fewster, 104–28; Hudson; Pearsall, "Middle English Romance and Its Audiences"; Taylor.

[22] Chaucer's stylistic and thematic indebtedness to Middle English romance is the subject of many excellent studies including Brewer, "Relationship"; Burrow, *Ricardian Poetry*, 12–23, and *Essays on Medieval Literature*, 60–78; Everett; Crosby. Two critics who argue for a lesser influence from English writing are Salter; Spearing, *Medieval to Renaissance*.

immaturity and sexuality in Geffrey underlines his anomalous status in relation to other pilgrims and to the genre of romance.

Well may the Host inquire "What man artow?" of this pilgrim without portrait or assigned social function (VII 695). Yet the Host's ensuing analysis takes "man" not in a directly social but rather in a sexualized sense by commenting on Geffrey's body and potential attractiveness to women:

> He in the waast is shape as wel as I;
> This were a popet in an arm t'enbrace
> For any womman smal and fair of face.
> He semeth elvyssh by his contenaunce,
> For unto no wight dooth he daliaunce.   (VII 700–704)

Given that the Host is a "large man" (I 753), these lines seem to project a small-scale rotundity to which a woman fond of dolls might respond.[23] The adjective "smal" is central to the passage, radiating its modification in three potential directions, that of the "womman" and of the "face" that may be hers or her poppet's. The Ellesmere manuscript places the virgule after "womman smal," suggesting the first alternative; Hengwrt divides the line after "womman" such that her small face may suit her to Geffrey's small stature or his small face may echo his diminutive body (fol. 213v and p. 849).[24] Appropriate to both Geffrey's "popet" body and his "elvyssh" countenance, "smal" links the childish connotation of dolls to the woman's embrace and the sexually charged nature of elves. The Host compounds this half-formed sexuality with a trace of feminine reticence: like Rosemounde who will "do no daliaunce" to her lover, Geffrey refuses his "daliaunce" to everyone—to the pilgrims, it seems, as well as to "any womman" who might attempt an embrace.[25] Here the unquestioned masculinity ascribed to the Host in the *General Prologue* ("of manhod hym lakkede right naught" [I 756]) reasserts

---

[23] On the lexical possibilities of *popet* see Patterson, "'What Man Artow?'" 129–31.

[24] Lee Patterson argues that the "face" is the poppet's rather than the woman's: "'What Man Artow?'" 129n.35.

[25] "To Rosemounde," *Riverside Chaucer*, 649. *Daliaunce*, although it can refer broadly to socializing, often characterizes sexually charged interactions (e.g., *Canterbury Tales*, I 211, IV 565, VI 66; *Romaunt of the Rose*, l. 2850).

itself in ragging Geffrey's manhood. Geffrey's quiet isolation contrasts with the Host's convivial leadership, his undefined estate
with the Host's capacity to lodge and manage all estates, yet the
Host's own answer to "What man artow?" deflects those social
differences into a comment on masculinity. Indeterminate social
status finds its expression in ambivalent gender status.

Estate and gender interpenetrate also in the Wife of Bath's prologue and tale, which confront the limitations placed on feminine
power in estates literature and romance. Alison's performance is
an instance of the mimicry treated in chapter 2, a strategic repetition of sanctioned positions on gender from the crucially different position of a feminine voice.[26] When she accuses her old
husbands,

> Thow seyst that droppyng houses, and eek smoke,
> And chidyng wyves maken men to flee
> Out of hir owene houses; a, benedicitee!
> What eyleth swich an old man for to chide?   (III 278–81)

she cites the stereotype within her performance of it, establishing
a link but also a distinction between the proverbial "chidyng
wyves" and her own chiding objection to the proverb. Charging
her helpless old husbands with the chiding she voices herself
restresses that she is impersonating a masculine discourse, dis-
locating it and voicing it from elsewhere. Such mimicry also operates at the level of genre on which I will concentrate. Alison sets
romance against satire for its contrasting estimation of women,
but the juxtaposition ultimately reveals a consonance between
the two generic visions of women's right to authority. That revelation leads to a sharpened sense of women's subordination in the
gender hierarchy, but also to gestures of insubordination in which
Alison models alternatives to her own conclusions.

---

[26] See chapter 2 under "Quoting against the Grain," and Dinshaw's discussion,
113–31, of the Wife of Bath's relation to clerical antifeminism in terms of Irigaray's
concept of mimicry. Dinshaw's conclusion is that Chaucer "recuperates the feminine *within* the solid structure of that [patriarchal] discourse" (116, her italics). An
earlier version of my discussion of the Wife of Bath and social rank was published
as "Alison's Incapacity."

Alison argues that her attempts to wield sovereignty are justified by the benefits she wins from it and the peace and happiness
that yielding to it will bring to men. Yet her vaunted abilities as a
"wys wyf" (III 231) are precisely those the estates satirists condemn, and her happy endings look illusory insofar as they draw on
romance. The inadequacies of her defense of women's sovereignty
inhere in the problematics of each term. "Women" signals, in
both estates literature and romance, statuses that are incompatible with authority. "Sovereignty" as the Wife uses it designates
authority, that is, a socially conceded right to exercise influence
and control the actions of others. But her own case as well as its
cultural context attests that women can achieve only a contested
and vulnerable power over men, an effective influence that is not
hierarchically sanctioned (see Lamphere). What Alison designates
as "sovereignty" vacillates, in part because her opposition to established "auctoritee" (III 1) can express itself only in exercising
feminine powers that do not enjoy cultural authority.

Romance and estates literature imagine women's capacity for
power differently in some respects. In romance, the demanding
standards of beloved ladies, after inspiring men to improve, are
complemented by the ultimate compliance that brings courtship
to fruition. Resourcefulness, sharp wit, and magical power tend to
be relegated to minor female figures such as Thessala of Chrétien
de Troyes's *Cligés* and Morgan le Fay in *Sir Gawain and the
Green Knight* and her many other manifestations. The admirable
women of romance wield their emotional sovereignty in ways
beneficial to men and pleasurable to audiences, deferring stasis for
a time but finally yielding in harmonious accord with male desire.
Antifeminist satire in contrast is nonnarrative, organized by an
authoritative voice that rigidifies and fragments femininity into a
set of discrete negative exempla on the nagging, mercenary dependence, and overbearing sexuality that characterize wives:

> And if that she be foul, thou seist that she
> Coveiteth every man that she may se. . . .
>
> Thou liknest [wommenes love] also to wilde fyr;
> The moore it brenneth, the moore it hath desir
> To consume every thyng that brent wole be.

"Bet is," quod he, "thyn habitacioun
Be with a leon or a foul dragoun,
Than with a womman usynge for to chyde."
(III 265–66, 373–75, 775–77)[27]

Estates literature beyond antifeminist satire, as outlined in this chapter's introduction, delineates women in general (and wives in particular) according to their sexuality, their bodily relation or absence of relation to men. The *Wife of Bath's Prologue* exemplifies the estates conception in substituting for the cloth-making trade of her portrait a "sexual economics" by which she extracts wealth from her husbands in exchange for domestic peace.[28]

Romance poets and satirists agree in conceding women a potential for excellence in domesticity and love, but satirists make the failure of that potential a chief argument for avoiding women: contrary to what the suitor expects, a woman will not delight him. Moreover, the qualities that in romance contribute to women's emotional excellence define their unworthiness in satire. Their greater fragility manifests itself in weeping and clinging, their capacity for love leads to torments of jealousy and sexual conflict, and their irrationality tyrannizes men like a child's or a badly trained animal's: "For as an hors I koude byte and whyne. / I koude pleyne, and yit was in the gilt, / Or elles often tyme hadde I been spilt" (III 386–88). Satirists thus argue that women's emotional power is harmful, aggressive, and falsely exercised instead of imagining with the romances that women may enjoy an emotional authority that derives from their feminine virtues. More fundamentally, both literary forms engage the issue of woman's power through her sexuality rather than through socioeconomic measures of achievement and skill. In so doing they identify sexu-

---

[27] Notes in the *Riverside Chaucer* document debts to works of Theophrastus, Jean de Meun, Matheolus, Jerome, and other writers which can be termed "clerical" in that they are important to the medieval antimatrimonial tradition, but that tradition is part of a wider literary antifeminism: see Bloch, *Medieval Misogyny*; Patterson, *Chaucer*, 280–321.

[28] See Delany. Alison's conflation of sex and gain in her marriages is significant to her identity; it is also important that, in the dynamic of those marriages, Alison does not herself produce the wealth she deploys. Wealth is something inert that she wins from men by subterfuge and force, not something she generates by cloth making.

ality as the basic component of women's social identity and eroti-
cize dominance and submission as a dynamic inherent in relations between men and women.

In her prologue the Wife of Bath addresses the issues of gender
and power as they are formulated in antifeminist satire. Her own
origin in the very texts she disputes forces her to shadowbox with
herself, receiving almost as many blows as she delivers. However
cleverly Alison attempts to parry satiric convictions—by celebrating the less-than-perfect life rather than accepting admonish-
ments to perfection, by claiming that the rational male should
yield reasonably to the less rational female—still the notion that
women's claims to authority over men are unjustified is inextricably woven into the generic fabric of her prologue. Alison's shift
to romance is thus a strategic one, challenging antifeminist versions of the issue by confronting them with a genre that celebrates
women's emotive power instead of undermining it. Romance is
the "profeminist" literature, it would appear, that can combat the
negative formulations of Matheolus and Walter Map.[29]

Initially romance does provide Alison with an argument to use
against the satirists. In that her tale lacks chivalric adventures
and features a crucially knowledgeable and capable female character, it is not a standard romance. But it answers to the phrase
Chaucer uses, according to Donald Howard, to designate his romances, "storial thyng that toucheth gentillesse" (I 3179; Howard, 52–53n). True to the genre are the setting in "th'olde dayes of
the Kyng Arthour" (III 857) and the educative process by which
women direct men's emotional and ethical development. Arthur's justice is tempered through the queen's mercy as is Theseus's through the "verray wommanhede" of weeping ladies who
plead for Palamon and Arcite (I 1748–61). The queen and the old
hag, as in romances generally, have special insight in matters of
love and morality that leads the knight to change for the better
and to achieve happiness in love.

Alison manipulates her romance with an eye to antifeminist
assertions, using her new genre to attract validity to the version of
women's sovereignty condemned by antifeminist writers. For

[29] Not only male writers pervasively assert that women's sexuality defines their
situation and that men should be sovereign over women: for examples from He-
loise, Margery Kempe, and Christine de Pisan see my "Alison's Incapacity," 22.

women's sovereignty is not identical in romance and in satire. Wives of satire seize tangible economic and physical power by force and subterfuge: "I have the power durynge al my lyf / Upon his propre body, and noght he"; "Atte ende I hadde the bettre in ech degree / By sleighte, or force, or by som maner thyng" (III 158–59, 404–5). Ladies of romance wield emotional authority over men who submit to them by reason of their excellence: Dorigen, Laudine, and Emelye do not solicit power over men; instead their suitors declare that their overwhelming merit places them in authority over their suitors' courtships and very lives. The Wife's tale, in referring to romance conventions, implies an equivalence between the unjustified tyranny of satire's wives and the meritorious supremacy of romance heroines. Yet there is no Dorigen or Emelye in her story. The hag is aggressive, manipulative, and sexually demanding in the best satiric vein, but her high and magical attributes—as queen of fairies, if we may identify her with the elf-queen of the tale's introduction (III 860), as goal of a quest for life, as moral guide, and finally as love object—obscure her antifeminist connections and work to validate her active exercise of power.

Even as romance dignifies the claim to women's sovereignty in this tale, frequent antifeminist touches vitiate the romantic elevation Alison seems to desire. The answers proposed to the queen's question "What thyng is it that wommen moost desiren" catalog feminine weaknesses, from "Somme seyde wommen loven best richesse" to "we kan no conseil hyde" (III 905, 925, 980). The animal metaphors for women (limed like birds, kicking like galled horses, booming like bitterns) also answer to the satiric conviction that women are profoundly irrational, sensual creatures.

Within the Wife's framing problematic of women's sovereignty, her juxtapositions of satire and romance amount to more than simple citation. They reveal the incongruity of the two generic visions and their shared inadequacy to her argument. The knight's trial culminates this process. Several shifts that may have seemed involuntary, from queenly authority to proverbial foibles, from fairy illusion to all-too-solid flesh, are here recuperated in a full return to romantic sensibility. The hierarchical display of the queen's assembly of judgment evokes fictional love courts, with the "queene hirself sittynge as a justise" (III 1028), and the answer she and her ladies accept from the knight seems to tally with courtly conventions about women's authority in matters of the heart. Yet the hag anticipates that the ladies will not gladly admit the knight's answer; even "the proudeste" will simply not "dar seye nay" (III 1017–19). Echoing her suspicion, the knight insists: "This is your mooste desir, thogh ye me kille" (III 1041). The implication of resistance marks a disparity between satiric sovereignty, actively claimed and energetically wielded, and the passive, apparently unwilled sovereignty of women in romance. To force the queen's ladies into accepting that "Wommen *desiren* to have sovereynetee" (III 1038) is to conflate the romance vision that has sanctioned women's unwilled authority with Alison's fiercer vision that woman consciously seek and enjoy it.

This assertion that women's power is always desired and always contested clarifies the insufficiency of Alison's two discourses for dramatizing a worthy sovereignty of secular women. Satire denies their worth. Romance seems a genre in which women's excellence confers authority, but the appearance proves false. The courted lady's temporary sovereignty is a function of the suitor's desire to build love into chivalric identity by demonstrating his capacity for adventure. Her mercy and compliance are the necessary closure to her ability to command devotion. That compliance and the tale's presentation from the knight's point of view, its evasion of punishment for the knight, and the queen's merely contingent authority (for which she "thanketh the kyng with al hir myght" [III 899]) offer a recognizably romantic fiction. The hag's power over her "walwing" knight is anomalous, more like the power of Morgan le Fay in *Sir Gawain and the Green Knight* than like that of a conventional beloved. But even the hag surrenders in the end. The joyful and thoroughly fanciful resolution that fulfills the knight's "worldly appetit" (III 1218) illustrates the most romance can render. Here, as in Lee Patterson's analysis of Alison's prologue, "her very verbalizations remain unavoidably dependent, feminine respeakings of a resolutely masculine idiom" (*Chaucer*, 313; see also Aers, 143–51; Hanning, "Textual Harassment").

Despite the respects in which the *Wife of Bath's Tale* does not manage to transcend its discourses, I would propose that the Wife jars them suggestively in two ways at least, first through organizing her tale around a crime of rape and second through dramatizing a certain mobility in genders that compromises the hierarchies her genres provide.

Rape is not absent from the history of romance, but it is hardly typical behavior for the genre's protagonists.[30] On the other hand, medieval and modern voices suggest that the rape and the forced marriage of the *Wife of Bath's Tale* do not depart from romance convention so much as demystify it. In a historical study of marriage practices, Georges Duby concludes that the Old French poetry of adultery and love service is based on a "fundamentally misogynous" conception of woman as merely a means to male self-advancement: "Woman was an object and, as such, contemptible" (*Medieval Marriage*, 108). Eugene Vance corroborates Duby's historical analysis by connecting early lyrics of adultery to romances featuring demanding ladies. Throughout, love's poetic expression is typically "le combat érotique," an aesthetic of antithesis recognizing the violence that is veiled by the mystified perfection of *fine amor* (see also R. F. Green, "*Familia Regis*" and "Chaucer's Victimized Women"). Feminine voices of the period extend the argument to the historical scene: the wife of Geoffrey de la Tour Landry warns that men's courtly importuning disguises their coerciveness (*Livre du Chevalier de la Tour Landry*, 246–28; *Book of the Knight of the Tower*, 163–64). Christine de Pisan repeats the warning in her *Epistre au dieu d'amours* and with particular force in the letter she attributes to Sebille de Monthault: lovers should be "loyaulx, secrez, voir disans, ce qu'ilz ne sont mie, ains scet on que communement sont fains et pour les dames decepvior dient ce qu'ilz ne pensent ne vouldroient faire" (loyal, discreet, truthful, which they are not at all; rather it is common knowledge that they are false and that to deceive women they say what they neither think nor desire to do) (*Oeuvres Poétiques*,

---

[30] L. H. Loomis, 29–31, cites a similar episode from *Sir Degaré* in her argument that Chaucer knew the Auchinleck MS. Degare's father, a fairy knight, meets a maiden lost in a forest and rapes her: "Þo noþing ne coude do ȝhe / But wep and criede and wolde fle; / And he anon gan hire atholde, / And dide his wille, what he wolde. / He binam hire here maidenhod . . ." (*Middle English Metrical Romances*, 291 [*Sir Degaré*, 107–11]).

3:169, 2:1–27). The Wife's tale concurs that sexual relations are power relations, whether men or women are on top. The rape in the Wife's tale is the limit case of differential power in sexual relations, and as such it speaks to the Wife's ongoing concern with sovereignty.

In the *Wife of Bath's Prologue* "sovereynetee" seems constantly to vacillate, but three major contradictions can be distinguished. Alison sometimes associates sovereignty with economic gain, "wynnyng" (III 416), yet she seems to win nothing from her fourth husband, gives up her gains to Jankyn, and makes the hag speak eloquently against the significance of wealth. At other points, coercion, including physical domination, renders Alison's metaphor "myself have been the whippe" (III 175) very nearly literal, but she moves from coercion to submissions and accommodations with her fourth and fifth husbands as does the hag with her knight. Finally, her conception of sovereignty requires the trust or the high opinion of her husbands: "Thou sholdest seye, 'Wyf, go wher thee liste . . . / I knowe yow for a trewe wyf, dame Alys,'" she instructs her old husbands, and Jankyn fulfills her desire in acceding, "Myn owene trewe wyf, / Do as thee lust the terme of al thy lyf" (III 318–20, 819–20). Nonetheless, the Wife cheerfully undermines her demand for trust and respect by asserting and demonstrating that women are untrustworthy: "half so boldely kan ther no man / Swere and lyen, as a womman kan" (III 227–28).

Why does Alison constantly alter and even cancel each of her versions of sovereignty? The solution is not that women's desire for power is nothing but a desire for love. Love is a relatively simple matter for the Wife, something she often gets from men. In contrast, women's sovereignty vacillates confusingly even in love's presence: with the "daungerous" Jankyn and knight (III 514, 1090) it works to perpetuate love, as if it were grounded in merit, but in her four earlier marriages it tyrannizes or substitutes for love, as if it were mere self-interest. The Wife's casual manipulation of her old husbands' devotion—"They loved me so wel, by God above, / That I ne tolde no deyntee of hir love" (III 207–8)—suggests that the question of power precedes and subsumes the question of men's love: it is sovereignty that "worldly wommen loven best" (III 1033). The object of this fundamental love is elusive, and its elusiveness partly accounts for its desirability, in accordance with Alison's psychological principle "Forbede us thyng, and that desiren we" (III 519). Female sovereignty, in any form, is the most heretical of her desires, unsustained in any of the conventional discourses on which she draws. Looking beyond these discourses necessarily leaves the Wife inarticulate, even about the meaning of the sovereignty she imagines. She desires to validate the forbidden but can hardly formulate what it is.

The persistence with which the Wife of Bath considers sex in terms of sovereignty recalls Catharine MacKinnon's argument that "male and female are created through the eroticization of dominance and submission" ("Feminism . . . Toward a Feminist Jurisprudence," 635). In the Wife's prologue and tale, the experience of sexuality takes place always in the context of masculine social authority. The Wife's contested control over her husbands, the knight's rape, his later concession of sovereignty, and his wife's ensuing obedience are all predicated on masculine ascendancy within sexuality and reveal that ascendancy even as they attempt to critique it. Sexuality is so fully subsumed within power relations as to be unimaginable in isolation from them.[31] Much of the literature of courtship endorses this state of affairs, as we have seen, but in narrating a story of rape the Wife pushes the power differential to its extreme and resists it with the sanction of law. The "cours of lawe" (III 892) that condemns the knight's rape also validates his discovery that women desire sovereignty: most immediately in the knight's case, they desire not to be raped.[32] At

[31] MacKinnon, although she uses sex and gender "relatively interchangeably" as do many writers, argues that "each element of the female *gender* stereotype is revealed as, in fact, *sexual*" such that "sex as gender and sex as sexuality are thus defined in terms of each other, but it is sexuality that determines gender, not the other way around" ("Feminism . . . Toward a Feminist Jurisprudence," 635; "Feminism . . . An Agenda for Theory," 530–31, her italics). For a contrasting position on the relation of gender to sex, see Butler, 7: "Gender ought not to be conceived merely as the cultural inscription of meaning on a pregiven sex (a juridical conception); gender must also designate the very apparatus of a production whereby the sexes themselves are established."

[32] Although in late medieval English legislation rape is both a sexual crime and a crime against property and family interests (see Post), the Wife's tale isolates the sexual offense against the maiden from other considerations by not representing a wronged husband or father in the criminal process.

the same time, the limit case of rape invokes official support (quickly diffused from the crime itself into the issue as a whole) for the knight's discovery that women desire sovereignty in all sexual relations.

Bringing the "cours of lawe" to bear on a sexual encounter argues further that sexuality is not sealed off from public life, is not merely a component of private subjectivity that has no social implications. Noting the division in estates literature between men's social and women's sexual functions, Lee Patterson asks whether subjectivity is then feminine: "If women were denied social definition, did this not mean that the realm of the *asocial*— of the internal, the individual, the subjective—was peculiarly theirs?" (*Chaucer*, 282 [his italics]). The Wife of Bath is indeed amply endowed with an emotive and reflective selfhood, but I understand the project of her prologue and tale to be one of resisting distinctions between the sexual and the social, the private and the public. Rape, as one instance in which sexual behavior clearly has social meaning, is consonant with the Wife's persistent claims that her own identity is bound up with that of other wives and that wives are beleaguered by clerical culture's antifeminism. Elsewhere I have argued that because Alison sees women's illiteracy as part of their subordination and herself attacks Jankyn's book as if that could redress cultural oppressions, her prologue and tale constitute the most substantial comment in Chaucer's works on the Rising of 1381 and the conditions surrounding it ("Writing Lesson of 1381"). Here I would add that gender, apparently a feature of private and subjective identity, is a vehicle for attempting to imagine transformations in women's social position.

Romance is the appropriate form for confronting an unknowable desire. Its "strategy of delay" holds narrative "on the threshold before the promised end, still in the wilderness of wandering, 'error,' or 'trial'" (Parker, 4–5). The hag's physical metamorphosis is only the most dazzling of many mutations demonstrating that genders are not fixed phenomena but fluid media through which new potential can be realized. Gender lines shift throughout the Wife's tale. The barber in Midas's story becomes a wife, the ladies' court of judgment replaces Arthur's, and the hag comes to speak like a cleric while her husband submits with wifely meekness to her "wise governance" (III 1231). These substitutions make women the active movers of plot, as they are not in most romances, where they may inspire chivalric activity but where that activity is itself the source of change. Gender displacements extend to the fairy realm, as the "elf-queene" and "hir joly compaignye" (III 860), who are all feminine when the knight encounters them (III 992), seem to metamorphose during Alison's introduction from "joly" dancers to potent incubi threatening women in the Arthurian countryside. The knight-rapist and the king both move from having power to surrendering it, while women throughout the tale move themselves into male purviews. The tale's exclusion of chivalric adventures reverses the prologue's effacement of Alison's cloth-making profession, emphasizing the dependence of men on women. Even the comic victory of friars over fairies in the tale's first lines is vitiated when the fairy wife's pillow lecture demonstrates her intimate knowledge of religious texts. Reassigning women to positions of authority traces the path of their transgression in the narrative itself. The power they exercise is not always benign or admirable, but the gender shifts themselves loosen the bond between maleness and authority that makes a worthy female sovereignty inconceivable.

The transgressiveness of such gender shifts, particularly in the context of an unlicensed feminine desire for sovereignty, allies the *Wife of Bath's Tale* to the carnivalesque, M. M. Bakhtin's productive conception of a complex of ideas and practices that stage confrontations between popular and elite culture, between the indulgent and the controlled body, pagan superstition and religious orthodoxy, and festival license and the rigors of law. Bakhtin argues that comic inversions of religious and regal authority (the crowned ass, the boy bishop, the mock priest) could amount to virtually philosophical reconsiderations of the sense of life in the late medieval and early modern period.[33] Yet these inversions

---

[33] Bakhtin, *Rabelais* and *Dialogic Imagination*, argued that a rigid separation developed in the Middle Ages between the poles of popular and official culture, and that only in the Renaissance, that moment of rupture and new beginning, did the carnivalesque bring popular ideology into relation with the official to critique and reform it, reaching beyond mere holiday escape to an insurgent rethinking of social organization. Whether or not there was in fact a time in the Middle Ages when popular culture did not interact with and modify the official structures of

are insistently material, as most fully manifested in the carnival body's outrageous appetites, bulk, and openness to the world. In contrast to the controlled, finished, polished individual that Bakhtin associates with both "classic aesthetics" and medieval "official" culture, the carnival body is "unfinished, outgrows itself, transgresses its own limits," not only to rebel against official constraints but also to represent a "collective ancestral body of all the people," a cyclical body that ambivalently combines renewal and degradation (*Rabelais*, 19, 25, 26; see Stallybrass and White, 1–26). Bakhtin's illustration of this body in figurines of "senile pregnant hags" who laughingly express both decay and fertility in "the epitome of incompleteness" particularly calls to mind the shapeshifters' transitions between mocking age and sexually submissive youth (*Rabelais*, 25–26). In the preceding chapter I proposed that the shapeshifters of romance use their double form to resist grounding their identities in bodily appearance. Shape-shifting can also represent a subversive potential of the feminine in the social order.[34]

Masquerade, in its traditional sense of dressing to disguise and parody, plays a central role in carnival behavior, and central to masquerade itself is transgression. Men dressed as women and women as men, seculars dressed as monks and nuns, children as adults, and humans as animals, all confound the distinctions on which organized social life proceeds.[35] In late medieval romances

---

Church and court, Chaucer is far from alone in staging such interactions: see Ganim, Gash, Cook.

[34] Medieval romance may seem an unlikely place to look for a carnivalesque sensibility, insofar as it is primarily a court literature that works out ideals and formulates concerns peculiar to those who rule. But historical as well as literary studies qualify the sharp separations Bakhtin posited between learned and popular, orthodox and superstitious, and high and low culture generally in the medieval period. On the mixed audience for fabliaux see Nykrog; Muscatine, *Old French Fabliaux*. The social composition of the audience for late medieval romance is a particular concern in Bennett, Coleman, Knight, and my *Insular Romance*. The commingling of popular and learned material in the Melusine analogues is the subject of Le Goff, *Time, Work, and Culture*, 205–22 ("Melusina: Mother and Pioneer").

[35] On crossdressing in romance, not taken up by Chaucer, see Perret. *Le Roman de Silence* particularly focuses on disguise, gender, and social strictures in its plot of a girl raised as a boy in order to protect her family's lineal rights.

the shapeshifters' masquerade of loathsomeness typically imitates the carnival body itself, the sensual excess and outsize physique that counter decency and restraint.[36] Dame Ragnell evokes strikingly that body's excess, its emphasis on orifices and indulgence, and its incompletion and openness to the world. Everything about her ugliness is oversized and voracious. Her bulging eyes and wide mouth, her snotty nose and cheeks wide as women's hips, her barrel body and enormous breasts produce an inverted *effictio* of extravagant ugliness; her protruding teeth and long nails make the spectacle of her gluttony "fulle foulle and nott curteys" (602; see also 228–51). Ragnell's gargantuan appetite extends to sex: "Thoughe I be foulle, yett am I gaye," she warns as she demands Gawain in marriage (300). The grotesque Ragnell penetrates courtly space, upending its protocols by dressing more richly than Guinevere, riding a beautifully caparisoned horse ("Ytt was no reason ne ryght") and holding a large public wedding rather than the small private one Guinevere suggests: "I wol be weddyd alle openly . . . And in the open halle wol I dyne" (251, 575, 579). Ragnell's aggressive, voracious body might be understood to alienate any disturbing qualities from the submissive, beautiful body that succeeds it, in a process that would finally authorize only the controlled courtly body. We have seen that such a reading would make shape-shifting sustain the stable equivalence of body and identity for women, but that the persistence of sexualized qualities in the ugly body resists its dismissal from the scene of femininity. Further resisting this dismissal are the grotesque body's penetration into the courtly world, revealing the limits of the court's control, and the invocation of a carnival sensibility in the very act of shifting the body from old to young, disgusting to pleasing, in that cyclical ambivalence which Bakhtin's laughing pregnant hags also illustrate.

The Wife of Bath, who masquerades in the split body of her tale's heroine, does not provide a description of the loathly body to match those of the tale's analogues. The absence of a detailed

[36] See chapter 2, pp. 85–92. The masculine connotations of Melusine's and Blonde Esmerees's serpent bodies are implicit in the scenes of their revelation and might supplement the outrage to social categories of commingling animal with human forms (English *Melusine*, 295–97; French *Mélusine*, 241–43; *Lybeaus Desconus*, Cotton MS, ll. 1984–2019; *Le Bel Inconnu*, ll. 3127–3211).

monstrousness in the *Wife of Bath's Tale* permits Alison's own body to fill the space, identifying her age and deterioration, her sexual appetite and aggressiveness with those of the "olde wyf." For Alison, like the shapeshifters of romance, is richly carnivalesque. Perhaps most telling is her persistent upending of her body to locate the essence of her attractiveness in "the beste *quoniam* myghte be," her *queynte*, her *bele chose*, her "chambre of Venus" (III 332, 444, 447, 510, 608, 618). Twice she associates the voracious mouth with sexual voracity, in her self-explanatory proverb "a likerous mouth moste han a likerous tayl" and in consoling her browbeaten husbands that "if I wolde selle my *bele chose*, / I koude walke as fressh as is a rose; / But I wol kepe it for youre owene tooth" (III 466, 447–49). In the *General Prologue* her large hips, bold face, and gap teeth also recall the carnival body's excess and openness; like the hag in the *Marriage of Sir Gawaine* "cladd in red scarlett" Alison wears red stockings and robes.[37] Her tale's prologue proposes inversions of power and reason in marriage that further invoke the reversals of festival and the Wife's own assertion that "myn entente nys but for to pleye" (III 192). Matched to her body is the unruly logic Chaucer derives from the *sermon joyeux*, the parody form that Lee Patterson has shown to be so useful in illuminating the Wife's manipulation of religious orthodoxy. Like the most orthodox preacher, the Wife takes a text—Paul's warning about the tribulations of marriage—but "as we would expect from a *sermon joyeux*, she unlocks the letter to discover an irreducible carnality" (*Chaucer*, 313).

Alison's unruly carnality both fills in the loathly lady's undetailed form and masquerades in her two extravagant bodies. The old wife's impeccable invocation of texts on gentility, poverty, and age extends the masquerade by providing Alison with a feminine voice that can cite authorities without distortion. Borrowing credibility from the tale's old wife as she borrows the capacity to shape-shift, Alison furthers her prologue's attempt to claim authority over men. Her festive transgressions, bodily and marital as they are, resonate with the public and social commentary of carnival. Particularly in an era when, as Natalie Davis notes, rela-

[37] The scarlet clothing is noted three times in the *Marriage of Sir Gawaine*, 237, 238, 239; Alison's red clothing at I 456 and III 559.

tions between the sexes could readily stand for the relations of
subject to lord, common to gentle, and Christian to Church, the
"disorderly woman" of mummings, charivaris, and literature is a
politically charged figure (124–52; see also Russo). Davis places
the Wife of Bath among many literary and historical instances of
unruly women who, depending on the context and case, may simply reassert prevailing social relations by temporarily suspending
them while illustrating the feminine irrationality that justifies
them, or who may additionally undermine the social order by
acting in ways not consonant with it. "Play with the unruly
woman," she concludes, "is partly a chance for temporary release
from the traditional and stable hierarchy; but it is also part of the
conflict over efforts to change the basic distribution of power
within society" (131). Whether Alison succeeds in mounting an
effective argument for women's sovereignty or only in dramatizing an outrageous challenge to women's subordination, the public
and festive register of her performance moves her sexuality onto
the social scene and denies the estates distinction between
worldly masculinity and domestic femininity.

   Also suggestive for Chaucer's work is Davis's evidence that the
"woman on top" in the early modern period could sanction social
disobedience for men, who rioted dressed as women and took female pseudonyms such as "Mère Folle" and "Lady Skimmington"
in uprisings against various government measures (147–50). Such
historical disguises draw energy from the disruptive claims to authority of figures like Alison as well as taking shelter behind the
identity of the less responsible and rational gender. As Chaucer's
own disguise, Alison talks back to important literary traditions to
which the poet and she are both in a subordinate relation. Alison's
disruptions of romance are Chaucer's as well, and more substantial by far than those attempted in the person of the decorous
Franklin.

   For my focus on the interplay of gender and social status,
Chaucer's crossdressing in Alison's feminine rebelliousness is
suggestive of the constraints hierarchy imposes on men, but more
salient is the ultimate collapse of Alison's specifically feminine
effort. The festive sexuality that pervades her performance celebrates the transgressive potential of women's sovereignty but also
expresses sovereignty as seized power rather than sanctioned au-

thority. Alison's restless metamorphoses, from antifeminist creation to romancer to clerical scholar and back to militant wife in her envoy, emphasize that each tradition on which she draws denies women authority. The inadequacy of her arguments, the shifting genders, and the flow of genres in her tale record the impossibility of her undertaking. To clarify the inconceivability of feminine authority is itself, however, to make a significant point about the place of gender in the social hierarchy.

Subtle Clerks and Uncanny Women

HE WONDERS of Chaucer's tales, his flying horse and healing sword, shape-shifting fairy, beloved elf-queen, and illusionist clerk, draw on some of the most familiar manifestations of magic in romance. Magic is a generic marker that signals the inferiority of romance in the hierarchy of genres. The persistent claim leveled against romance magic is that it evades the genuine concerns of the world in favor of seductive falsehoods. Louise Fradenberg begins a study of the *Wife of Bath's Tale* with Bishop Hurd's account of the "magic of the old romances" dissolved when reason "drove them off the scene, and would endure these *lying wonders*, neither in their own proper shape, nor as masked in figures."[1] Hurd's association of magic and falsehood echoes that of medieval writers for whom religious literature offered truth and salvation in place of the fable, folly, and lies of romances. In *Insular Romance* I have argued that the "lying wonders" of romance can comment on political and social concerns; here I argue that magic becomes in romance a means of expressing gender difference. Participating in the cultural construction of gender and at the same time moving against its restraints, the deployment of magic in romance is far from irrelevant to worldly concerns.

Magic is for the Middle Ages on a continuum with philosophy and science, but in romance it can be rather narrowly defined as the manifestation of powers that are not directly attributable to Christian faith, yet are so far beyond the ordinary course of nature as to be inexplicable according to its laws (see Kieckhefer; Peters; Thorndike; on romances see Carasso-Bulow; Kelly, 146–204).

---

[1] Fradenberg, "Wife of Bath's Passing Fancy," 31 (his italics). Fradenberg, 34n.9, points out the similarity of Auerbach's view that "the courtly romance is not reality shaped and set forth by art, but an escape into fable and fairy tale" (*Mimesis*, 138).

Shape-shifting, divination, and the fabrication of objects that extend human capacities are common expressions of magic in romance. The *House of Fame* divides its description of magical powers into three categories, those of illusion, spell casting, and natural magic:

> Ther saugh I pleye jugelours,
> Magiciens, and tregetours,
> And Phitonesses, charmeresses,
> Olde wicches, sorceresses,
> That use exorsisacions,
> And eke these fumygacions;
> And clerkes eke, which konne wel
> Al this magik naturel,
> That craftely doon her ententes. . . .
> Ther saugh I Colle tregetour
> Upon a table of sycamour
> Pleye an uncouth thyng to telle—
> Y saugh him carien a wynd-melle
> Under a walsh-note shale.   (1259–67, 1277–81)

"Colle tregetour" and the opening group of entertainers "pleye," whereas the clerks of natural magic "konne wel" how to use astrology "craftely" to accomplish their will (here, to control health). Set against both groups of men are the women who use spells and rituals, and whose source of knowledge is occulted, attributed neither to skill nor to study. Although all three groups are obviously allied to some degree, the general distinction drawn here between masculine skill and knowledge and the more occulted feminine power that I will call uncanniness persists in the romance genre.

From the perspective of gender, magic has two characteristic expressions in romance. Magic associated with masculine concerns and characters is learned, is clearly hostile or helpful, and strives to confer on the individual subject an autonomy and completeness that we have seen to be chimerical in masculine identity as romance develops it. In association with the feminine, magic expresses the ambiguous danger and pleasure of intimacy between the sexes. The mirror brought to Cambyuskan's court points toward this distinction. The emissary who brings the mir-

ror from the "kyng of Arabe and of Inde" (V 110) at first explains
to Cambyuskan that it will reflect approaching adversity "Unto
youre regne or to youreself also, / And openly who is youre freend
or foo" (V 135–36), but goes on to present the mirror to Canacee
because it can show "any lady bright" what her suitor's true feelings are (V 137–45).

As the mirror slips from appearing to be a gift for Cambyuskan
to being instead Canacee's gift, a single token defines masculine
concerns as public and feminine concerns as intimate. Further,
the mirror is broadly appropriate to woman in signifying for medieval writers her identification with her external appearance, with
the beauty that makes her the object of the male gaze. The mirror
carried by Oiseuse in the *Romance of the Rose* can equally stand
for woman as image and for the feminine role as mirror to men in
courtship, preparing for the connection between the pool of Nar-
cissus and the lady's eyes.[2] For Luce Irigaray too the mirror is an
image for woman, specifically as perceived by man: the mirror
indicates that man knows himself both by observing what he is
not, in the objectified woman, and by seeing himself reflected in
woman (*Speculum*, 133–46). The mirror as the emissary first represents it to Cambyuskan elides the feminine by reflecting men to
men directly and by predicting affairs of state rather than revealing affairs of the heart. This first version of the mirror's capacity
expresses the tendency of masculine magic in romance to seek a
self-sufficiency and control beyond the usual contingencies of social and intimate relations. Feminine magic, as suggested by the
insights about suitors that Canacee's gift can show to any lady,
reintroduces the complexities of relationship and puts suitors at a
disadvantage even as it serves intimacy. For Irigaray the feminine
mirror is concave, taking its shape from the woman's face and
challenging as well as reflecting the masculine: "But perhaps
through this specular surface which sustains discourse is found
not the void of nothingness but the dazzle of multifaceted speleol-
ogy. A scintillating and incandescent concavity, of language also,
that threatens to set fire to fetish-objects and gilded eyes" (*Speculum*, 143). The woman-mirror, at first providing the validating re-

---

[2] For the mirror's association with the "stereotypical courtly lady" and further
possibilities for the mirror's meanings see Hult, 221–23 (quotation at 222).

flection of man, becomes a burning glass capable of destroying what it has sustained. In romances, women who wield magical power typically are men's sustaining intimates and their endangering opposites, in uncanny combinations of the alien and the familiar.

"ARTES THAT BEEN CURIOUS"

One sort of magic in romance is practiced by "clerkes that been lykerous / To reden artes that been curious" (V 1119–20). The arcane knowledge of these clerks expresses and promises access to the autonomy that male characters seek in romance. Magic of this kind responds to two problematic aspects of masculine identity in romance as outlined in the first chapter above. The ideological demand that a knight or aspirant to knighthood achieve an independent, self-contained, heterosexual identity generates courtships that figure identity as a process of alienation from woman, the foreign, the animal; all that can be made exterior to masculinity marks off where it is to be found. Identity is thus purchased at the cost of isolation and diminishment. The chivalric communities of romance, by recognizing their members in relation and opposition to one another, constrain self-determination from another direction. Identity becomes subject to reputation in the chivalric sphere, and contrarily to narcissistic isolation in the sphere of courtship. The "artes that been curious" attempt to alleviate the constraints on heterosexual masculinity by serving that role's claim to autonomy and self-determination. Although magic finally has little to do with masculine achievements, the desires it expresses importantly characterize masculinity in romance.

Clerical magic resembles applied science in attempting to control the natural world and extend human capabilities. Romances typically attribute the fabrications of magicians to their wisdom and wide learning as well as their specific training in magic. Merriam Sherwood provides examples of automatons such as flying horses and warning devices that are fine machines operated by magic, and notes the medieval association between such creations and the Orient, a place of both science and wonders. Robert Hanning discusses marvels in romance with reference to the term *engin*, which reflects the admixture in clerical magic of technique and artfulness in meanings that range from "machine" and "invention" to "cleverness" and "deception" (*Individual*, 105–38). For Chaucer the term of choice is "subtil," also widely applied in romances to clerks of magic. *Cleomadés* compares the magical gifts presented on the king's birthday to similar wonders made by Virgil such as the mirror in Rome to which Chaucer refers (V 231):

> Mout ot en Virgile sage honme
> Et soutieu, car il fist a Ronme
> Une chose mout engingneuse
> Mout soutieu et mout merveilleuse. . . .   (1723–26)

[Virgil was a very wise and subtle man, for he made in Rome a most clever thing, most subtle and marvelous.]

Virgil's subtlety includes working "par nigromance," by conjuring of spirits, as do the men who constructed the king's gifts: "clerc furent de grant afaire / d'astronomie et d'ingromance" (they were clerks of high station in astronomy and necromancy) (1735, 1830–31). Fabricating Chaucer's flying horse, "maad moore subtilly" than the crowd can comprehend, required its maker to know "ful many a seel and many a bond" (V 222, 131). The "subtil clerk" of the *Franklin's Tale*, also called a "magicien" and a "philosophre," is similarly learned in astronomy although he uses "magyk natureel" rather than invoking spirits (e.g., V 1125, 1184, 1261, 1572). For these subtle clerks magic facilitates the application of scientific theory to particular uses. Clerical magic has masculine associations with learning and worldly effectiveness, and its practitioners are predominantly male.

Chaucer's tales leave unanswered just what kind of magic their philosophers are practicing. It has been proposed that the Clerk of Orleans is merely a "tregetour," a banquet-hall illusionist who only calculates when a high tide will occur, but to so argue is to choose one assertion about his magic from a conflicting set of assertions in the tale.[3] Aurelius's brother remembers the Clerk of Orleans as one who was learning the "particuler sciences" of "magyk natureel," preparing for the astronomical calculations

---

[3] Background for the allusions to "tregetours" (V 1141) is provided by L. H. Loomis, "Secular Dramatics," and by Braswell. On the possibility of a high tide covering the rocks, see Spearing, ed., *Franklin's Prologue and Tale*, 16, 50–54, and Luengo.

the Clerk later performs (V 1122, 1125). However, the brother expects the Clerk to accomplish only a tregetour's mechanical illusion (V 1138–64). The narrator also describes his magic as mere sleight of hand in his censorious account of the "illusion / By . . . apparence or jogelrye" that the rocks have disappeared (V 1264–65), but the Clerk's prescience about his visitors—"he tolde hem al that was in hire entente" (V 1178)—suggests remarkable powers of divination. This range of information leaves the Clerk's magic in some measure undefinable, as do the conflicting explanations in the *Squire's Tale* for the magical gifts. The foreign knight who declares that the horse's maker "knew ful many a seel and many a bond" (V 131) has not clarified for editors whether natural magic or conjuration is at issue; the assembled crowd anticipates Aurelius's brother by invoking "an apparence ymaad by som magyk, / As jogelours pleyen at thise feestes grete" (V 218–19).[4] The conflicting explanations again obscure the nature of the magical operations performed.

Obscuring how magic functions is one way of insisting on its inaccessibility to ordinary understanding and its superiority to everyday contingencies. Yet narrators are also at pains to establish some degree of detachment from clerical magic. The double movement of insisting on the validity of magic and yet disengaging from it, which parallels the gendered function of clerical magic as a source of masculine autonomy that does not finally guarantee it, returns us to the problems of tone in the Squire's and Franklin's tales.

The Squire's thinly developed relation to his tale argues that features of tone such as the narrator's attitude toward the "lewed peple" (V 221) and the startling juxtapositions of wonder and demystifying explanation are better referred to the tale itself than to the Squire's psychology.[5] Jennifer Goodman has shown that the *Squire's Tale* draws on late medieval composite romances for its

---

[4] On natural magic versus conjuration as the referents of "many a seel and many a bond" see the notes to V 131 in the *Squire's Tale, Variorum Edition,* and in the *Riverside Chaucer.*

[5] Recent assessments of Chaucer's plans for Fragment V in relation to manuscript discrepancies are Lawton, 106–29; Pearsall, *Canterbury Tales,* 14–23; and Cooper, *Canterbury Tales,* 217–18, 230–32. The dramatic reading of the *Squire's Tale* as a distortion of romance suited to a young and inexperienced teller is illustrated by Miller.

projected vast scale, its interlaced adventures of several family members, its motifs (even when these may have more distant Oriental analogues), and its "distinctive taste for a combination of the fantastic and minute realism" (130; see also Hornstein). Even closer to the *Squire's Tale* than the English composite romances cited by Goodman are Girard d'Amiens's *Meliacin* and, to a lesser extent, Adenet le Roi's *Cleomadés*.[6] These works illustrate a generic attitude to magic that does not depend on a particular narrator's psychology. A first tendency in narrating clerical magic is to insist on its mystery as well as its science. Concluding the lengthy account of Virgil's fabrications that provides background for the magical gifts to the king, *Cleomadés*'s narrator comments on "lewed peple":

> Gent de petit entendement
> Demandent a la fois conment
> Tels choses pueent estre faites
> Que je vous ai ici retraites,
> Aucun en sont tout esbahi.
> Et savez vous que je leur di?
> Je leur di que nigromancie
> Est mout merveilleuse clergie,
> Car mainte merveille en a on
> Faite pieç'a, bien le set on.   (1639–48)

[People of little understanding ask all at once how such things as I have described to you here can be made, and some are completely in fear of them. And do you know what I say to them? I say to them that necromancy is a most wonderful study, because from it many marvels have been made for a long time, as is well known.]

Far from explaining clerical magic, the narrator insists on its inexplicability, on the "merveille" of "merveilleuse clergie" that

---

[6] *Meliacin* and *Cleomadés* arise from two different versions of an ultimately Oriental tale, according to their editors: *Cleomadés*, 610–41; Aebischer. Girard d'Amiens and Adenet le Roi both appear to have visited England under Edward I, and Froissart's reference to *Cleomadés* in his *Espinette amoureuse*, written just after his years in service to Queen Philippa, has suggested that the romance may have been current in England in Chaucer's youth. Oriental associations of the *Squire's Tale* (but not its derivation from composite romance) were outlined by Braddy and more recently by Metlitzki, 140–60.

places it beyond ordinary comprehension. Wonder, rather than attempted explanation, is the right response.

The *Squire's Tale* also takes this position. The Squire's throng begins by expressing wonder at each gift:

> But everemoore hir mooste wonder was
> How that it koude gon, and was of bras . . .   (V 199–200)
>
> And somme of hem wondred on the mirour . . .   (V 225)
>
> And oother folk han wondred on the swerd . . .   (V 236)
>
> Tho speeke they of Canacees ryng,
> And seyden alle that swich a wonder thyng
> Of craft of rynges herde they nevere noon . . .   (V 247–49)

But subsequently the people displace wonder with scientific explanations, historical analogies, and concrete fears. Concealed enemy soldiers in the horse, the science of optics, and the technology of glassmaking and "hardyng of metal" (V 243) reduce clerical magic to the merely learned; a few brief allusions to Greek myth and "fairye" (V 201) divorce "merveille" from "clergie" and relegate the former to the long ago and far away. The narrator's position, here as in *Cleomadés*, is that the answer to how such things can be made is beyond the reach of such explanations: these things "been maad moore subtilly / Than they kan in hir lewednesse comprehende" (V 222–23). Narrator and people finally return to wonder in the passage describing how to operate the brass horse:

> Swich wondryng was ther on this hors of bras
> That syn the grete sege of Troie was,
> Theras men wondreden on an hors also,
> Ne was ther swich a wondryng as was tho.   (V 306–9)

The clarity of the instruction to "Trille this pyn, and he wol vanysshe anoon" contends with the narrator's "The hors vanysshed, I noot in what manere" (V 328, 342) as if to insist on a residual mystery within the masterful construction. This close echoes the wonder first experienced when the "strange knyght" arrived: "In al the halle ne was ther spoken a word / For merveille of this knyght; hym to biholde / Ful bisily they wayten, yonge and olde"

(V 89, 86–88). Silence and "merveille" acknowledge the superiority of clerical magic to ordinary understanding.

Despite the narrator's insistence on the wonder of clerical magic, there is also a hint of detachment in the closing observation that the "hors vanysshed, I noot in what manere, / Out of hir sighte; ye gete namoore of me" (V 342–43). This is less the silence of wonder than of dismissal.[7] *Cleomadés* ends the list of Virgil's wonders on a still more detached note: "De ce plus vous ne parleroie, / Qui croire m'en veut si m'en croie / Et qui ne le veut si le laist" (I won't speak to you of this any more; whoever wants to can believe me and whoever doesn't want to can drop it) (1835–37). The *Franklin's Tale* moves from detachment to condemnation of "swiche illusiouns and swiche meschaunces / As hethen folk useden in thilke dayes" (V 1292–93). I have argued above that, in conjunction with other features of his narration, the Franklin's condemnation of magic can be read as a criticism of the romance genre's commitment to "lying wonders," but romance narrators do express a range of reservations about magic that contrast with their insistence on wonder. *Meliacin* illustrates a detachment similar to that in the *Franklin's Tale*:

> En icel tenz en augories
> Creoit on et en sorceries,
> En avisions et en mençonges.
> Et li clerc haut homme restoient
> Qui de ces ars s'entremetoient.
> Et quant il estoient trouvé
> Bon clerc et sage et esprouvé,
> Phylozophes les apeloient
> Cil qui lor granz oevres looient. . . .
> Des deablies qu'il usoient
> Et de lor mauvèses aprises
> S'en estoient lor oevres mises
> En auctorité et em pris.   (172–80, 186–89)

[At that time people believed in auguries and sorcery, in visions and lies. And the clerks who set themselves to these arts held high re-

---

[7] Stillwell, 177, 181, argues that violations of "unity of tone" (the crowd's amazement, the narrator's demurrals) distinguish the *Squire's Tale* from "a typical romance"; I believe shifts in tone, narrative detachment, and other ironic effects are characteristic of romance.

spect. And when they were found to be good clerks, wise and proven,
people who praised their great works called them philosophers. . . .
On account of the deviltries they practiced and their evil knowledge
their works were held in authority and high esteem.]

The location of lies and sorceries in a pagan past together with the
condemnation of philosophers' "evil knowledge" anticipates the
Franklin's comments on his philosopher's "japes and his wrecch-
ednesse / Of swich a supersticious cursednesse" (V 1271–72). And
yet in both cases the story outruns the commentary. In *Meliacin*
there are good magicians (two whose gifts win them daughters of
the king in marriage) who are distinguished from the bad (the
third magician, whose ugliness expresses a treacherous heart).
The story's emplotted version of the merit of philosophers escapes the comments on their uniformly evil ways, just as
Chaucer's depiction of the Clerk's scientifically orthodox astrological calculations moves beyond the comments on his "supersticious cursednesse."[8]

In summary, there is a double focus to the presentation of clerical magic in romance that both strives to preserve wonder from
the demystifications of the ignorant and, contrarily, assumes
tones of detachment, doubt, and even condemnation. That both
wonder and detachment characterize narration echoes the role of
clerical magic as a source of great power that does not crucially
drive masculine self-advancement or determine events.

The power of clerical magic lies in expanding the realm of possibility. Rather than propelling protagonists beyond the competitive chivalric circle altogether, clerical magic offers assistance in
meeting the concrete challenges presented there. The *Franklin's
Tale* introduces the expansive identity of magic with a trompe
l'oeil description in which the border between reality and illusion
is at first imperceptible:

> Doun of his hors Aurelius lighte anon,
> And with this magicien forth is he gon

---

[8] On the accuracy of the scientific description see Eade; on the tone of the condemnation, Eade notes that "neither Chaucer nor anyone else could reasonably
describe the Toledo Tables as designed for 'supersticious cursedness'" (69). On a
book of divination assembled and partly written for Richard II, the *Libellus Geo-
mancie*, see Mathew, 40–41.

Hoom to his hous, and maden hem wel at ese.
Hem lakked no vitaille that myghte hem plese.
So wel arrayed hous as ther was oon
Aurelius in his lyf saugh nevere noon.
 He shewed hym, er he wente to sopeer,
Forestes, parkes ful of wilde deer;
Ther saugh he hertes with hir hornes hye,
The gretteste that evere were seyn with ye. (V 1183–92)

The forests and parks seem on first reading to be features of the magician's well-arrayed property rather than of his art, since the account postpones the information that "yet remoeved they nevere out of the hous / Whil they saugh al this sighte merveillous" (V 1205–6). The gradual progress from the initial sight of forests and parks which could be taken for real estate to the evident illusion of Dorigen dancing with Aurelius proposes that magic can expand reality toward the fulfillment of desire. The magician grounds this proposal in his clerical learning by making his presentation "in his studie, ther as his bookes be" (V 1207, 1214). A similar continuum from the real to its magical extension is evident in the horse of the *Squire's Tale*, which combines an appearance "so horsly, and so quyk of ye / As it a gentil Poilleys courser were" (V 194–95) with extraordinary speed, endurance, and maneuverability. Again the presentation focuses on desires fulfilled in the horse's capacity to "beren youre body into every place / To which youre herte wilneth for to pace" (V 119–20).

Beyond these concrete benefits, magic offers protagonists access to the exotic. For readers, too, magic is the central expression of Oriental and Celtic exoticism in romance. Because romance associates the exotic with the feminine, as Canacee's adventure will illustrate, the genre invites readers to align themselves with masculine protagonists whose encounters with the alien in all its manifestations express desires for self-extension and completion as well as for control.

Jacques Le Goff studies the Orient as "le monde clos de l'exotisme onirique de l'Occident médiévale" (the closed world of the medieval West's exotic dreams) and associates it with the Celtic world as a second "horizon onirique" ("L'Occident médiéval," 246, 263). These are dreamed places in their conjoined inaccessibility and desirability, sites for the projection of European fears and longings. R. W. Southern and Anthime Fourrier specify the Orient as a place of scientific and mechanical marvels such as gems of wonderful power, strange races of animals and humans, and automatons; the Breton world by contrast partakes of "la féerie et le mystère" (Fourrier, 12; see also Sherwood, 571–72, 574–75). Romances both manage and indulge the exotic in generating images of it, just as romances' plots invite protagonists to appropriate the exotic to their own desires. The Clerk of Orleans's magic cannot be written off in the narrator's references to heathen tricks, but the Clerk and his magic are nonetheless creations of Christian poetic art that serve its purposes. In the *Squire's Tale* also, literary representation of the exotic is less a matter of rejection than of a narrative distancing that asserts control over the exotic. Even *occupatio* can work to contain the challenge of foreign custom:

> I wol nat tellen of hir strange sewes,
> Ne of hir swannes, ne of hire heronsewes.
> Eek in that lond, as tellen knyghtes olde,
> Ther is som mete that is ful deynte holde
> That in this lond men recche of it but smal;
> Ther nys no man that may reporten al.   (V 67–72)

"Strange sewes" and "som mete" evoke ignorance and repulsion as does the refusal to go into detail, but the narrator suppresses those responses by asserting that efficient storytelling governs the evasion. The cultural distance between narrator and Tartar court redoubles when into that already exotic space rides an emissary from Middle India whose words and bearing recall the other "horizon onirique," the Celtic: "Gawayn, with his olde curteisye, / Though he were comen ayeyn out of Fairye, / Ne koude hym nat amende with a word" (V 95–97; see Whiting). This hyperbole, even as it layers one exotic world on another, draws on familiar conventions about Gawain and courtly speech that make the superlatively rich and strange scene of the *Squire's Tale* accessible to its readers.

For Edward Said, the literary constitution of exoticism as a site of desire and control adumbrates the colonial encounter. Said labels the cultural idea of the East "*Orientalism*, a way of coming to terms with the Orient that is based on the Orient's special place

in European Western experience. The Orient is . . . its cultural
contestant, and one of its deepest and most recurring images of
the Other." Inventing literary images "was always a way of controlling the redoutable Orient" through "domestications of the
exotic," Said argues (1, 60). John Fyler independently describes
the narrative process in the *Squire's Tale* as "domesticating the
exotic" and stresses the desire to appropriate that complements
the desire for control. Only partially successful, the tale's tendency to demystify its marvels "shows how fully romance reflects
a basic human desire for reintegration, for abolishing the distance
caused by alienating categories; and it also shows how vigorously
such categories resist their own dissolution" ("Domesticating the
Exotic," 21). To introduce gender into this valuable framework for
considering the exotic, we should note that romance attributes
the longing for reintegration to male characters and resistant
alienness to female ones, such that the desired and elusive exotic
constitutes a sexually charged dynamic central to courtship.

    Canacee's much-stressed womanhood signals not only her dis-
tance from the male narrator or author but also the relation between femininity and other aspects more obviously alien to masculinity such as the foreign and the animal. The multiplication of
exotic registers in Canacee's adventure is governed by its association with women in several generalizing statements that frame
the episode: Canacee is "ful mesurable, as wommen be"; her sympathy arises from her gentleness and "verray wommanly benignytee"; she and all her women lament the falcon's plight; the
mew constructed for the falcon is lined in blue velvet "in signe of
trouthe that is in wommen sene" (V 362, 486, 633, 645). Fyler
notes the appropriateness of this gendered narration to the tale's
concern with all forms of the exotic: "When a young noble male
European imagines the sentiments of a *gentil* female bird 'of
fremde land' (429), as these are made evident in her colloquy with
a Mongolian princess, we are assured that a basic impulse of romance, asserting and then overcoming distance, is being pushed
to its farthest limits" ("Domesticating the Exotic," 13). Canacee's
encounter with the falcon makes the exotic available in a series of
metaphorical shifts from animal to human and from species to
species. The falcon speaks "in hir haukes ledene" of her bird
suitor who, a tiger in doubleness, falls to his knees in false prom-

ises to her (V 478, 543–44). In such passages the magical ring seems to be translating from several registers of the exotic at once.[9] Indeed, Chaucer has translated the whole story from *Anelida and Arcite* to the wild kingdom (Alfred David points out that the falcon's tale is "the identical story recycled—with feathers") so that the ring can retranslate it into human speech (110). Identified with the lamenting falcon through her gentle sympathetic femininity, Canacee is an instance of the exotic for the narrator. Within the tale as well her relation to clerical magic differs from the masculine relation in that she moves toward subjective knowledge of relationships in her adventure, rather than toward a masculine appropriation of the exotic into self-advancement. Her adventure will be resolved through masculine intervention, "by mediacion of Cambalus," and through the chivalric courtship for her hand waged by "Cambalo, / That faught in lystes with the bretheren two / For Canacee er that he myghte hire wynne" (V 656, 667–69).[10]

For male protagonists, romance figures an evocation and control of the exotic that answers desires for autonomy. The emissary's account in the *Squire's Tale* emphasizes that the magical gifts have pragmatic uses. The devices, however mysterious in themselves, will perform predictably for their owners: "This is a verray sooth, withouten glose; / It failleth nat whils it is in youre hoold," the emissary declares of the sword (V 166–67). Clerical magic is similarly facilitating in the *Franklin's Tale*. Aurelius is cut off from Dorigen not only by her demand for a supernatural performance but more generally by the hierarchizing differences courtship asserts between men and women. Clerical magic responds to the alienating limitations of courtship and the inaccessibility of woman by providing access to an exotic field that overlaps with that of the feminine in its strangeness and surpassing of rational explanation. The *Knight's Tale* identifies the exotic

[9] Further examples are the tiger who would weep if he could (V 419–22) and the exemplum of caged birds (V 607–20) in which "tenor and vehicle, number and gender keep reversing and dissolving into each other" (Fyler, "Domesticating the Exotic," 17).

[10] The overlapping names of Canacee's brother and suitor, whether or not they imply an exotic acceptance of incest, bring the tale back from its excursion into the alien feminine to the masculine characters' relations with one another.

with the feminine most overtly, in the narrator's refusal to recount Emelye's rite of bathing: "But hou she dide hir ryte I dar nat
telle / But it be any thing in general; / And yet it were a game to
heeren al" (I 2284–86). The evasion is not paralleled in the accounts of Palamon's and Arcite's rites in the temples of Venus and
Mars, suggesting that Emelye's gender intensifies her rite's exoticism. At the same time, the narrator's aside that "it were a game
to heeren al" indicates that appropriation is as good as accom-
plished, identifying the feminine with the exotic both as mystery
and as target for narrative domestication. A similar identification
is implicit in the *Franklin's Tale*. Aurelius turns to supernatural
powers to overcome the vast distance he perceives between his
humble suit and Dorigen's resistance. Entreating Phoebus
Apollo's aid in completing Dorigen's task, Aurelius evokes a gendered heaven in which the feminine moon follows after the masculine sun in her desire to mirror his rays (V 1045–51). This image
of a heavenly masculine autonomy finds earthly expression in the
Clerk's ability to manipulate his knowledge of the moon:

> [He] knew the arisyng of his moone weel,
> And in whos face, and terme, and everydeel;
> And knew ful weel the moones mansioun
> Acordaunt to his operacioun. . . .   (V 1287–90)

The Clerk's manipulation of "his moon" replaces Apollo's influence over Lucina as the means of accomplishing Dorigen's task,
while the moon's importance to the Clerk's illusion sustains the
association between the distant heavens and the feminine gender.
In allying himself with the magician's astrological manipulations,
Aurelius gains an experience of the exotic that parallels the success he hopes to achieve with Dorigen. In romance generally,
magic is a compensatory exotic that extends men's capacities in
the direction of their desires, toward the alien space that femininity most importantly occupies. Insofar as this self-expansion depends on the aid of magicians—and Aurelius's dependence is particularly clear at the tale's close—it is recuperated into masculine
interrelations. The magician's reappropriation of his horse, together with the hero's bride upon it, similarly reminds Meliacin
and Cleomadés that their access to magic is contingent on the
magician's will. Although a struggle of masculine wills is central

to these plots as to that of the *Franklin's Tale*, the attraction of magic for striving suitors records a desire to control the exotic and incorporate it into identity despite identity's very foundation on expelling the exotic into the realm of the Other.

Clerical magic proposes an escape from a related paradox of masculine identity explored in the first chapter, according to which identity depends on recognition by the chivalric community yet the demand of the community is for a self-established identity independent of all others. Identity is caught between contrary demands of reputation and autonomy, so that masculine desire takes on such convolutions as Aurelius expresses in his complaint to Dorigen: "I wolde that day that youre Arveragus / Wente over the see, that I, Aurelius, / Hadde went ther nevere I sholde have come agayn" (V 969–71). Although Arveragus has undertaken the journey "to seke in armes worshipe and honour" (V 811), in Aurelius's lament his rival's lonely self-hazarding models independent chivalric identity in contrast to Aurelius's involvement in rivalry and the dependence of his success on usurping Arveragus's place. One source of the lyric lover's perpetual sorrow is not simply his choice of a distant and difficult object but his involvement in rigorously social measures of merit that compromise the ideal of an autonomous self even as they confer social recognition on the effort to construct that self.

Aligning himself with Arveragus and competing with him for Dorigen, Aurelius responds to the elements in Dorigen's reply that would make his courtship most analogous to that of Arveragus: her resistance and her promise to love him "best of any man" (V 997) if he accomplishes a supremely difficult task. Although Dorigen's concern is for his rival's safety, to Aurelius the task resembles Arveragus's long courtship and "many a labour, many a greet emprise" (V 732) through which he won Dorigen. In this light the task of removing the rocks along Brittany's coast would surpass conventional achievements in kind and difficulty, demonstrating Aurelius's superior worthiness. Aurelius measures his position and actions against those of Arveragus in his initial and final interviews with Dorigen (e.g., V 1526–44, 1604–5), but the "monstre or merveille" (V 1344) that the magician produces for Aurelius frees him temporarily from comparison. When Aurelius

reports that "I have do so as ye comanded me" (V 1333), it seems
that magic has raised individual achievement beyond the reach of
competition.

Yet magic does not finally provide the freedom from interpersonal contingencies that it seemed to promise. The feat itself is
suspect, an illusion whose duration of "a wowke or two" (V 1161,
1295) is ephemeral next to the tale's chosen measure of meaningful time, "a yeer or tweyne" (V 809, 813, 1062, 1102). By the time
it is performed, the feat is irrelevant to Arveragus's safety, it involves Aurelius in a further competition among men rather than
setting him beyond rivalry, and it does not bring Aurelius union
with Dorigen despite having fulfilled her command in the eyes of
all concerned. These developments follow the genre's understanding of how magic is related to heroic endeavor. Helen Cooper has shown in a survey of romances and lays that the magical
objects, potions, and capabilities introduced as aids and solutions
tend not to be called upon, to be unimportant to plot, or not to
function. She concludes that magic illuminates and exacerbates
personal quandaries rather than evading them as may be the case
in ballad and fairy tale: "the process of turning tale into romance
requires something more. Magic that does not work, by definition, has little to do with plot; but it can be used in a different
way—used psychologically, rather than magically" ("Magic,"
134). On the Clerk of Orleans's feat she remarks that "the question at issue is not whether the magic has worked or not, but how
this will make everybody behave" (141). In a fine study of chivalric consciousness Anne Middleton makes the similar point that
the Franklin discredits magic in his tale because "the will to produce such heart-ravishing appearances is seen as destructive
rather than creative of communal faith and accord. In his tale
patience and pity are the only salutary forms of 'magic natureel'" ("War by Other Means," 130). The genre's resistance to
magical solutions in favor of interpersonal negotiations returns
protagonists from the illusion of transcendence to the demands of
community.

The magical gifts in the *Squire's Tale* also seem prepared to
enhance human capacities beyond compare, but the tale's analogues go on to reveal that the gifts have little significance to
events. The analogues could well illustrate Philippe Ménard's ob-

servation on Chrétien de Troyes's use of marvels: "tout au long de ces romans le réel est singulièrement présent et le merveilleux furtif" (throughout these romances the real is strikingly present and the magical is fleeting) ("Chrétien de Troyes et le merveilleux," 58; see also Carasso-Bulow). The horse and sword have specifically gendered power in that both are metonymic for chivalric masculinity. Their broader cultural associations with male sexuality and willfulness underlie more prominent and genre-specific associations with knighthood, adventure, and noble rule. Horsemanship is the costly skill that distinguishes the highest military ranks; the sword is a similarly prestigious possession associated with ascendancy to knighthood.[11] Often given names of their own, a knight's horse and sword stand for his capacity to sustain and forward his chivalric privileges. The magical horse of the *Squire's Tale* prepares for far-flung adventures and miraculous escapes, again expanding the individual protagonist's capacities in the direction of autonomy. The magical sword expands the ordinary properties of swords in the relevant direction for chivalric plots, in that it adumbrates forgiveness as well as force. Like Cambyuskan who is "pitous and just, alwey yliche" (V 20), the sword promises to express mercy as well as power. Yet in so doing the sword turns from being a token of autonomous invincibility to reintroducing chivalric relationship, and even to recalling that wounding as well as healing establishes relations among knights. The flying horse also turns from providing independence in *Meliacin* and *Cleomadés*: its maker quickly reappropriates it to his own evil designs, and the young lovers must spend years going about the world by ordinary means in search of their kidnapped sweethearts. A little statue of a man with a trumpet that replaces the magical sword in *Meliacin* and *Cleomadés* is just as marginal to events: in *Meliacin* the figure apparently fails to warn of treachery and in *Cleomadés* it blows its warning trumpet when the young prince first gets on the horse and again when his bride is stolen, but everyone is too excited to notice.[12] In both cases magic again

[11] Some cultural associations for horses are traced in Robertson, 30, 194, 253–55, 394, 476. On horses and swords in relation to knighthood see Keen, 16, 47, 50, 64–65, 71–75, 103.

[12] *Cleomadés*, ll. 2407–24, 5661–66; in *Meliacin* the figure does help Meliacin's father resist an invasion (73–74).

returns protagonists from the promise of independence to the constraints of life in a chivalric community.

Clerical magic has many further uses in romance, from expressing the parallel alchemy of poetry writing to resisting Christian hegemony. Insofar as clerical magic directs itself to masculine identity in romance, it addresses the tension between a private desire for autonomy and a chivalric community that assigns identity in relation to others. It further responds to a desire for the exotic arising from the alienation of the feminine that characterizes chivalric courtship. But clerical magic illuminates rather than revises the masculine predicament, clarifying the difference between private desire and public demand and the distance between courtly suitor and exotic beloved.

UNCANNY WOMEN

Women who wield magical power in romances are the intimates of male protagonists, their lovers and mothers and aunts. Male clerics and enchanters provide aid or resistance in magic that is uncomplicated by intimacy. Although clerical magic can establish deeper connections between men than the merely professional, as Aurelius's closing interaction with the Clerk of Orleans illustrates, these connections, like the magic that instigates them, are unambiguous in their expressions and implications. Women's magic has an element of ambivalence that expresses femininity's compounded attraction and danger in romance. Whereas men master magic as an exceptionally difficult science that they can then freely deploy, women's magic is less often learned than inherited, imposed by enchantment, or of unexplained origin, and not always under their control.

Of course there are some partial exceptions to this generalization. The ugly magicians in *Cleomadés* and *Meliacin* demand marriage in return for their art as do the feminine grotesques who seek intimacy in other romances, but the ugly magicians' motives are unambiguously evil rather than potentially or partially benevolent. Merlin changes his shape, a typical expression of feminine magic's ambiguity, but his learned identity and his involvement in public and political matters contrast with the more hidden workings and intimate preoccupations of uncanny women. The few masculine fairies of romance, whose otherworldly origin and inborn rather than clerical magic are more typical of the genre's feminine figures, are restricted to the roles of lost father and peripheral challenger.[13] A few women such as Morgan le Fay and Melior of *Partonope of Blois* receive clerical training in magic, but Morgan is hostile and helpful by turns or even simultaneously, and Melior's power has a crucial limitation that puts it in her lover's control rather than her own.[14] The differences between magical effects attributed to clerks and to women in several Middle English romances provide a context for considering how the *Wife of Bath's Tale* involves magic in its depiction of gender.

One might suppose that a fairy mistress or spell-casting mother is simply superior to a mortal one, her protection more extensive and her beauty nearer perfection. But in these romances superiority is only half the story. Sometimes a magical mistress's protection is contingent on a prohibition that is broken: Sir Launfal tells of Tryamour, Raymondin peeks at Melusine on a Saturday, Partonope whips out a lantern to see what Melior looks like, and whether willingly or unwillingly, the lady vanishes. Her magical protection has a catch. Richard Coeur de Lion's mother, a beautiful infidel, is a good wife and mother until forced by her husband to see the elevation of the Host, upon which she flies up through the roof and disappears forever. Or, as in Dame Ragnell and the lady of Synadoun in *Lybeaus Desconus*, a beautiful shape may belatedly revise a "forshapen" body that is repulsively animal. Melusine's misshapen children as well as her own weekly transformation into a lamia, half serpent and half woman, betray the incompleteness of enchanting beauty. *Sir Gawain and the Green Knight* juxtaposes the aged Morgan to the young wife who may be

---

[13] Harf-Lancner surveys male fairies, 63–74; for an overview of Merlin's appearances see MacDonald.

[14] R. S. Loomis, 105, quotes Mark Twain's Connecticut Yankee on Morgan's contradictory manifestations: "I have seen a good many kinds of women in my time, but she laid it over them all for variety." Paton provides a wealth of detail, although my argument opposes her thesis that the fairy of romance is "superior to human blemish, contingency, or necessity, in short, altogether unlimited in her power" (5). Harf-Lancner's premise is that fairies are of two types, that of the conquering and controlling Morgan who ravishes heroes to the otherworld and that of the submissive Melusine who marries a mortal and serves him with her magic; my argument is that conquest and submission, benevolence and malevolence, and other oppositions are more importantly confounded than distinguished in fairies of romance.

her double, and finally traces the adventure's seductive dangers to an aunt to whose chimneyside Gawain is invited to come home. Does Morgan more accurately threaten Gawain's life or nurture his growth? Are Dame Ragnell and the Wife of Bath's old hag truly ugly and aggressive or truly beautiful and obedient? Such bivalence is irreducible in romance and it is gendered feminine. Through an uncanniness that opposes yet is subsumed within intimacy, romances express the difference that marks the idea of woman, the marginal position of woman in narrative, and her resistance to both appropriation and dismissal.

Sigmund Freud's essay on the uncanny, "Das Unheimliche," comments on contradictions within femininity in the course of a much broader discussion of the psychological bases for artistic effects. Freud's translator points out that her "canny" means "cozy," "gentle," "familiar," "safe," but also "endowed with magical or occult powers," that is to say, "uncanny" (219, 222). Similarly, Freud notes that "*heimlich* is a word the meaning of which develops in the direction of ambivalence, until it finally coincides with its opposite, *unheimlich*," or uncanny (226). The negative term arises and resides within the positive. This lexicographical enfolding resonates with representations of the feminine in romance, where the lover's intimacy with woman is nonetheless estranged by gender difference. Here is a first element of woman's difference in romance, that within her intimacies there is something occulted and unpredictable. Both the gorgeous fairy mistress who vanishes and the repulsively "forshapen" woman who declares her love dramatize the contradictions inherent in the desired and alien feminine.

Freud relates the aesthetic perception of uncanniness in literature and in experience to the process of repression: "the uncanny [*unheimlich*] is something which is secretly familiar [*heimlich-heimisch*], which has undergone repression and then returned from it." Freud illustrates with the common declaration of male patients "that they feel there is something uncanny about the female genital organs. This *unheimlich* place, however, is the entrance to the former *Heim* [home] of all human beings, to the place where each one of us lived once upon a time and in the beginning" (245). The return of the repressed has wider implications for romance as a literature of masculine identity-formation, but

for my immediate concern with the articulation of feminine uncanniness, Freud's illustration suggests that we consider the lexical field of Middle English *queynt*. In addition to its occasional
euphemistic reference to female genitalia, *queynt* encompasses
some of the same meanings and ambivalences as the modern
canny/uncanny.

The coexistence of positive and negative valences in *queynt*
can be broadly illustrated in uses of the formula "queynt of
ginne," which signifies trickery or spell casting when applied to
male adversaries, and great skill when applied to protagonists.
Lybeaus Desconus seeks to rescue the lady of Synadoun from
two magicians who have immured her in a "palys queynte of
ginne . . . be nygremauncye / Y-makeþ of fayrye" (Cotton MS,
1701, 1705–6) The magicians taunt the merely mortal Lybeaus to
fight his best by using the same formula: "Fyȝte þou most wyth
vs! / Queynte þou art of gynne / Yf þou þat lady wynne" (Cotton
MS, 1836–38).[15] Very occasionally heroes are "queynt" in the
sense of clever or subtle rather than simply strong and skillful, but
it is primarily in women that "queyntise" moves easily from
refinement to deception and spell casting. In *William of Palerne*,
the queen who at her marriage is "corteys and convenabul and . . .
comen . . . of gret kin, and koynt hireselve"—that is, irreproach-
ably aristocratic—is soon transforming her stepson into a were-
wolf "with hire connyng and hire queynt charmes" (4089–90,
4136). All the court ladies and demoiselles of *Kyng Alisaunder*
who dress "in faire atyre, in dyuers queyntise" (Laud MS, 173) are
fashionable and pleasing, as is Bertilak's lady when she takes her
place in church "coyntly" (*Sir Gawain*, 934). On the other hand,
Morgan's "koyntyse of clergye, bi craftes wel lerned" tricks Gawain in a mode he calls feminine: "myn honoured ladyez" are
typical in that they have "koyntly bigyled" him "þurȝ wyles of
wymmen" (2447, 2412–15). Gawain voices a slippage between
the term's positive and negative connotations, a slippage that coincides with the move from woman's decorative appearance to
her hidden nature. In medieval rather than Freudian terms,

---

[15] Contrast such fabliau protagonists as the Miller's Nicholas, whose "queynte
cast" (I 3605) is clever rather than confrontational. Another intriguing exception
to the gendered connotations of *queynte* is Dame Ragnell's assertion that men use
"flatryng and glosyng and queynte gyn" to court women (*Weddynge of Sir Gawen*,
l. 416).

Adam's long-lost trust in Eve returns to fallen man, weaned from that trust, as an uncanny experience of indeterminately pleasing and misleading "queintise." In Gawain's postlapsarian perception, woman is disconsonant with man because disconsonant in her very nature.

Some romances insist on the alienness enclosed in the apparently accessible mistress's body through prohibitions on looking, touching, and speaking that limit lovers' access and eventually threaten to deny access altogether. Melior's magic craft was itself concealed, practiced only in a chamber "preuely" for her father's household, "þorowe wych mony man was blynte." She can conceal Partonope and herself from the public eye as long as she remains concealed from Partonope; her power ends "for ye haue sene me a-yen my will."[16] Launfal's Tryamour is available to him in any "derne stede": "Well priuyly I woll come to þe / No man alyue ne schall me se" (354–57). She too moves away when exposed by the lover, although she eventually revises her withdrawal by feasting the male gaze—"Sche dede of here mantyll on þe flet / Þat men shuld here beholde the bet"—and blinding the doubting Guinevere (979–80). In these texts the attempt to restrict access seems as inherently feminine as the lover's disobedience or curiosity seems masculine: Raymondin finally looks at Melusine on a Saturday by poking a hole in the door of her retreat with his sword. The knights who persuade Richard Coeur de Lion's father to detain Cassodorien in church until the elevation of the Host promise that "þou schalt se a queynte brayd" (*Richard*, 216). The "queynte" response they anticipate might lexically refer to a trickiness, or hiddenness, or elegance, or sorcery in Cassodorien that will now be seen by the assembled knights. The ambivalence of the term *queynte* stresses her unknowability within the articulation of male curiosity.

The "queynte fantasye" Alison attributes to all women in her prologue makes axiomatic their difference from the men who pursue or refuse them:

> I trowe I loved hym best, for that he
> Was of his love daungerous to me.

---

[16] *Partonope*, ll. 5936, 5945, 5979. Melior's account of her magical practices uses many images of concealment and secrecy (ll. 5933–79).

> We wommen han, if that I shal not lye,
> In this matere a queynte fantasye:
> Wayte what thyng we may nat lightly have,
> Therafter wol we crie al day and crave.
> Forbede us thyng, and that desiren we;
> Preesse on us faste, and thanne wol we fle. . . .
> This knoweth every womman that is wys.
>
> (III 513–20, 524)

Here as throughout the *Wife of Bath's Prologue*, woman's desire appears to be irreducibly at odds with her situation. But wise women deploy a second-order "queyntise" to achieve their ends: Alison wins the "daungerous" Jankyn in marriage with falsehoods and veiled allusions, the first of which, "I bar hym on honde he hadde enchanted me" (III 575), preempts masculine wariness of woman's uncanny charms. When duplicity becomes her mode of interaction, difference has fissured the feminine itself.

In feminine magic, romance mystifies the antifeminist topos of woman as contradiction and self-contradiction. The old hag's courtship in Alison's tale reworks the canny deceptions Alison uses to win Jankyn into the uncanny ability to shape-shift. According to Freud's model, the hag's shape-shifting can draw an uncanny effect from a plot in which "the distinction between imagination and reality is effaced, as when something that we have hitherto regarded as imaginary appears before us in reality. . . . It is this factor which contributes not a little to the uncanny effect attaching to magical practices" ("Uncanny," 244).[17] Moreover, when the masculine wish becomes substance, the accessible body remains *unheimlich* insofar as repression has distanced it from familiarity—or, in the medieval terms suggested above, the reincarnated Eve cannot return man to prelapsarian trust but instead embodies an uncanny vacillation between accessibility and strangeness. The hag's second shape, together with her supplementary arguments concerning low birth and poverty, do not ac-

---

[17] Freud's essay restricts uncanny effects in fiction almost entirely to works that "move in the world of common reality" such that introducing the supernatural provides a disorienting contrast similar to that produced by lived experience (250). However, he notes that the class of uncanny effects "which proceeds from repressed complexes is more resistant and remains as powerful in fiction as in real experience" (251).

complish substitutions but only destabilizations. This is perhaps
more evident in the hag's words than in her body. Her curtain
lecture does not favor lowborn poverty over gentle wealth but
questions the validity of divisions between these categories, reinterpreting the distinction between poverty and wealth, for example, through paradoxes that resist distinction: "he that noght
hath, ne coveiteth have, / Is riche, although ye holde hym but a
knave" (III 1189–90). Wealth and poverty become mobile doubles
of one another rather than isolated states. The hag's bodily transformation is analogous:

> And whan the knyght saugh verraily al this,
> That she so fair was, and so yong therto,
> For joye he hente hire in his armes two.
> His herte bathed in a bath of blisse.
> A thousand tyme a-rewe he gan hire kisse,
> And she obeyed hym in every thyng
> That myghte doon hym plesance or likyng.   (III 1250–56)

How distinct is this young and fair appearance from the ugly old
age that it revises? Despite the fairy's claim to a prelapsarian
perfection, to equal any wife "syn that the world was newe"
(III 1244), a residual presence of the old body within the new is to
be suspected. The metaphor for the knight's joy, "his herte bathed
in a bath," carries the Wife of Bath's fallen body back on the scene,
and the assertion that "she obeyed hym in every thyng" slips into
the Wife's combative prayer for "grace t'overbyde hem that we
wedde" (III 1260). The knight's bliss does not encompass the full
narrative effect of the transformation. As with the argument
about gentility and wealth, submissive beauty becomes in this
shape-shifting a category that admits its opposite, as low birth has
invaded gentility and poverty has paradoxically become a species
of wealth. Shape-shifting pleases the "worldly appetit" (III 1218)
of the knight but again emphasizes the uncanny indeterminacy
of the feminine.[18] We have seen a similar process at work in
the search for "what thyng that worldly wommen loven best"

---

[18] Heng, "Feminine Knots," argues that in *Sir Gawain* femininity is "plural,
heterogenous, and provisional, elusively reforming elsewhere just as it might seem
most fixedly locatable" (502).

(III 1033), in which the cacophony of possible answers yields to a single response, yet "sovereignty" is itself multiple and indeterminate in meaning. For the *Wife of Bath's Tale* as for other Middle English romances, woman's uncanniness lies in her difference from men but also in an inner differing that defies understanding.

One consequence for this femininity is displacement to the periphery of the narrative. The strangeness inherent in the uncanny becomes emplotted; woman instigates or occasions masculine discoveries and developments whose scene is marked off from and by femininity. Sir Thopas exaggerates the effect in requiring only the idea of an elf-queen for inspiration. In the course of their second interview Gawain takes the Green Knight to be his ally (confessor, host, and fellow knight all in one) and traces the threat and shame of the adventure to the quaint beguiling of "myn honoured ladyez." The relation Gawain finds between them and biblical temptresses who specialize in pratfalls further contrasts them to the Green Knight, who articulates Gawain's adventure as a happy fall into proven excellence among knights.[19] Twice refusing to be reconciled with his feminine adversaries, Gawain makes evident that the homosocial power of this last encounter is based in discounting women: best to love them well and not listen to them, Gawain concludes, "luf hom wel, and leue hem not" (2421).[20] The lady's green girdle is but a trace denoting an absence; despite its earlier status as a feminine garment, now the Green Knight declares "hit is my wede þat þou werez, þat ilke wouen girdel." Negotiating the girdle's signification takes place between the two men, and ultimately it joins the men of the Round Table together in a new brotherhood (2358, 2516–20). These closing negotiations transform Morgan's uncanny intervention into an instance of dif-

[19] For some critics Gawain's speech is out of keeping with his courtesy and the poem's thematic structure. Mingled appreciation and wariness do, however, characterize Gawain's encounters with Bertilak's wife, and the moral and gendered distance taken from women in Gawain's speech counterbalances the common ground of chivalric morality that Gawain and the Green Knight share in the closing encounter. Sheila Fisher reviews critical reactions to the speech, 92–93 and 105n.

[20] Sedgwick demonstrates the importance in modern literature of bonds between men that are formed in rivalries over women.

ference not so much from as within man: the uncanny contradictoriness attributed to woman brings to light more meaningful
tensions in chivalric identity. Knotting the girdle crosswise over
his surcoat as a heraldic bend, Gawain charges the pentangle
worn "in bytoknyng of trawþe" with "þe token of vntrawþe þat I
am tan inne" (626, 2509). His "vntrawþe" modifies his "trawþe"
as his own self-difference; woman becomes the adventure through
which his self-difference was revealed to him.

Similar narrative developments characterize other romances in
which uncanny women exercise their arts. Melior articulates her
own silencing when, after losing her magical ability, she becomes
the object of many suits and laments to herself that "Men mowe
speke and sende with penne and Inke / What they wole, and
women mow but þinke" (*Partonope*, 10783–84). Sidelined, she
can only hope that Partonope will be able to win her hand in the
decisive tournament. Dame Tryamour of *Sir Launfal* keeps her
magical power yet makes of herself a mere surface, a body whose
only gestures are to reveal itself (riding into court and removing
her mantle) or conceal itself (blinding Guinevere and departing).
Tryamour does deliver a speech defending Launfal from Guinevere's accusations, but the speech merely glosses the decisive visual proof that Launfal has no need of another lover. For some
readers, Marie de France's *Lanval* and the two Middle English
works related to it are wish-fulfillment fantasies that express
Launfal's masculinity; for other readers, the works' Celtic motifs
and narrative structures are primary.[21] Whether one construes the
need that brings the fairy mistress into being as Launfal's or the
narrative's, it is a curious irony that the forces generating her
must finally make her the object of the court's gaze in order to
establish Launfal's identity as a knight of honor and substance.
Such narrative objectifications and silencings make a space for
the dramatization of masculine interactions, self-difference, and
self-development that are the deepest concerns of romance.

The context of romances in which women wield magical power
highlights a resistance in the *Wife of Bath's Tale* to effacing fe-

[21] Good examples of psychologically oriented readings are Spearing, "Marie de
France and Her Middle English Adapters"; Hanning and Ferrante, ed., *Lais of Marie
de France*, 123–25. Examples of analyses focused on narrative patterns are Ménard,
Les Lais de Marie de France, and Sienaert.

male characters and concerns. In contrast, *The Weddynge of Sir Gawen and Dame Ragnell* exaggerates to the point of burlesque the opportunities provided by the plot for subordinating the apparently powerful woman to masculine interactions. To mention only the most salient efforts in this direction, Arthur's adversary Sir Gromer Somer Jour poses the question of what women most desire not in response to a crime against women's sovereignty but to take Arthur's life over a land dispute; the question has no educative intent and indeed is meant to be unanswerable. Sovereignty is not a meaningful problem but a rhetorical ploy, a way of encompassing all possible answers to the question under a single term. As Dame Ragnell puts it, "there is one thyng is alle oure fantasye . . . For where we haue souereynte alle is ourys"; Arthur presents the answer after all other possibilities as the trump that will "rule the, Gomer syre" (420, 425, 472). Ragnell then demands Gawain's hand of Arthur, focusing the plot on the devotion between Arthur and Gawain: "for your love I wolle nott spare," Gawain promises Arthur, and Arthur responds, "My worshypp and my lyf thou savyst for-euere, / Therfore my loue shalle nott frome the dyssevyr" (371, 375–76). Ragnell must win sovereignty over her husband to break the spell on her body, but she subsequently attributes the question to her wicked stepmother and makes a conventionally feminine plea for mercy on Sir Gromer, denying that her goal was really to win a sovereign position. The *Weddynge of Sir Gawen* drives the uncanny woman from the high status her lifesaving knowledge might assign by conceiving that knowledge as a mere trick of rhetoric, by orienting the plot around male animosity and friendship, and by identifying sovereignty simply as a spell-breaker rather than a condition Ragnell herself seeks.

In each respect the *Wife of Bath's Tale* by contrast allows prominence to issues that the text defines as feminine: the worth of women's sovereignty, its relation to rape and marriage, and whether obedience somehow resides within it. Incorporating these issues gives them weight even though their problematic, transgressive framing reasserts the subordination implicit in the romance conception of femininity. The tale's attraction to the subordinated feminine puts a comic spin on the transition "this knyght, of which my tale is specially" (III 983) as it pulls us away from the long excursus on women's multiple desires. Further, in contrast to Dame Ragnell, who in the end denounces her grotesque body and demands as involuntary manifestations of her stepmother's spell, Chaucer's hag focuses contradictory feminine traits in one figure. She unites a Morganic power over life and death, a submissive, protective desire like Melior's or Tryamour's to marry and to please, and an educative role with the recreant knight that the queen also occupies in the tale. The hag's multiply charged identity compels attention even as it illustrates the unresolvable contradictions that relegate the feminine to liminal positions in romance.

A decisive distancing of the feminine does, however, take place in the *Wife of Bath's Tale* through the association of magic with a lost past. "I speke of manye hundred yeres ago" (III 863), the Wife begins, and the elf-queen is the first instance of the past's distant uncanniness. Louise Fradenberg has shown in the course of placing the *Wife of Bath's Tale* at the conjunction of feudal and capitalist worlds that the romance genre and the concept of woman share absence and alienness at that conjunction, when "the new 'everyday reality' will construct the category of the past as coterminous with the equally fantasmatic category of the woman" ("Wife of Bath's Passing Fancy," 33). Within the already nostalgic world of romance, the hag's time-bending transformation from old to young removes her even further from "everyday reality." The anonymous maiden's fleeting and violated body at the tale's beginning is finally more substantial than the fairies' shifting and disappearing ones.

Yet women's uncanniness represents a complication in the narrative processes that use the feminine to define and concentrate on the masculine. I have argued, for example, that the hag's aged body lingers residually in the young body designed for the knight, such that the knight's bliss does not encompass the reactions invited by the tale's end. Freud's account of an uncanny experience with women can extend this point. "As I was walking, one hot summer afternoon, through the deserted streets of a provincial town in Italy which was unknown to me, I found myself in a quarter of whose character I could not long remain in doubt. Nothing but painted women were to be seen at the windows of the small houses, and I hastened to leave the narrow street at the next turning. But after having wandered about for a time without enquiring my way, I suddenly found myself back in the same street, where my presence was now beginning to excite attention. I hurried away once more, only to arrive by another *détour* at the same place yet a third time. Now, however, a feeling overcame me which I can only describe as uncanny," he continues, and he locates the source of that feeling in his "helplessness," more precisely in "an unintended recurrence of the same situation" ("Uncanny," 237).

Freud's narrative shares three features with adventures of romance that I have been examining. To begin with the second in the order I have followed, women appear to be peripheral to narrative significance. The perspective is that of the disoriented traveler, and the articulated significance of his adventure is "unintended recurrence"—that is, neither desire for the painted women nor the women themselves figure in the adventure's importance. But would the experience of recurrence have been uncanny if painted women had not been its unintended goal? If the triple return had been to the post office or a central square, would the episode not have been irritating or simply unmemorable rather than disturbing? Women are not so clearly insignificant to this adventure as they are displaced from their centrality at the point of triple return by the interpretive claim that the returns were unintended and were themselves, as process, the source of uncanniness.

Despite the interpretive claim, Freud's narrative effectively configures the women in two ways familiar from romance, through difference from the adventurer and from themselves. Their inviting paint and their self-exposure in the windows are in conflict with the traveler's involition and with their own domestic situation—in a "provincial" town, a "narrow" street, inside their "small" houses. The eruption of woman's sexuality in this foreign yet domestic scene is a return of the repressed analogous to the traveler's uncontrolled return to their small houses. In romance, uncanniness could describe any moment when women seem not to be fully domestic and appropriated, nor clearly beyond the pale morally and socially, but moving somewhere in between.

That indeterminacy makes uncanny women resistant to dismissal and to appropriation alike. In Freud's adventure, dismissing the painted women from significance by locating uncanniness in "unintended recurrence" requires suppressing the possibility of masculine desire, indeed requires suppressing masculine subjectivity altogether. The traveler's reaction to these provincial women is apparently irrelevant, yet their transgressive sexuality resists erasure from the calculus of uncanny effects. Gawain attempts to dismiss uncanny women from his adventure in similar fashion, by aligning the "honoured ladyez" with temptresses of the past and asserting his independent experience of "cowarddyse and couetyse." These are masculine failures, Gawain declares, sins against "larges and lewté that longez to kny3tez," the business of Bertilak and himself rather than of women (2374, 2381). Bertilak invites Gawain's interpretation by presenting his own actions as if they were independent of Morgan's designs: "I wro3t it myseluen," he says of the lady's temptations, and "I halde þe polysed of þat ply3t" (2361, 2393). The text's contradictory indications, that Morgan designed the adventure and that her relation to Gawain encompasses enmity and familiarity both, express the limitations of Gawain's and Bertilak's claims.

Uncanniness equally resists inclusion. Chaucer's *Knight's Tale*, although not strictly invoking feminine magic, builds a tension between expressed masculine interpretations and wider textual implications that centers on the scene in Diana's temple.[22] Diana does not promise aid to Emelye, reinforcing the submission to marriage that the gods will decree, but Diana's message takes an uncanny power from her knowledge of what is "writen and confermed" (I 2389) before Mars's gift of victory to Palamon and the dispute among the gods have taken place. The following chapter frames in terms of adventure the tale's effort to fit Emelye and Diana into the Athenian world picture, and the countermovement that denies their full appropriation.

Magical ability frustrates as well as forwards women's constitution as private treasure and public ornament for men in romance. For example, feminine magic expresses and is even inter-

---

[22] On a number of literary associations between Diana and fairies in medieval literature, see Paton, 228–47.

changeable with the potential for sexual license. Raymondin's brother, persuading Raymondin that he must find out what Melusine is doing on Saturdays, says the rumor is that either she is a fairy or she is committing adultery: "I wot not to whiche of bothe I shal byleue," the brother concludes, but the two accusations might be considered one, that Melusine is not entirely known to her husband, not entirely in his charge (296). Melior falls under similar suspicion for not allowing Partonope to see her. Apparently succumbing to his mother's suspicion that Melior may be concealing a devilish shape, Partonope confesses to the bishop, "Off a synne I moste me shryue. / A loue I haue, wyche in my lyue / Wyth myne eyen yette neuer I seye" (5756–58).[23] The fairy mistress in the Launfal texts exemplifies inappropriation of another kind, in that she sets her status as treasure against her status as ornament. She is totally available to Sir Launfal in secret places but adamantly unavailable in public. Saving Launfal entails reversing those conditions, withdrawing from Launfal in private for the space of a year but then unveiling her body to the court. Perhaps all such oppositions can be dissolved in the fairyland to which they escape, as in the unmagical perpetuity of Melior's marriage to Partonope, but in the romantic space preceding resolution, women's magic complicates their intimacies with men.

Although the *Wife of Bath's Tale* begins by relegating the elf-queen to a distant past and ends by asserting her appropriation to the knight's desires, an association between magic and sexual license pushes against containment. At the outset the Celtic fairies and their Christian exorcists come to resemble one another as if the task of exorcism were not quite achieved: the friars who visit all the elfin haunts are oddly weightless, "as thikke as motes in the sonne-beem" (III 868), and their sexual aggressiveness is a vestige of wilder spirits:

> For ther as wont to walken was an elf
> Ther walketh now the lymytour hymself. . . .
> Wommen may go saufly up and doun.
> In every bussh or under every tree

---

[23] Marie de France reverses the genders in this plot of suspicion and shape-shifting in *Bisclavret* (*Lais*, 61–71).

> Ther is noon oother incubus but he,
> And he ne wol doon hem but dishonour.
>
> (III 873–74, 878–81)

The friar follows in the footsteps of an elf who persists in the
Christian image of the incubus and its imitator the friar. Sexuality
moves irrepressibly across genders from the elf-queen and her
company (ladies all when they later appear) to the ravishing friar
and knight, and back again to the hag who smiles as her captive
husband "walweth and he turneth to and fro" (III 1085). These
crossgenderings recall the carnival spirit in which the feminine
grotesque usurps masculine sexual aggressiveness.[24] The hag's
ability to enforce sovereignty, in physical terms at least, further
associates woman's empowerment with an unrestrained exercise
of female sexuality. The connection between feminine magic and
sexual license emphasizes the freedom from containment that
each implies. Even at the tale's conclusion this fairy wife like others of romance is not entirely in her husband's control, bound
only by her own will to obey.

In Middle English romances, then, the possibility of intimacy
with woman does not cancel her strangeness. These narratives
trace the manifold difference in woman, her consequent liminal-
ity, yet also her consequent resistance to dismissal on the one
hand and to appropriation on the other. Uncanniness expresses
particularly well the troubling oppositions that mark the feminine at the deepest levels of conception: we might say that shape-
shifting naturalizes woman's contradictoriness, and that magical
power essentializes her otherness. Feminine uncanniness is en-
folded in intimacy as the *unheimlich* depends for its sense on the
heimlich: woman once familiar and domestic now also disturb-
ingly *unheimlich*—not at home, on the margins, undomesticated,
unfamiliar.

[24] See chapter 3, pp. 126–31.

CHAPTER V

Adventure

DVENTURE is the critical term most specific to romance, indicating the arbitrary, the random, and the unmotivated that divide the experience of romance from the clear necessities of epic struggle, the transcendent assurance of hagiography, and the instructive designs of chronicle. The French noun *aventure* has from before the twelfth century implications of fate and foreordination, as does its use in English, but its dominant later medieval meanings revolve around chance and accident (see Godefroy, Kurath). Romance draws on both senses of the noun in foregrounding the unexplained strangeness of adventurous encounters yet intimating that they have a hidden design. Morton Bloomfield, using adventure to define the difference between romance and other genres, recognizes this double sense of adventure in describing "inexplicable events which seem to have their center above and beyond the poem. . . . Something is happening about which we cannot be clear" (106). Magic and divine forces have a place in adventure not only to signify that apparently random encounters partake of some larger mysterious design but also to heighten the value of characters' success at encountering the unknown. Douglas Kelly argues that it is not merely "aventure" but "aventure merveilleuse" that marks romance, that there is an exceptional quality about the unmotivated challenge whether in its magical or divine origin, its reversal of natural law, or merely its extreme difficulty (146–204). Only beginning with the wonder of talking to birds, the Squire promises to go on "To speken of aventures and of batailles / That nevere yet was herd so grete mervailles" (V 659–60). Thopas's dream of an elf-queen, the Wife of Bath's knight's encounter with a shape-shifting creature, and the "monstre or merveille" of the disappearing rocks in the *Franklin's Tale* (V 1344) instantiate the extraordinary nature of adventure in many romances.

Adventure is so deeply associated with romance as to become
virtually synonymous with it, particularly in lays using Celtic
material. Marie de France's description of the Bretons making lays
to record important adventures ("pur remambrance les firent /
Des aventures k'il oïrent," *Prologue*, 35–36) yields to her designating her own accounts directly as adventures in such formulations
as "Vos mosterai une aventure" (I will show you an adventure)
and "L'aventure d'un autre lai, / Cum ele avint, vus cunterai" (I
will tell you the adventure of another lay just as it happened)
(*Guigemar*, 24; *Lanval*, 1–2). The Gawain poet similarly calls his
work "þis laye" and "an outtrage awenture" in the same passage
(*Sir Gawain*, 29–30). The *Franklin's Prologue* is sensitive to this
conjunction, perhaps specifically to its formulation in the prologues to *Sir Orfeo* and *Lai le Freine*, in recounting that "Thise
olde gentil Britouns in hir dayes / Of diverse aventures maden
layes" (V 709–10).[1] In equating their full narrative scope with adventure, the lays expand the concept from the narrower sense
some romances convey of a specific test of merit occurring outside the bounds of the daily life of courts. Guy of Warwick
"wendeþ in-to fer lond, / More of auentours for to fond," and Colgrevance "rade allane" (rode alone) in *Ywain and Gawain* "forto
seke aventurs . . . My body to asai and fande" (*Guy*, Auchinleck
MS, 1063–64; *Ywain and Gawain*, 154–55, 316). But the dragon
that attacks England in *Guy of Warwick*, the theft of Herodis from
her own garden in *Sir Orfeo*, and the fairy mistress who seeks out
Sir Launfal illustrate that the challenging and transforming wonders of adventure need not be solicited on arduous journeys. Jill
Mann's analysis of Malory's procedure could, stated in its general
terms, apply to much of romance and to Chaucer's use of it: for
Malory, Mann argues, adventure is not a specific encounter isolated within a "special period of time" but refers instead to "the
mystery and power in the ordinary operations of chance" that require of the adventurer "an attempt to stretch the self to embrace
the utmost reach of possible events" ("'Taking the Adventure,'"
89–90). A marvel of some kind may emphasize the mystery of
chance, but an ongoing responsiveness to unforeseen challenges
constitutes the sense of adventure. Aurelius's shifting responses

---

[1] To the *Franklin's Prologue* compare *Freine*, ll. 1–20, and the prologues to *Sir Orfeo* in Harley 3810 and Ashmole 61 (Bliss edition).

to his situation are more importantly his adventure than the illusion sought in Orleans; the knight's change of heart in the *Wife of Bath's Tale* is a more significant transformation than his wife's change of shape.

Adventures commingle unpredictable hazard with concrete gain. In some lights the adventures young men undertake seem extravagant, even wasteful. Leaving the safety of home or court to find trouble is a sort of conspicuous consumption for knights that lies beyond the means and understanding of their inferiors. Guy's and Colgrevance's active search for adventure is a class-specific behavior distinguished by its gratuitousness as well as its dangers. Sir Thopas's insistence on sleeping outdoors plays up this will to expose oneself: "And for he was a knyght auntrous, / He nolde slepen in noon hous, / But liggen in his hoode" (VII 909–10). The knights' uncommon self-risking takes institutional form in the openness of Arthur's court to pleas and challenges from strangers: in *Sir Gawain and the Green Knight*, Arthur declares "þurȝ nobelay" (through his nobility) that he will not eat on Christmas until he has heard of or met with "sum auenturus þyng" (91, 93). Yet adventure does bring tangible rewards. Indeed, Michael Nerlich's *Ideology of Adventure* argues compellingly that the knight-errant is direct ancestor to the merchant-adventurer, and that the twelfth century is thus the source of an ideology of adventure characteristic of the modern world. This ideology, according to Nerlich, interprets adventure in opposed but overlapping terms as both a virtually philosophical search for revelatory experience and, in contrast, a great risk taken with a view to great material profit. Instances of the term *aventure* used to designate rents, incomes, and return on investment are attested from the thirteenth century, but even in the earliest romances knights are already winning wives, titles, and lands through their success at adventure.[2] The marriage projected as the Squire's fragment ends, the signs of masculine rivalry between Arveragus, Aurelius, and the

---

[2] Compare the merchant's speech reported by the Canon's Yeoman: "Us moste putte oure good in aventure. / A marchant, pardee, may nat ay endure, / Trusteth me wel, in his prosperitee" (VIII 946–48). Nerlich's argument on risk, profit, and adventure in romance is indebted to Köhler's *Ideal und Wirklichkeit in der höfischen Epik*. See also Fradenberg, *City, Marriage, Tournament*, 244–64; and, on Chaucer's specific revisions to emphasize gain in the *Knight's Tale*, Stock (esp. 217–19).

Clerk of Orleans, and the politically charged relations of Theseus and the lovers over how to "darreyne" Emelye (I 1609, 1853) point to the substantial benefits at stake in these plots.

This chapter takes two perspectives on the ways gender figures in adventure. The first section traces the alien and appropriated status of the feminine in the *Knight's Tale*. Adventure's imbrication of concrete gain and unpredictable hazard points to this first gendered interaction in adventure: often undertaken on the chance of winning a woman in marriage, adventure as often proves to be not a departure from woman but an experience, if only metonymic, of her femininity. Bertilak's wife teaches Gawain that the "lel layk of luf" is the very "lettrure of armes": "Hit is þe tytelet token and tyxt of her werkkez, / How ledes for her lele luf hor lyuez han auntered" (1513, 1515–16). Gawain might reply that his adventure demands chastity rather than love, but it nonetheless draws him into substantial and telling contact with the feminine rather than leading him away from it. Moreover, in romance the experiences of woman and of adventure similarly commingle challenge and accommodation. Encounters with threatening, magical, or exotic forces, like encounters between men and women, do not tend to be simply adversarial. Bevis of Hampton defeats a pagan giant, Ascopart, who then follows him across Europe as faithfully and meekly as Guy of Warwick's lion follows him. In *Sir Gawain and the Green Knight* the magic that seems to doom Gawain proves to be strangely benevolent. Courtship, whose vocabulary is so often that of combat, is the central adventure of many romances. The adversarial alterity of women's resistance resonates with the unpredictable and exotic forces encountered in other adventures, forces that like the beloved both resist and attract the hero. These adversaries may remain irreversibly strange, yet adventure often culminates not simply in conquest but in appropriation—in marrying the woman, seizing the enemy's lands and titles, converting the pagan, taming the animal. At the culmination as throughout, adventure's validity inheres in that alienness which provides occasions for self-testing and self-discovery.

The chapter closes by returning to the question of crossgendering that introduced the first chapter. Male characters take on an apparently feminine vulnerability in making themselves available to adventure. Guigemar's slumber as the magic boat carries him to his future love in Marie de France's lay, Gawain's white neck bared to the Green Knight's ax, and countless lovers' importunities that prepare for Aurelius's to Dorigen and Palamon's and Arcite's to Emelye demonstrate that adventure demands a conjoined boldness and subjection. The encounter with femininity that adventure figures seems to require men to behave in some ways like women. Conversely, women, so involved in the idea of adventure, can have adventures themselves. These occur in the shadow of masculine endeavor and conflict with it. Women's oppositional experience, while ultimately bending to the course of men's adventures, establishes a feminine subjectivity that questions and relativizes those adventures. Through the gender reversals and expansions of adventure, romances complicate their own dominant paradigms of masculine and feminine behavior.

ADVENTURE AND THE FEMININE IN
THE *KNIGHT'S TALE*

The *Knight's Tale* is not so evidently indebted to the adventures of romance as other tales; here the lovers do not ride out in imitation of the "knyght auntrous" as does Sir Thopas, nor are they confronted with magical gifts and tests as are Cambyuskan's children and the Wife of Bath's knight. The lovers do undertake in the tournament a "greet emprise" (V 732) to win Emelye as do Arveragus and Aurelius to win Dorigen, but the tale's persistent concern with ordering and Theseus's concluding assertion of a preordained design are not consonant with the sense of chance that informs adventure. In Lee Patterson's memorable formulation, "the shape of the narrative argues that what appears to be 'aventure' or 'cas' is in fact 'destynee.' . . . Events that might in other stories be considered to be random are here revealed to be part of a master plan that has been, we are encouraged to think, in force from the beginning" (*Chaucer*, 208). A. C. Spearing argues that "we must recognize in Chaucer, wherever we look, a contempt for romance of all kinds" (*Medieval to Renaissance*, 36). A. J. Minnis, Derek Brewer, Robert Frank, and J. A. Burrow have also noted Chaucer's lack of interest in or sympathy for romance, especially for its narrative illogicalities and unmotivated marvels.[3] Much in the *Knight's Tale* is not best understood in terms of romance; for example, emphasizing Chaucer's classicism illuminates ideas about order and justice in the tale, and focusing on the use of Boccaccio's *Teseida* clarifies Chaucer's narrative strategies. Readers have nonetheless long recognized that the romance genre informs the *Knight's Tale* more fully than does any other genre. Spearing concurs with earlier critics in calling the tale a "classical" or "philosophical romance," a generic modification that simplifies and clarifies plot and makes wonders explicable or historicizes them "as part of the religion of the classical past" (*Medieval to Renaissance*, 38–39; see also Minnis; Frost; Halverson). Chaucer's generic revisions, in this view, free the *Knight's Tale* from disorder and irrationality, precisely the qualities that characterize romance from the classical perspective.

Yet I will argue that adventure offers a way into the *Knight's Tale*'s affiliations with romance, and that Chaucer's sense of adventure's illogicalities and marvels contributes to his treatment of gender, social order, and destiny in the *Knight's Tale*.[4] The scene in Diana's temple, which seems from classical and Boccaccian perspectives to be marred by a number of compositional weaknesses, is particularly meaningful when considered in terms of romance. In this scene and beyond, romance informs the tale's representation of Emelye as an occasion for adventure. Both Emelye and Diana contradict the tale's governing ideals and structures and do so in the unmotivated mode of adventure. Emelye expresses a desire not to love or be loved that may seem simply coy, but that does not make easy sense in relation to her other manifestations in the tale. Diana's manifestations are similarly imponderable. Around both figures Chaucer has generated illogicalities from Boccaccio's more coherent presentation. The omens Diana shows Emelye, for example, predict a future that Diana should not know. Chaucer attributes an unexplained prescience to Diana by temporally relocating the scene in her temple: rather than following the gods' determinations as in the *Teseida*, it occurs just before Arcite's prayer to Mars and the ensuing dispute among the

---

[3] Minnis, 7–8, 133; Brewer, *Symbolic Stories*, 92–97, 99; Frank, 111–33; Burrow, "*Canterbury Tales*," 109.

[4] An earlier version of the following discussion was published as "Medieval Romance and Feminine Difference."

gods. This and several similar compositional adjustments to the *Teseida* might be thought careless or insignificant for their illogicality, but I would like to reconsider them as aspects of a romance sensibility that permeates the *Knight's Tale*.

In the *Knight's Tale*, *aventure* evokes both the Boethian hierarchy of apparent causes, as a near synonym for "sort" and "fortune," and the generic field of romance, as the term of choice for substantial encounters with the unforeseen. The former sense operates in lines such as "Were it by aventure or destynee" and "For fallyng nys nat but an aventure" (I 1465, 2722); the latter in Arcite's "For which I tolde thee myn aventure" and "Thyne is the victorie of this aventure" (I 1160, 1235).[5] The significance of adventure in romance differs from, indeed reverses, the significance assigned it in Boethian philosophy, where all apparent accidents are subsumed in a providential design. In romance there may well be a sense of design, even a belated explanation of the marvelous adventure, but the sense of mystery predominates over the philosophical drive to clarify.[6] The scene in Diana's temple particularly endorses adventure's romance associations over its rationalized philosophical ones.

The mystery inherent in romance adventure associates the feminine with adventure itself. Romance establishes a masculine narrative perspective that specifies the feminine as that which is beyond the lover's experiential knowledge and the plot's discursive anticipation. Jean-Charles Huchet resists the early critical position that by representing women romances enhanced the status of historical women; he argues that "la prise en compte de la femme par le roman ne s'est jamais donnée pour la reconnaissance de la spécifité d'une différence, mais pour l'introduction en son sein d'une métaphore de l'alterité qui permette de parler et au roman de s'écrire" (in taking women into account, romance is not seeking to recognize their specific difference, but to adopt a meta-

[5] On *aventure* as a synonym for *fortune* see Patch. Mann argues for the predominance of a Boethian sense of *aventure* in the *Knight's Tale* in "Chance and Destiny."

[6] Many romances illustrate that *aventure* encompasses a suppressed sense of *fortune* and *destinee* as in the *Knight's Tale*: Kelly, 154–59, cites examples from *Mélusine*, the *Roman de Troie, Amadas et Ydoine*, the *Chevalier a la Mance*, and others; see also Wilmotte, 116–17, on the *Roman de Troie*.

phor of alterity that permits speech, and permits romance to be written) (*Roman médiéval*, 218). As the "metaphor of alterity," woman is the locus of the impossible demand, the uncanny intuition, the unimaginable passion. Narrative and lover move toward encompassing her through adventure: in countless romances women who, like Emelye, embody love and impersonate Venus occasion plots concerning their lovers' courtship and experience of love.

Courtship in the *Knight's Tale* begins with Palamon and Arcite interpreting their own desire as the onslaught of a life-threatening adventure. As we have seen in chapter 2, from their first sight of Emelye the lovers perceive her attractiveness as aggression. Their unreturned gaze upon her becomes her act upon them: "I was hurt right now thurghout myn ye / Into myn herte, that wol my bane be," Palamon declares, and Arcite later echoes, "Ye sleen me with youre eyen, Emelye! / Ye been the cause wherfore that I dye" (I 1096–97, 1567–68). The narrator's presentation is rhetorically consonant with the lovers' in these respects. He praises Emelye's beauty; he compares her to an angel and cannot judge between the rose and her complexion, rather as Palamon compares her to Venus and cannot distinguish between her womanhood and divinity; and he concurs with the lovers' sense of victimization by love: "with that sighte hir beautee hurte hym so, / That, if that Palamon was wounded sore, / Arcite is hurt as muche as he, or moore" (I 1114–16). In terms of romance's conventions of courtship, whether the *Knight's Tale* narrator is at every moment the Knight or entirely a Chaucerian narrator created before the composition of the *General Prologue* or a complexly mingled presence is not relevant. The narrating voice is importantly masculine throughout, and when Emelye first appears, the consonance of narrator and lovers helps naturalize the lovers' sense of victimization and license their consequent passivity toward Emelye herself.

Palamon and Arcite experience Emelye in lyrical self-absorption for some years. It may seem that their imprisonment enforces a distant and unchanging experience of desire, but their prison "evene joynant to the gardyn wal" (I 1060) has more metaphorical than circumstantial meaning (Kolve, 85–105). Later the disguised Arcite enforces silence on himself, expressing his love only in the

name Philostrate and in complaints voiced alone. Palamon and
Arcite perceive Emelye as all-powerful and free in contrast to
their own imprisonment by love, but the distance they maintain
from her identifies the experience of love as their own and not
hers. Why exclude her? For a Gaston Paris or a C. S. Lewis the
lady's apartness encouraged the lover's improvement; recent and
not entirely incompatible interpretations are that the lady's apartness allows lovers to project what is lacking in themselves onto
the concrete distance separating them from their goal, or into the
unresponsive passivity of the beloved lady.[7] In the latter readings
the lover's sense of improvement may be delusory, but the distance between lover and lady remains crucial to the claim that
male desire is an improving experience. Palamon and Arcite are
willing to die to determine whether Emelye is "my lady" or "thy
lady" before she has responded in any way to their love (I 1581,
1617, 1619). In the end each man does win Emelye's answering
devotion, Arcite at the time of his victory and death and Palamon
at his marriage. For the space of the plot, however, the difference
between the masculine and the feminine experience of courtship
generates adventure. Her lovers' detachment determines a social
passivity in Emelye as in other courted ladies, but feminine passivity is less important to understanding romance than is the
striking difference that woman embodies in the genre despite her
relative inaction, despite a process of courtship that absents her
from the narrative and reconstitutes her to the specifications of
her lovers' desire.[8]

   In her configuration as a ground of adventure for male protagonists the beloved lady acquires an oppositional identity that challenges their courtship. Emelye's most overt opposition, her assertion to Diana that "I / Desire to ben a mayden al my lyf, / Ne

[7] To Lewis and Paris compare Rey-Flaud; Johnson, 3–20; Huchet, *Roman médiéval*.

[8] Minnis, 133, argues that Emelye's passivity is importantly pagan rather than
courtly and that it "becomes comprehensible only if it is placed in its historical
perspective and related to her fatalism." I argue that the classical and Boethian
material in the *Knight's Tale* interacts with paradigms of courtship drawn from
romance. The classicizing impulse heightens Emelye's passivity and her lovers'
detachment over the norms of romance, revealing the genre's tendency to sub-
sume the feminine within the masculine experience of love.

nevere wol I be no love ne wyf" (I 2304–6), exemplifies a perpetual contradictoriness that makes her finally indecipherable. Emelye is the most evident instance of a multivoiced ambiguity that characterizes the *Knight's Tale* and that for romance has its origin in gender difference. Theseus as well as Emelye speaks differently from the lovers, but Theseus's perspective is normative insofar as it tallies with the narrator's perspective and invokes common sense, chivalry, and an idea of order.

Emelye's resistance, like adventure itself, is unmotivated: acquiescing to Theseus's plan for giving her away but then praying to remain a virgin, lamenting Arcite's death but then loving Palamon, she is as diffused in her scattered manifestations as the subdivided heroine of the *Romance of the Rose*. Several explanations might be proposed for Emelye's dispersed gestures, and I review them briefly in sequence to suggest that Emelye is constituted by unverifiability, rather than by the text's validation of one explanation over another.

Some readers conclude that Emelye "fears the primal curse of childbearing" and "is afraid to enter on the next stage of life, marriage, with all that that signifies": she is an affectionate but timid young woman.[9] Boccaccio's Emilia, so young that "non chiede amore intero" (she does not seek a mature love) (bk. 3, st. 19) fits this explanation in asking Diana for protection from both men yet admitting that, if she must have one, "io nol so in me stessa nomare, / tanto ciascun piacevole mi pare" (I don't know myself how to choose, each one seems so pleasing to me) (bk. 7, st. 85). Emelye, in contrast, is unexplained. Given that she represents virginity as her chosen way of life and expresses no desire for her suitors, her prayer is in itself unambiguous and considered, however much it differs from her expressions elsewhere. But in the absence of textual cues it is possible to imagine her motive to be a momentary fear or coyness.

On the scant evidence of the tale, we could just as plausibly (or implausibly) say that Emelye is Athenian in manner but still Amazonian within, behaving properly to all appearances but tacitly maintaining her independence and her "compaignye" of

---

[9] Harrison, 112; Brooks and Fowler, 127; Kolve, 122, agrees that Emelye is not a "dedicated virgin" but a "young girl not yet awakened to love" in the temple scene.

maidens for as long as possible (I 2307). In this view the public plea for mercy on Palamon and Arcite in which Emelye participates would illustrate the braking function of "verray wommanhede" (I 1748) in chivalric literature as in history, a function that provides masculine war making and justicing with opportunities for peacemaking and mercy. Emelye's private prayer for virginity would in contrast recall the independence of Amazonian life that for Boccaccio was unnaturally masculine in requiring "virile animo . . . uomini fatti, non femine" (viril courage . . . deeds of men, not of women) (bk. 1, st. 24). If the prayer does express an Amazonian sensibility, it neutralizes Boccaccio's condemnation by encompassing a "womanly" request for "love and pees bitwixe hem two" (I 2317) and by aligning isolation from men with chastity and maidenhood rather than with "virile" aggression.

A third version of Emelye's behavior might be based in the couplet that glosses the "freendlich ye" she casts on Arcite at the end of the tournament: "For wommen, as to speken in comune, / Thei folwen alle the favour of Fortune" (I 2680–82). The couplet does not appear in several manuscripts including Hengwrt, Ellesmere, and Cambridge Gg.iv.27; if it is Chaucer's, it seems to come to us *sous rature*, or it might represent an early copyist's attempt to make sense of Emelye.[10] Linking Emelye to Fortune explains her reversals as inexplicable—no more than accidents—and at the same time integrates her inexplicability into the tale's broader concern with the place of accidents in the providential scheme. In this reading Emelye presides over the circular tournament ground as Fortune over her wheel, or at most as Venus over lovers and Diana over maidens: apparently mistresses but finally handmaidens of destiny. The couplet's dubious authority is appropriate both to the tale's evasion elsewhere of interpretive comment on Emelye and to the suppressed but still operative role of misogyny in romance, where the challenge a beloved lady embodies can seem at once an inspiration and a capricious folly typical of womanhood.

These explanations are obviously not compatible in most respects, and they illustrate how Emelye's unmotivated nature can

---

[10] See Manly and Rickert, 3:434n; and John H. Fisher's account of more recent theories of transmission.

make her a site for our projections of motive as she is for her lovers' (e.g., "Venus, if it be thy wil / Yow in this gardyn thus to transfigure"; "She that dooth me al this wo endure / Ne reccheth nevere wher I synke or fleete," I 1104–5, 2396–97). Explaining Emelye's few manifestations in terms of each other is so conjectural that her significance is surely not in any unified personality but in her very contradictions. That is where all critical attempts to understand her coincide: she is changeable, and in that she is feminine—she is like "wommen . . . in comune." In relation to her lovers she is both attractive and resistant, elusive and threatening, as befits the terrain of adventure in romance.

The scene in Diana's temple clarifies that Emelye's strangeness is not idiosyncratic but feminine. Complementing Emelye's desire that Palamon's and Arcite's love be extinguished or turned away from her are indications that her opposition is related to her gender, to a community of difference. Her only words in the tale are spoken as part of a maidens' ritual that sets her apart from men. The narrator's refusal to describe Emelye's rite of bathing could express a distance from the pagan past, as Spearing and Minnis argue (Spearing, *Medieval to Renaissance*, 41–42; Minnis, 108–9). But since other pagan rites and myths are described without demur, the narrator's "I dar nat telle" (I 2284) suggests that in this case gender distances him from the rite. His refusal resonates with Actaeon's punishment for seeing Diana bathing. The narrator avoids making Actaeon's error, as if recalling the painted depiction on the temple wall:

> Ther saugh I Attheon an hert ymaked,
> For vengeaunce that he saugh Diane al naked;
> I saugh how that his houndes have hym caught
> And freeten hym, for that they knewe hym naught.
>
> (I 2065–68)

Emelye's bathing ritualizes a division between female and male that her Amazonian past, her prayer for virginity, and Diana's vengeance on Actaeon reinforce. Although the assertion that "it were a game to heeren al" (I 2286) does not take the situation seriously, the rite's gendered oppositions continue in a closing explanation cast in the masculine: "To hym that meneth wel it were no charge; / But it is good a man been at his large" (I 2287–88). The meaning of "at his large" is problematic (out of prison? free to imagine?), but more important is the vaguely antagonistic distance between the maidens in Diana's temple and the masculine observer who edits out Emelye's body. The prohibition implicit in "I dar nat telle" and the transgressive pleasure in "it were a game to heeren al" both recognize feminine separateness and adumbrate its violation.

I believe that the gendered narration in the temple scene invokes the sexual connotation of the word *queynte*, which is repeated five times in Emelye's prayer and its answering omens. Larry Benson has argued that *queynte* cannot carry a prurient second meaning in this scene because the term can be a sexual euphemism only when the context invites it: "If we are led to expect the obscenity and hear *queynte* instead, we have a pun. Unless we are led to expect the obscenity, no pun is possible with this word" ("'Queynte' Punnings," 45). *Queynte* has primary meanings that are not euphemistic, like the modern *Peter* or *pussy*. Benson argues that, since the word *queynte* does not function euphemistically by replacing a sexual term in the temple of Diana scene, *queynte* means here only "strange" and "extinguished":

> But sodeynly she saugh a sighte queynte,
> For right anon oon of the fyres queynte
> And quyked agayn, and after that anon
> That oother fyr was queynt and al agon;
> And as it queynte it made a whistelynge. . . .   (I 2333–37)

The context does not equate the word with its sexual referent, but such referents do not always behave so politely as to sit still until expressly invited to come forward. I believe that punning occurs in this passage despite the double obstacle of syntax (*queynte* in adjectival and verbal form rather than nominal) and the absence of obscene meaning for entire phrases. According to Benson, punning is impossible in these circumstances, but his closing paragraph illustrates on the contrary that a generally suitable context invites obscene connotations: "Should [those finding obscene puns in Chaucer] publish, should they expose themselves in public, let us screw up our courage. Let us say with the accused in *Trial by Jury*: 'Be firm, be firm, my pecker.' And let us collectively put an end to the punsters!" ("'Queynte' Punnings," 47). "Let us screw up our courage," for example, is only an approximate pun, depending for its obscene implication on context and the euphemistic sense of the morpheme *screw* alone, not on the phrase's syntax ("screw up") or an evident obscene meaning for the entire phrase. But the exhortation is clearly a double entendre and would make an entirely recognizable medieval one: Charles Muscatine notes Gautier le Leu's puns on *con* within verbs such as *consentit* and *conquis*; Frederick Ahl analyzes many approximate puns in Ovid, Isidore of Seville, and other Latin authors; R. A. Shoaf writes of "the dual and duel of sounds" in John the carpenter's unconscious pun "Allas, now comth Nowelis flood" (I 3818).[11]

I suggest that in Diana's temple double meaning does arise from the conjunction of context and the morpheme *queynte*. The narrator's opening recognition of gender difference and his double assertion that "I dar nat telle . . . and yet it were a game to heeren al" prepare rhetorically for a pun. The context is that of a prayer for virginity that is being answered in the negative; Emelye admits the relevance of her lovers' "hoote love and hir desir" (I 2319) but seeks to withhold her body from them as from the sight of all men during these rites. Even (or especially) her refusal itself invites the unruly connotation from the morpheme's many repetitions. If the passage were modern and the omens were talking pussycats, even the most sober readers might sense a surreptitious unveiling of the female body that was earlier forbidden to us. The tale's normative perspective is masculine, Emelye's rites are feminine, and the disparity between perspective and rites makes Diana's temple a scene of difference that clarifies woman's absence from the masculine experience of love in romance.

Outside the temple Emelye is Theseus's "suster" and Arcite's "wyf" (I 1833, 3062, 3075), recuperated into the program of courtship that Palamon and Arcite initiate and Theseus modifies. Only in the temple does she dissent from courtship, in the company of maidens and the presence of Diana. The context of Emelye's resistance suggests that her gender accounts for the disparity between her perceptions and those of her suitors.

To this analysis it might be objected that Emelye aligns herself

---

[11] Muscatine, *Old French Fabliaux*, 115 (see also 105–51); Ahl; Shoaf, "The Play of Puns," 54. Culler provides a useful reconsideration of theoretical and critical approaches to puns.

with Actaeon, in praying to Diana, "As keepe me fro thy ven-
geaunce and thyn ire, / That Attheon aboughte cruelly" (I 2302–
3). In a scene illustrating particular gender divisions, the equivalence Emelye finds between her fate and Actaeon's may seem out
of place, but in effect the story of Actaeon reiterates gender difference with peculiar force. The trope of invoking the divinity's
own record while asking for divine protection parallels Palamon's request that Venus aid him "For thilke love thow haddest
to Adoon" (I 2224) and Arcite's request that Mars "rewe upon
my pyne / For thilke peyne and thilke hoote fir / In which thow
whilom brendest" with desire for Venus (I 2382–84). The two men
ask for aid in winning Emelye with reference to stories of divine
passion, and Emelye asks for aid in remaining a virgin with reference to a story of divine chastity. Still, it might seem more appropriate for Emelye to imagine herself as a new Daphne than as
a new Actaeon. How is his situation like Emelye's? In terms of
Palamon's and Arcite's courtship, Emelye's fear of Actaeon's
fate reinterprets the familiar poetic image of courtship as hart
hunting, illustrated in the allegorical frame for the *Book of the
Duchess* (348–86, 1311–13) and in many contemporary works
(Thiébaux, 115–27, 144–66, 244–46). The image of lover-hunters
in pursuit of the women's heart reverses the aggression that Palamon and Arcite have attributed to Emelye's wounding beauty.
More important, the specific instance of Actaeon's death alters
the conventional image of love's hunt from a desirable to a horri-
fying situation: according to the story Emelye chooses, her very
identity is in jeopardy, her pursuing lovers bestial and unable to
perceive her humanity. The parallel Emelye draws between herself and Actaeon is not gender-neutral in terms of her situation;
indeed, Emelye's reinterpretation of love's hunt by means of Actaeon's story sets her again in gender-determined opposition to
the lovers.

The scene in Diana's temple is further set against the normative
masculine world of the tale by the goddess's uncanny prescience.
Like a heavenly Cassandra, Diana is unable to affect the course of
events that she foresees. She recounts Emelye's fate as a decision
beyond herself and seems forbidden even to articulate all she
knows, yet her knowledge is peculiarly complete. One of the fires

on Diana's altar seems to go out, then burns again; the other fire goes out and bloody drops run from the extinguished sticks. Emelye weeps in alarm and Diana comes to console her,

> And seyde, "Doghter, stynt thyn hevynesse.
> Among the goddes hye it is affermed,
> And by eterne word writen and confermed,
> Thou shalt ben wedded unto oon of tho
> That han for thee so muchel care and wo,
> But unto which of hem I may nat telle.
> Farwel, for I ne may no lenger dwelle.
> The fires which that on myn auter brenne
> Shulle thee declaren, er that thou go henne,
> Thyn aventure of love, as in this cas."   (I 2348–57)

Boccaccio's gloss to the omens notes that the first fire represents Palamon's briefly quenched and then rekindled hopes when Arcite wins the tournament but then dies, and the second fire represents Arcite's death.[12] This meaning is easy to deduce, recalling similar wonders in the *Aeneid*, *Metamorphoses*, and *Inferno*, but it is obscured in the *Knight's Tale* by a double displacement: Diana's words connecting the two suitors to the two fires follow the omens' appearance on the altar, rather than preceding it as in the *Teseida*; and Chaucer has shifted the whole scene in Diana's temple from its chronologically plausible site in the *Teseida* to a much earlier moment, before Arcite's prayer to Mars, the dispute between Venus and Mars in heaven, and Saturn's ominous forecast of a solution that will settle the dispute.

Yet, as in the *Teseida*, Diana asserts that the fires on her altar reveal the future. I believe that Chaucer's relocation of the scene responds to a romance imagining of the "aventure of love," and particularly to adventure's components of the mysterious and the unmotivated. Diana's foreknowledge does not submit to rational explanation. Some editors propose that Chaucer relocates Boccaccio's scene in order to place it at Diana's astrological "houre in-

---

[12] For the text of Boccaccio's gloss see *Teseida*, 484; see also the *Riverside Chaucer* explanatory note to I 2339–40; and Boccaccio, *Chaucer's Boccaccio*, trans. Havely, 133–35, 209nn. Pratt argued against Chaucer's knowledge of Boccaccio's glosses; Boitani, 190–97, makes the case for Chaucer's knowledge of the glosses.

equal" (I 2271), between the hours of Venus and Mars.[13] I have not found any analysis of the resulting prevenience of Diana's omens, omens that in Boccaccio merely report the solution that has just been worked out among the gods. We might dismiss the omens' revelations in Chaucer as a compositional error introduced by the relocation of the scene, but Chaucer's further relocation of Diana's speech, to follow rather than precede the omens, suggests that his reorderings are deliberate attempts to render the omens wonderfully strange, and strangely out of place.

Deliberateness is perhaps the wrong characterization for a compositional process that introduces inconsistencies and errors into a handsomely ordered tale. This process more sensitive to mystery than to accuracy might account as well for the erroneous translation of Boccaccio's "Fu mondo il tempio e di bei drappi ornato" (the temple was clean and decorated with fine hangings) (bk. 7, st. 72) into the wonderfully evocative "Smokynge the temple, ful of clothes faire" (I 2281). Most editors posit that Chaucer mistook *fu mondo* for *fumando* (smoking); in contrast, J.A.W. Bennett suggests a deliberate attempt to condense Boccaccio's long account of sacrificial fires into one phrase (136). Between simple mistakes and deliberate revisions is the romantic possibility of meaningful error, an errant uncanniness that helps make Diana's temple a site of women's difference. According to Spearing, the *Knight's Tale* has a "classical simplicity and rationality of structure" in which there are "no narrative complications, no irrelevancies, none of that procedure by digression that is the typical method of medieval romance" (*Medieval to Renaissance*, 39). Certainly the *Knight's Tale* is handsomely designed, and its romance "complications" and "irrelevancies" are part of that design, introducing oppositional voices that interrogate the tale's most fully articulated visions.[14] Just as Emelye's desire not to be

[13] Editors also note the inversion of order within the scene, Diana's speech following rather than preceding the omens; on both reorderings see the comments in the *Canterbury Tales* edition of Tyrwhitt and Clarke, 1:208; and the *Knight's Tale* editions of Bennett, 135–37; and Spearing, ed., *Knight's Tale*, 181; see also Kovetz.

[14] A complication similar to Diana's foreknowledge but without narrative implications is the depiction of Caesar's and Nero's deaths on the walls of Mars's temple (I 2031–38).

loved confuses the image of courtship in the tale, Diana's reply disrupts the progression of surrounding episodes, not only chronologically but metaphysically. Diana should not know the outcome at this moment, and more important, she should not know it at *any* moment.

Diana's assertion that there is an "eterne word writen and confermed" does have precedent in the *Knight's Tale*. Often characters vacillate between resigning themselves fatalistically to a fixed destiny and applying to capricious gods who may be swayed to intervene in earthly events. Arcite muses that love has wounded him so terribly "that shapen was my deeth erst than my sherte" (I 1566), yet he asks Mars to intervene in the tournament. Palamon believes that the future is "writen in the table of atthamaunt" (I 1305) but prays for Venus's intercession. Reading the *Knight's Tale* for its classicizing but Christian perspective, Minnis and others make sense of the tale's metaphysical scheme by establishing a distinction between the capricious accidents that the gods seem to control and God's serene providence that guides the universe but that even Theseus's final speech can barely articulate. Thus Theseus's positive vision of a "wise purveiaunce" (I 3011) informing the universe can be reconciled with the squabble among the gods and the resolution cobbled together by Saturn: from Chaucer's Christian perspective, as in Theseus's partial understanding, events apparently at the whim of the gods are in fact providentially designed. The characters in the tale, Minnis concludes, are "benighted pagans . . . wasting their devotions on false gods. The implicit Christian standard in *The Knight's Tale* is thereby indicated, and a focus provided for Christian distrust of the 'rytes of payens'" (135; see also Kolve, 136–49).

Diana's words to Emelye break down these metaphysical distinctions. Providence is within Diana's purview, an "eterne word writen and confirmed" in the *pagan* heavens, "among the goddes hye." Her access to this eternal word and the accuracy of her omens are at odds with the strife-torn and capricious behavior of the gods in surrounding scenes. Those gods exist chronologically in relation to the world, arguing and weeping into the lists until Saturn brings about his catastrophe, whereas Diana is already living in a harmonious sempiternal order in which all is foreseen and foreordained.

Diana is Emelye's celestial complement, feminine in romance's terms through her contradictory manifestations as well as her articulated contradiction of the celestial order that is projected elsewhere in the tale. Outside the temple, Diana like Emelye seems in consonance with the orderly Athenian court that Theseus heads, "for after Mars he serveth now Dyane" (I 1682) in sociable hunting parties. Diana's oratory is located between the temples of Mars and Venus and is built "of alabastre whit and reed coral" (I 1910), suggesting that she may mediate between the lovers who fight under the red banner of Mars and the white banner of Venus. Retrospectively it seems that Emelye's red and white complexion and the red and white flowers she wove together in her green garden adumbrated a concord in marriage that Diana's temple expresses in its very architecture.[15] But Diana's connections to concord, mediation, and stasis are countered in the images of her vengeance and changeability: she stands on a phasing moon; she transforms her victims. In a final contradiction, the temple's images of change are themselves reversed in Diana's knowledge of the eternal word.

Diana's foreknowledge is so disruptive of the tale's metaphysical design that critics tend not to notice or believe in the omens' prediction of Palamon's and Arcite's fates, glossing the fires and the bleeding sticks instead as representations of Hymen's and Venus's torch, "the blood shed in menstruation, defloration and childbirth," or "the loss of virginity."[16] If the omens predicted only Emelye's marriage, Diana would still know a future to which she should not have access, but denying the omens' relation to Palamon and Arcite mutes the scene's disturbing prescience to some degree. I would like to emphasize that prescience, because it is a complication that typifies the procedure of romance. Like Emelye's resistance to love, Diana's foreknowledge exemplifies

[15] Blanch and Wasserman argue for the "ontological unity of white and red" in the *Knight's Tale* (184 et passim).

[16] Brooks and Fowler, 127; Spearing, ed., *Knight's Tale*, 181. There is a muted suggestion that Venus in some sense knows the outcome as well, in that her omen to Palamon "shewed a delay" (I 2268) that presages the lapse of time between tournament and marriage. Although Venus does not elsewhere seem prescient (perhaps because of her association with Palamon rather than a feminine cult), her omen suggests like Diana's a gender-related foreknowledge.

the genre's juxtaposition of contradictory voices. Such juxtaposition, writes Stephen Nichols, "calls into question the very possibility of erecting a unified philosophical system within the romance narrative. The dialectical indeterminacy of romance made it by nature a genre subversive of the privileged discourse requisite for unity in the totalizing systems favored by medieval society" (50–51).

Two privileged discourses are at issue in Diana's temple, that of chivalric courtship and that of metaphysical order. Although the *Knight's Tale* cannot be treated solely in terms of the romance genre, courtship and social order are central concerns of that genre, not least because they are central to the validation of the nobility as the estate that "does justice and keeps it."[17] In romance (as in wider cultural expressions) the nobility's ordering and rationalizing identity is specifically masculine. Chivalric courtship designs sexual relations and dynastic succession around masculine endeavor: Palamon, Arcite, and Theseus all assume that Emelye will marry and disagree only on how to "darreyne hire" (I 1609, 1853). Social and metaphysical ordering in romance involves distinguishing what is just, virtuous, or Christian from the unjust, evil, or pagan. Again Palamon, Arcite, and Theseus are aligned in their preoccupation with such distinctions, from the first dispute over priority in love to the final discourse on heavenly and earthly order.

It is particularly Chaucer's identification of feminine positions located outside the masculine designs of courtship and social order that expresses in the *Knight's Tale* the romantic sense of adventure. Emelye's experience of courtship differs from that of her lovers: she prefers not to be won and prays to remain a virgin. Her prayer immediately meets omens of refusal that Emelye might indeed understand as a phallic drama of impregnation. In these smoky omens the romance dynamic of feminine aloofness overcome by persistent courtship is elevated to the status of holy mystery and foreordained design. Yet Emelye's pleading for virginity and her terrified weeping at the omens reveal in courtship

[17] Benoît de Sainte-Maure, *Chronique des ducs de Normandie*, quoted in Duby, *Three Orders*, 273. Halverson discusses the *Knight's Tale* in terms of the ordering function of the second estate. A provocative recent discussion of dynastic succession in romance is Bloch, *Etymologies*.

a coerciveness that contradicts Palamon's and Arcite's stances of
respectful worship. Similarly, Diana's serene prescience disturbs
the tale's metaphysical distinction between the classical gods and
Christian providence. Her words collapse the antique heavens
into the medieval Christian universe, according a providential design to the former and leaking intimations of chaos into the latter.
The *Knight's Tale* becomes, here as elsewhere, not just an anti-
quarian exercise but a subversively anachronistic exploration of
accident and disorder in all or any time.

The feminine ritual in Diana's temple contradicts the tale's rituals of courtship and justice, not in open argument and refutation
but surprisingly and mysteriously. In such adventures romance
questions its every ideal and refuses a reductive evasion of difference. To deny the *Knight's Tale* its romantic complications and
irrelevancies is to mute the tale's most profound interrogations
and to elide its gendered oppositions.

CROSSGENDERING IN ADVENTURE

Adventure also challenges the gendered oppositions it stages.
Male characters experience, particularly in adventures of love, an
apparently feminine subjection and passivity. Female characters
transgress their more typical quiescence to experience challenging adventures themselves. Crossing gender boundaries in these
ways does not finally threaten the heterosexual binary but does
assert a certain mobility in gendered behavior. Adventure, I will
argue, provides men with a positive experience of femininity by
protecting them from the taint of resembling women. Women's
adventures are peculiarly at odds with, and concealed within, the
dominant adventures of their lovers. In narrating feminine adventures, romances propose a distinctiveness but also a certain parity
between masculine and feminine experience.

Masculine adventures hold the dominant position in romance
and yet ask men to take on personal qualities associated with
women. Chapter 1 traces how virtues such as compassion may
seem to be feminine but come to be understood as subordinate
aspects of masculinity, identifying the masculine with the universal experience. The same chapter argues that courtship is closely
modeled on chivalric competition, incorporating the pursuit of

love into other masculine interactions. Adventure is often a clearly masculine pursuit in which to be helpless is not to be feminine. Cleomadés swept away by the magical horse, or Gawain and his fellows but "berdlez chylder" before the Green Knight (280), do not appear feminine in their incapacities. They are immature aspirants facing the unknown; as Fredric Jameson notes, "a casual glance at the traditional heroes of romance . . . suggests that the hero's dominant trait is naiveté or inexperience, and that his most characteristic posture is that of bewilderment" ("Magical Narratives," 139). When this inexperienced youth faces the "aventure merveilleuse" that is most fully embodied in women, however, he risks appearing not simply naive but feminine. Yvain in need of Lunete's help to win Laudine's hand, Arcite serving Emelye anonymously and expressing his woe only to himself, Aurelius languishing for two years in bed for love of Dorigen, and all such "drooping courtly lovers" seem to have taken on feminine traits in becoming lovers of women.[18]

It is certainly the case that a range of writers (and genres) find contact with women to be a substantial threat to masculinity. For Orderic Vitalis the threat is not one to which the active and militant men of earlier times were subject. At the end of the eleventh century young men first "grew long and luxurious locks like women, and loved to deck themselves in long, over-tight shirts and tunics. . . . Our wanton youth is sunk in effeminacy [femineam mollitiem], and courtiers, fawning, seek the favours of women with every kind of lewdness" (4:188–89; see Farmer). Contact with women brings on effeminate imitation of them as well as luxurious desire for them. The *Parson's Tale* similarly critiques men's dress, claiming that when men wear fashionably tight hose "the buttokes of hem faren as it were the hyndre part of a she-ape in the fulle of the moone" (X 423). The male body when dressed to reveal its sexuality appears instead inappropriately crossgen-

---

[18] The quotation is from Hansen, 17; Hansen's argument for the "feminization" of courtly lovers contrasts interestingly with that of Jill Mann in *Geoffrey Chaucer*: for Hansen, feminization is "a dramatized state of social, psychological, and discursive crisis wherein men occupy positions and/or perform functions already occupied and performed . . . by women" (16); for Mann feminization improves men and "does not marginalise woman, but centralises her, making her experience the exemplar for male heroism" (182).

dered. Both passages argue that masculine display is unavoidably if inadvertently feminine.[19] John Gower declares in *Vox Clamantis* that knights afflicted with sexual desire ("amoris voluptas") adopt womanish ways ("femineos mores") and consign their reason to the role of an abased handmaiden: again, feminine imagery expresses the distortion of masculinity that contact with women risks.[20] The diverse contexts of these medieval pronouncements endorse Sigmund Freud's perception of a durable, even transhistorical masculine fear of feminine sexuality: "Perhaps this dread is based on the fact that woman is different from man, for ever incomprehensible and mysterious, strange and therefore apparently hostile. The man is afraid of being weakened by the woman, infected with her femininity. . . . In all this there is nothing obsolete, nothing which is not still alive among ourselves" ("The Taboo of Virginity," 198–99).

Rather than simply expressing this danger of infection by femininity, romances imagine the "incomprehensible and mysterious" woman successfully confronted through adventure. I have argued with regard to the *Knight's Tale* that courtly behaviors serve a similar protective and distancing function for male lovers. The love to which courtship submits young men is intensely ideological and self-isolating, largely removing them from engagement with the feminine. For Palamon and Arcite, idealizing Emelye distances the threat that her adversarial voice might indeed pose to their suit. Courtship and adventure overlap in this respect, adventure serving not only to distance suitors quite literally from contact with women but also to provide them with a productively metonymic experience of the feminine in their encounters with the unknown. Examples from two Middle English adaptations of

---

[19] Lacan attributes this effect to the woman's masquerading response to desire: "The fact that femininity takes refuge in this mask . . . has the strange consequence that, in the human being, virile display itself appears as feminine" (85). On masquerade, see chapter 2, pp. 85–92.

[20] Gower, *Vox Clamantis*, bk. 5, ll. 225–40. Roger Bacon endorses the teaching attributed to Aristotle "quod coitus est destructio corporum et abbreviatio vitae, et corruptio virtutum, legis transgressio, femineos mores generat" (that sexual intercourse brings about the destruction of the body, the shortening of life, the corruption of virtues, the transgression of law, and the adoption of effeminate manners): pt. 7, sec. 3, chap. 5 (2:273). See also Wack.

highly artful French texts can illustrate how persistently adventure transforms the threat of feminization into productive masculine self-expansion.

Ywain and Gawain and *Lybeaus Desconus* differ strikingly from their French antecedents, Chrétien de Troyes's *Yvain* and Renaut de Beaujeu's *Le Bel Inconnu*. Their differences are most visibly losses: Derek Pearsall notes that *Ywain and Gawain* "is less interested in sentiment, and not at all interested in Chrétien's psychological speculations"; similarly, *Lybeaus Desconus* "is a good example of the way in which passionate erotic romance in French is emasculated into innocent knockabout in English" ("Development," 103, 113). Despite their quickened pace, directness, and relative simplicity of expression, however, the English texts find ways to convey the neutralizing of a feminine threat to masculinity.

In *Yvain* the subordinations of courting Laudine are part of the larger adventure of the magic spring that Laudine's husband defended and Yvain subsequently defends against his mocker Kay in view of all Arthur's court. Winning Laudine's hand substitutes for the trophy Yvain had hoped to seize from Esclados when pursuing him back to his castle (*Yvain*, ll. 891–99). Yvain's marriage and hospitality to Arthur put him in charge of Laudine's body and land, an outcome the court understands as Yvain's victory. *Ywain and Gawain*, while halving the length of Chrétien's episode, places heightened emphasis on Ywain's shaming of Kay and the role of his marriage in his success: Ywain tells Arthur's courtiers "With þe knight how þat he sped, / And how he had þe lady wed" and invites them to "wend with me to my purchace, / And se my kastel and my towre" (1361–62, 1368–69).[21] Despite their differences in subtlety and elaboration, both works incorporate Yvain's subordination to Laudine into his ultimate success at achieving the adventure of the magic spring.

Gawain most directly articulates the risk that intimacy poses to masculinity in urging Yvain to join him at tournaments after his marriage:

> "Comant! seroiz vos or de çax,"
> Ce disoit mes sire Gauvains,

---

[21] Compare the less obviously self-vaunting passage in *Yvain*, ll. 2297–2304.

> "qui por leur fames valent mains?
> Honiz soit de sainte Marie
> qui por anpirier se marie!"   (2486–90)

["What, are you going to be one of those," said my lord Gawain, "who is worth less on account of his wife? May he be shamed by Saint Mary who grows worse for marrying!"]

> "Þat knyght es nothing to set by,
> Þat leves al his chevalry
> And ligges bekeand in his bed,
> When he haves a lady wed."   (1457–60)

Here is the danger of feminine contact articulated by Orderic and Freud, but *Yvain*'s plot develops a positive space for Laudine's influence. What undoes Yvain's identity altogether in madness is not marriage to Laudine but forgetting to return to her, and what reestablishes his merit is a series of adventures that take into account the distress of women, the right and wrong of competing claims, and the pressure of time, three concerns that were lacking in his insouciant life with Gawain and that were implicit in his wife's reproach for his forgetfulness. Yvain's adventures take place in the absence of Laudine but respond to her in metonymic interactions with other potential wives and women in distress. These interactions are, moreover, constructive sources of self-definition for Yvain, who reshapes his identity into the "Chevalier au lÿon . . . / qui met sa poinne a conseillier / celes qui d'aïe ont mestier" (the Knight with the Lion, who strives to help women in need).[22] Far from eliding this argument in its condensations, *Ywain and Gawain* emphasizes the place of feminine influence in Ywain's transformation. For example, the English redactor adds a speech soon after Ywain returns to his senses from madness, articulating his loss of identity and its relation to his loss of Alundyne:

> I was a man, now am I nane;
> Whilom I was a nobil knyght
> And a man of mekyl myght;

[22] *Yvain*, ll. 4810–12; cf. *Ywain and Gawain*, ll. 2804–6: "þe knight with þe lyown: / He helpes al in word and dede, / Þat unto him has any nede."

> I had knyghtes of my menȝe
> And of reches grete plente;
> I had a ful fayre seignory,
> And al I lost for my foly.
> Mi maste sorow als sal þou here:
> I lost a lady þat was me dere.   (2116–24)

Alundyne's loss is both the greatest of all and a curiously belated notation following Ywain's account of losing manhood and knighthood and property "for my foly." This rhetorical structure manages simultaneously to suggest and to suppress the possibility that Alundyne's loss is pivotal to Ywain's loss of manhood. The speech encapsulates the plot's analogous procedure of placing Laudine at the origin of Yvain's madness but displacing her from the chivalric adventures that culminate in regaining her. She represents all that Yvain strives for, but at such a remove that achieving her is equivalent to masculine achievement in general. As the English text clarifies at the lovers' reconciliation, "þe knyght with þe liown / Es turned now to Syr Ywayn / And has his lordship al ogayn" (4020–22). In a different register, Chrétien's profoundly ironic presentation of both Yvain's courtship before marriage and his reconciliation with Laudine establishes an affective distance between the lovers that displaces Laudine to the periphery of Yvain's wider program of achievements. For the English redactor, irony appeared not so crucial to Chrétien's endeavor as did the more deeply emplotted indications that, negotiated through adventure, relations with women can consolidate masculine identity and control.

The final adventure in *Lybeaus Desconus* illustrates in small compass the unmanning that femininity accomplishes but also the incorporation of that reversal into productive masculine achievement. At the decisive moment in his fight with two magicians who have imprisoned the lady of Synadoun, Lybeaus turns from the slain body of one to hunt for the other, who has disappeared after Lybeaus wounded him. A huge serpent with a woman's face bursts into the hall and advances on a Lybeaus now frozen with fear:

> So sore hym gan agryse
> Þat he ne myȝt aryse

> Þauȝ hyt hadde y-bene all a-fere!
> And er Lybeauus hyt wyste,
> Þe warm wyth mouþ hym kyste
> All aboute hys swyre.   (Cotton MS, 2002–7)

The kiss transforms the serpent into the lady of Synadoun, who reveals that only a kiss from Gawain or one of his kin could break the magicians' spell and that her transformation indicates that both magicians are dead (Cotton MS, 2020–31, 2064–67).

Lybeaus's passivity and fear before the serpent are startlingly inappropriate to the combat he was engaging (what if the serpent had proved to be the second magician returning to kill Lybeaus?) yet his passivity and fear are necessary to the adventure's happy resolution in that they prevent him from killing or driving off the enchanted woman. She, in turn, quickly glosses Lybeaus's incapacity as a heroic action she must reward:

> And for þou sauyst my lyf,
> Casteles ten and fyf
> J ȝeue þe wyth-outen ende,
> And Y to be þy wyf,
> Ay wyth-out stryf,
> Ȝyf hyt ys Artours wylle.   (Cotton MS, 2032–37)

Lybeaus's momentary incapacity thus leads to establishing his identity as Gawain's son and to winning a wife and property. The corresponding scene in *Le Bel Inconnu* is less important to cross-gendering the young knight: he moves to attack the serpent but it makes signs of submission that stay his hand; the knight is suspicious of the kiss and repudiates it (ll. 3127–3211). *Le Bel Inconnu* develops a pervasive threat to the Inconnu's masculinity through his vacillation between two lovers, the lady of Synadoun and a fairy mistress. *Lybeaus Desconus* dismisses the fairy mistress as a mere troublemaker (Cotton MS, 1423–34) but preserves the challenge to masculinity in revising the lady of Synadoun's rescue.

The *Knight's Tale* draws on this widely expressed understanding that adventure engages the mysterious feminine, not deleteriously but in a positive process of masculine gain and self-definition. Adventure's trajectory of achievement faces down the

danger of lost manhood. Arcite, for example, begins the tale as a
Theban warrior but becomes a pseudonymous courtier unable
even to declare his love. His incapacitation derives from his love
as if by infection from Emelye's own passivity. But Theseus
frames and diminishes the lovers' bootless suffering in his speech
of pardon and reminiscence: "A man moot ben a fool, or yong or
oold— / I woot it by myself ful yore agon, / For in my tyme a
servant was I oon" (I 1812–14). His tolerant irony tallies with that
of the tale's narrator and recalls the voices of Chrétien, Renaut,
and many others. In that detached perspective love is appropriate
to youth, part of the masculine experience, and subordinate
within Theseus's mature masculinity. The tournament will begin
the process of containment by transmuting the lovers' desire into
the terms of chivalric endeavor and closing their courtship in
marriage.

We have seen how Palamon and Arcite's love for Emelye challenges and finally enriches their friendship and their standing as
knights. Evading contact with her, the lovers submit themselves
in isolation to the new affective experience Emelye represents. In
accepting the unpredictable fortunes of the tournament, the lovers again submit not so much to her will as to the unknown in
adventure; they take up an inquiring and responsive stance toward a mysterious universe. Arcite's death speech derives this responsiveness from his love for Emelye:

> Allas, the wo! Allas, the peynes stronge
> That I for yow have suffred, and so longe!
> Allas, the deeth! Allas, myn Emelye!
> Allas, departynge of oure compaignye!
> Allas, myn hertes queene! Allas, my wyf,
> Myn hertes lady, endere of my lyf!
> What is this world? What asketh men to have?
> Now with his love, now in his colde grave
> Allone, withouten any compaignye.   (I 2771–79)

The extraordinary beauty of this passage's formal construction—
its sorrowful anaphora on "allas" made lyrical in perfectly iambic
lines, its shift from exclamation to question made urgent by the
shift from iambic to first-syllable stress on "what" and "now,"

and its striking return to iambic liquidity in the last line's echo of "allas" in "allone"—confers a dignity on Arcite's speech that is in striking rhetorical contrast to the immediately preceding account of his body's disintegration. Arcite's lament to Emelye earns its high rhetorical status by conjoining the commitment to love that persists as his body collapses to a search for meaning in the accidents of his life. This search contrasts to his earlier conviction that he could make assertions about how Fortune and the gods operate. Whether his conviction of the moment was that the gods provide for humans "Wel bettre than they kan hemself devyse" or that Mars should answer his prayer and "do that I tomorwe have victorie" (I 1254, 2405), here in his only interview with Emelye Arcite's assurance first yields to interrogation. His deeply affective sense of mystery in this speech springs from his experience of love and provides him the full experience of adventure. Arcite's speech complements Palamon's eventual consolidation of his victory in marriage; taken together, the youths' encounters with love in adventure both render them helpless before the unknown and productively shape their identities.

Many further aspects of the *Knight's Tale* and other tales draw on the strategies by which romance represents and controls the dangers of femininity through adventure. Aurelius's relation to Arveragus recalls Palamon and Arcite's to Theseus; each man in the *Franklin's Tale* negotiates his subordination to love within a larger process of self-definition. John Fyler has extended the connection between courtship and adventure to the *Squire's Tale* in proposing that the Squire's youthful love informs his attempt at "Domesticating the Exotic," appropriating the adventures of Mongols, women, and birds by telling his tale. Thopas and the Wife of Bath's knight both love an elf-queen, quintessential figure for the disarming alienness of women and adventures. *Sir Thopas*'s suspended narration fixes Thopas in perpetual passivity, his unresolved love-longing and his retreat from Oliphaunt retroactively casting a suspicious femininity onto such details as his climbing into the saddle, his small sides, and his white skin (VII 725, 797, 836). This parodic tactic in *Sir Thopas* recognizes that male characters do undergo some crossgendering in romances, however firmly it may be suppressed under the sign of an enhanced masculinity. Such crossgendering enlarges the space for imagining intimacy between two genders that romance defines first of all in opposition to one another.

If adventure is the masculine experience of a mysterious and often overtly feminine unpredictability, can it be said that women have adventures of the same kind? Certainly they can act in consonance with their lovers: Marie de France's Guigemar and his lover both wear chastity tokens and find each other through a magic boat, William of Palerne and his lover Melior together disguise themselves in bearskins to escape her arranged marriage, and Florete even helps her husband to kill a dragon in *Floriant et Florete*. Ydoine of *Amadas et Ydoine* demonstrates her loyalty to Amadas, preserves her chastity for him, and rescues him from madness before they are finally married. In such plots women's actions, ostensibly at least, answer their lovers' desires by paralleling and repeating their actions. But there is a countertendency in romances that imagines women's experience in opposition to men's, not just in the static resistance to men's desire that drives courtship but in challenges that differ from and even contradict those faced by men. Women's adventures, as I will call these oppositional experiences, complicate the predominantly masculine orientation of romance and enrich the image of femininity that romance projects.

One of the alterations Chaucer makes to Boccaccio's scene in Diana's temple allows for a double reading of her omens. In the *Teseida*, Emilia notes that "per Arcita ci si pone / l'una, e l'altra poi per Palemone" (for Arcita one [fire] has been set and the other for Palemone) and she asks Diana specifically to show her which of the two she will marry, if that is to be her fate. Diana's maidens reply that Emilia will indeed marry and that the fires will answer Emilia's question: "tosto vedrai ciò che per te s'aspetta . . . ma celato / poco ti sia qual debbia esser di loro" (you will soon see what lies ahead for you . . . but it will be partly hidden from you which one of them it is to be) (bk. 7, sts. 86–89). Boccaccio's gloss noting which fire stands for which man is virtually superfluous, the briefly quenched and then rekindled flame that represents Palemone contrasting evidently to the bleeding sticks and extinguished flame that represents Arcita. In Chaucer's version, as we have seen, neither Emelye nor Diana indicates that the fires represent the lovers; Diana says more obscurely that "I may not telle" to whom Emelye will be married but that the fires show "Thyn aventure of love" (I 2357).

Although the most evident reading of the fires remains their revelation of Palamon's and Arcite's fates, Chaucer's refusal to specify what the fires represent licenses readings that have to do instead with Emelye's fate, her own "aventure of love" (I 2357). As well as the defloration and childbirth that modern critics find in the bleeding sticks of the second fire, both fires could represent the outcome of Emelye's desire "noght to ben a wyf" even as they represent her lovers' contrary desire to win her. The briefly quenched fire would then stand for her hope for maidenhood threatened in Arcite's victory but rekindled by his death; the extinguished and bleeding fire would stand for the loss of that hope in her marriage to Palamon.[23] Emelye's adventure would then involve recognizing that her will to independence must submit to the pressure of events. Jill Mann argues that such is the trajectory of adventure itself, as Theseus illustrates most fully in his "readiness to move with the course of events, to match their change with his own. . . . And this responsiveness encompasses not only human beings but also events, the 'aventures' which the romance hero allows to dictate the pattern of his life, accepting the destiny they forge" (*Geoffrey Chaucer*, 176, 178). According to Mann, Emelye models the feminine patience and pliancy in adventure that Theseus imitates.

In discerning the stance of submissiveness that adventure requires, Mann reveals an important connection between Emelye's and male characters' experiences in the *Knight's Tale*, but I do not see in Emelye's adventure the full equivalence, indeed the priority, that Mann finds in it (*Geoffrey Chaucer*, 180–82). It is true that Emelye recognizes in her prayer that she may "nedes have oon of hem two" (I 2324) despite her desire for virginity, and that

[23] Susan Arvay has suggested this reading to me; its strengths are that it accounts for both fires in terms of Emelye's desire and matches the chronology of events (whereas the fires as they represent the lovers' fates are temporally reversed). If the fires can represent her fate in terms of her expressed wish for virginity in the temple, the ensuing contradictions of her smile of favor to Arcite and her happy marriage with Palamon remain unresolved.

she does finally accommodate herself to marriage, as Theseus
does to Arcite's unforeseen treachery, Palamon's escape, and Arcite's death. What distinguishes Emelye's adventure is that it is
both like men's and consistently encompassed by men's adventures. Theseus's response to Arcite's death is richly articulated;
Emelye's appears only in an *occupatio* that notes we will not hear
"what she spak, ne what was hir desir" (I 2944). Theseus requests
her consent to marriage—"Lat se now of youre wommanly pitee"
(I 3083)—but that pity is first and most importantly his own.
Chapter 1 argues that the *Knight's Tale* ascribes pity to women in
order to suggest its subordinate role in masculine justicing. The
tale's last scene even more than its earlier ones locates pity first of
all in Theseus's own urge to turn Arcite's death to good; Emelye's
accord is a highly circumscribed, even preordained recognition of
Theseus's thoughtful gesture. "Lene me youre hond, for this is
oure accord," he prefaces his request (I 3081). Like the omens that
most evidently refer to her lovers' hopes but might also refer to
her own, Emelye's "aventure of love" is both at odds with and
contained within the more fully articulated adventures of male
characters.

Two lays of Marie de France, *Eliduc* and *Fresne*, can illustrate
how characteristically women's adventures both differ from and
take place within men's. Eliduc, in disfavor with his king, leaves
his wife at home and falls in love with the daughter of a king he
serves in Logres. Torn with regret for wronging his wife but unable to give up his love for the maiden, Eliduc brings her back to
his country where she falls into a deathlike trance on hearing that
he is already married. Eliduc's wife finds the hermitage where he
has been lamenting over the maiden's body, sees a weasel revive
its dead companion by placing a red flower in its mouth, and restores the maiden with the same flower. Then she reassures the
maiden that Eliduc loves her despite his deception, asks Eliduc's
permission to take the veil, and retreats to allow the two of them
to marry. After some time Eliduc also retreats to religious life and
the second wife joins the first in her establishment.

This lay begins and ends with a struggle over its naming. Titled
Eliduc in the unique manuscript, Harley 978, the text nonetheless
opens by asserting the priority of the women's names over the
man's:

> D'eles deus ad li lais a nun
> *Guildeluëc ha Guilliadun.*
> *Elidus* fu primes nomez,
> Mes ore est li nuns remuez,
> Kar des dames est avenu
> L'aventure dunt li lais fu. . . .   (21–26)[24]

[From the two of them the lay is called *Guildeluëc and Guilliadun.*
At first it was called *Eliduc* but now the name is changed, because
the adventure the lay is about happened to the women.]

The assertion that the adventure is the women's, already countered by the title chosen in the manuscript, surrenders to compromise in the lay's closing lines: "De l'aventure de ces treis / Li
aunciën Bretun curteis / Firent le lai pur remembrer" (the old
courtly Bretons made a lay to commemorate the adventure of
these three) (1181–83). In its conflicting sites of naming, this lay
both raises and suppresses the possibility of a distinction between
Eliduc's experience and that of Guildeluëc and Guilliadun.

   The suppressed distinction between the women's adventure
and the man's encourages a double reading of the lay's pivotal
marvel, the deathlike trance of the maiden broken by the wife's
discovery of a way to restore her. The more evident reading centers on the two women's conflicting relations with Eliduc and the
dilemma of his divided allegiance. In this reading the wife's great
generosity and pliancy toward her husband's new love resolves
the dilemma. The weasel lamenting its dead companion and reviving it with the magical flower recalls the main plot and indicates its resolution: in Robert Hanning and Joan Ferrante's reading, "the lover who grieves for his dead mate seems to represent
Eliduc, but the 'flower' *he* finds to bring her back to life is his
wife's charity" (*Lais of Marie de France,* 225n [their italics]). Deborah Nelson similarly argues that the wife's gesture has Eliduc as
its object: in grieving for and resuscitating Guilliadun, the wife
"makes the sacrifice necessary for his salvation" from adultery
and falseness (40).

---

[24] Rychner's note, *Lais,* 281, argues that "aventure" can be both the subject of
"est avenu" and the object of "cunterai" in the following line, "Si cum avint vus
cunterai" (just as it happened I will tell it to you).

At the same time, the two weasels are grammatically feminine and do not necessarily represent a heterosexual couple: "une musteile" is killed by the wife's valet as it runs through the chapel and across the maiden's body; then "sa cumpaine" laments over her and fetches the reviving flower (ll. 1032–53). The weasels' grammatical gender calls to mind Guildeluëc and Guilliadun and the wife's own lament for the maiden on finding her body: "Ele cumencet a plurer / E la meschine regreter" (she began to weep and mourn for the maiden) (1029–30). The wife's sorrow for Guilliadun's apparent death prepares for their retreat from the world together at the end of the lay:

> El la receut cum sa serur
> E mut li porta grant honur.
> De Deu servir l'amonesta
> E sun ordre li enseigna.
> Deu priouent pur lur ami
> Qu'il li feïst bone merci,
> E il pur eles repreiot.   (1167–73)

[She received her as a sister and showed her great honor. She urged her to serve God and taught her the rules of her order. They prayed to God that he show mercy to their friend, and he prayed for them too.]

If the two weasels can represent the wife and maiden, they point to a meaning that pushes Eliduc aside in favor of their feminine similarity in name, in affective relation to Eliduc, and subsequently in spiritual sisterhood.[25] The feminine adventure of the lay would then be a discovery that charitable cooperation links women productively within the imperatives of heterosexual relations. That is, Guildeluëc is both a submissive wife to Eliduc in reviving his lover and withdrawing from marriage, and a feminine companion to Guilliadun in mourning her, reviving her, and eventually living happily with her. The women's second identity as companions resides within their first identity as Eliduc's lovers,

---

[25] Eliduc could perhaps be represented in the valet who strikes the weasel senseless as she runs across Guilliadun's body (as Guilliadun is stricken by hearing that Eliduc is married). Gautier d'Arras's slightly later work *Ille et Galeron* relates a similar plot concerning the son of Eliduc, attesting to the influence of Marie's lay or its avatars.

determining the lay's titular and closing suppression of its claim that "des dames est avenu / l'aventure dunt li lais fu" (the adventure of the lay happened to the women). But the double, gender-crossing possibilities for reading the marvel of the weasels' companionship endorses feminine community in a plot most clearly about feminine sacrifice.

Marie's only lay titled for a woman, *Fresne*, provides its heroine with a similarly double experience of heterosexual love and feminine community. Fresne's mother, having slandered a neighboring woman by saying that the woman's twins must be the result of adultery, feels compelled to abandon one of the twin girls she subsequently bears. Raised in a convent, the abandoned Fresne loves and agrees to live with the young nobleman Gurun, but eventually Gurun's followers convince him to marry a legitimate heiress, Fresne's twin sister Codre. Fresne makes no protest, courteously prepares the house, and because Gurun's bedcovering is old she decorates the wedding bed with the silken cloth in which she was wrapped when abandoned; "Pur lui honurer le feseit" (she did it to honor him).[26] The girls' mother recognizes the cloth and reveals Fresne's parentage; Fresne is married to Gurun and her sister is richly married to another.

This plot, like that of *Eliduc*, expresses the value of submissiveness in love. Fresne and Guildeluëc, by yielding to Gurun's and Eliduc's new bond with another woman, prepare for happy resolutions to their beleaguered situations. In *Fresne* it is the framing situation of the mother's slander and ultimate reunion with her daughter that introduces a second value for Fresne's crucial gesture. Placing her brocade on the marriage bed honors Gurun's new wife as well as Gurun, canceling the potential rivalry between Fresne and Codre and reversing the slander their mother committed against her neighbor when she bore twins. Here the silken cloth becomes a token of acceptance rather than of division and loss as it was when Fresne was abandoned in consequence of the mother's slander. The mother's lament at the birth of her twins prepares for this meaning: "jeo meïsmes me jugai, / De tutes femmes mesparlai" (I condemned myself in speaking badly of womankind) (79–80); in the Middle English version, "Ich have

---

[26] *Fresne*, l. 405. The end of the Middle English *Lai le Freine* is lacking in the Auchinleck manuscript.

yʒouen min owen dome. / Forboden bite ich woman / To speken
ani oþer harm opon" (90–92). Fresne, asserting her feminine allegiance with Codre, recuperates the relation her mother's slander
destroyed.

In *Fresne* as in *Eliduc* and the *Knight's Tale*, women's "aventure of love" is most evidently their submission to the trajectory
of male desire, but within that adventure lies another concerning
the value of women's interrelations. Emelye, in contrast to Palamon and Arcite, goes to her temple not alone but with "Hir
maydens, that she thider with hire ladde" (I 2275). At other pivotal moments women act in concert as well. The widows of
Thebes kneeling two by two, the interceding women in the grove
where Palamon and Arcite are fighting, and of course the Amazons whose defeat opens the tale provide a context for Emelye's
prayer to Diana that she be allowed to remain "of thy compaignye" (I 2307). Emelye's allegiance to women is, in the plot of
the *Knight's Tale*, incompatible with the desires of Theseus and
her lovers. Its value is thus less evident than in *Eliduc* and *Fresne*,
where feminine community is a shadowed potential that sustains
the more salient concerns of courtship and marriage. The conflict
between Emelye's allegiance to women and men's desires has the
effect of devaluing the former, indeed of rendering it virtually irrelevant to the course of events. Her allegiance nonetheless entails representing in the *Knight's Tale* a distinctively feminine experience of community that contrasts with yet persists within the
experience of heterosexual courtship.

That women's adventures are distinguishable from men's sustains gender difference, estranging women in the ways chapter 2
explores. At the same time, representing women's adventures
makes a space for imagining a feminine subjectivity. Canacee's
experience is both highly exotic and sympathetically patterned on
knightly adventures. The *Squire's Tale* transmutes riding out
alone from court to wilderness into Canacee's walking out with
female companions along flowery paths in a park. Like her brothers, Canacee is led to adventure by her magical gift; her own exotic encounter is a muted version of masculine adventure in that
she hears a story of turbulent love rather than participating directly in its events. The encounter demands her sympathy and
healing knowledge, a compassion the falcon calls "wommanly,"
but it is "Cambalus, / The kynges sone" who will get the falcon's

lover back for her (V 486, 656–67). Brother and sister both aid the falcon, the former in action and the latter in her attentive sympathy. As in Marie's lays and the *Knight's Tale*, women's particular experience of adventure involves forming feminine allegiances within a context of masculine endeavor.

Another recurring feature of women's subjectivity as represented in their adventures is the high value they place on preserving their chastity for their lovers. Ydoine, married against her will in *Amadas et Ydoine*, uses sorcery and tears to persuade her husband not to consummate their marriage; in *Erec et Enide* the faithful wife warns Erec of one count's designs on her and resists marriage to a second count after Erec's apparent death. Dorigen's situation illustrates that the feminine endeavor to preserve chastity may be, again, both in consonance with and opposed to the course of events in which men's adventures engage them. At stake in Dorigen's case is the conflict between a bodily faith and a faith to pledged word, such that Aurelius can remind Dorigen of her oath to love him with the formula "I speke it for the honour of yow" (V 1331) while Dorigen understands herself to be faced with "deeth or elles dishonour" (V 1358). In her view, surrendering her body to Aurelius would dishonor her, rather than preserve her honor by fulfilling her word.

This distinction between a feminine commitment to chastity and more public masculine commitments has wide social currency. Chaucer's use of Jerome's *Adversus Jovinianum* for Dorigen's reflections on "deeth or elles dishonour" explicitly raises the issue of whether her feminine sensibility can be distinguished from the prescriptions of a masculine tradition. As befits that tradition's gender polarities, Dorigen has not had a successful time with words; pledging her "trouthe" to Aurelius has betrayed her into a painful situation. Now she traces Jerome's argument that her concern should be with her bodily honor: in killing herself she "wol be trewe unto Arveragus" (V 1424). Dorigen, however, comes to resist this line of thinking. She refers to a feminine community, "many a noble wyf" (V 1364) whom she proposes to herself as her sisters in suicide, but she remains divided from them in not killing herself, nor apparently desiring to do so. A certain detachment marks her recollection of "thise stories" (V 1367), a distance not only of time and space but, I have argued in chapter 3, of alienation from the patristic version of womanhood that Chaucer's use of Jerome evokes. Her lengthy and ever-widening list of examples both urges and uneasily interrogates the parity between Jerome's stories and her own. Distancing herself from the suicide that would guarantee her honor, she puts her chastity at risk before Arveragus does.

But in avoiding suicide Dorigen does not reject her devotion to chastity. She laments Arveragus's command and attributes valuing verbal troth to him only in declaring she acts "as myn housbonde bad, / My trouthe for to holde—allas, allas!" (V 1512–13) She is alienated from her husband's exhortation as well as from Jerome's. Arveragus indeed more clearly asks her to act against her commitment to chastity in demanding her crossgendered commitment to the pledged word. Dorigen is to behave like a man instead of following a man's counsel to suicide. Her crossgendered guise does finally preserve her chastity, but a disparity opens between her subjectivity and masculine values as she resists suicide yet continues to value her chastity rather than her oath to Aurelius. The disparity restores the gender-specific sense of "man" to Arveragus's universal maxim "Trouthe is the hyeste thyng that man may kepe" (V 1479). The muted difference between Dorigen's and Arveragus's experience of "this aventure" (V 1483) constructs a feminine sensibility that opposes but finally participates in the tale's predominantly masculine negotiations. Like other women's adventures in romance, Dorigen's reveals the gendered specificity of men's experience by contrasting with it, yet also requires that she accommodate her sensibility to men's desires.

Both arguments of this chapter concern experiences of adventure that are peculiar to one gender and common within it. Palamon and Arcite share perceptions of Emelye that define their masculinity and set them apart from her femininity. Emelye and Dorigen alike have adventures that parallel yet differ from and even oppose the trajectory of masculine adventures. I emphasize the gendered distinctiveness of men's and women's adventures in order to pursue my wider argument that romances participate in defining heterosexuality as the oppositional and even adversarial differentiation of masculinity from femininity. Here I can only suggest that within the constraints of the heterosexual paradigm there is also room for a diversity of experience that remains im-

portantly gendered. Theseus's, Palamon's, and Arcite's responses
to Emelye may all be in distinct contrast with one another yet
may all express aspects of masculine identity. Emelye and Dorigen could illustrate contrasting degrees of pliancy and resistance, chastity and submission that remain markers of femininity. Here I have stressed the similarities that unite the experiences
attributed to men and contrast them to women's experiences in
romance. Likewise, I have sought the common ground among diverse literary texts in order to argue for the influence of a romance
sensibility in Chaucer's *Canterbury Tales*. Yet romances are so
diverse, and their generic boundaries so fluid, that I could as well
have worked out the contrasts as the similarities among Chaucer's tales with regard to romance.

Arcite's dying speech, which I have characterized above as his
fullest experience of adventure, holds a place in the *Knight's Tale*
that is emblematic of both the space for and the constraints on
romance in the *Canterbury Tales*. Arcite's sense of life's mystery
as he dies soon yields to Theseus's closing statement of philosophical assurance and soon after to the bluntly physical universe of
the *Miller's Tale*, in which Arcite's touching apprehension of an
eternity "Allone, withouten any compaignye" describes a student
fortunate enough to have a room to himself (I 2779, 3204). Low in
generic status in relation to philosophy and epic, romance has
nonetheless an important place among the genres that make up
this "noble storie" (I 3111). Commingled with those higher genres, romance in the *Knight's Tale* does not enjoy the high profile
of fabliau in the *Miller's Tale* or saint's legend in the *Second
Nun's Tale*. Perhaps medieval writers conceive romance to be a
feminine genre to imply not only its relatively low status but further its elusiveness, its protean capacity to reshape itself in relation to other genres. Like the version of the feminine it promotes,
romance evades definition, thrives in subordination, embodies
contradictions and mystery, and stages a richly affective experience for its admirers. And like its image of women, the genre deserves our efforts to discern its identity, value its difference, and
describe its place in the ideological formations of the late Middle
Ages.

BIBLIOGRAPHY

❧

The following abbreviations are used in the bibliography:

C.F.M.A.   Classiques français du moyen âge
E.E.T.S.   Early English Text Society
  o.s.   original series
  e.s.   extra series
  s.s.   supplementary series
SA   *Sources and Analogues of Chaucer's "Canterbury Tales"*
S.A.T.F.   Société des anciens textes français

PRIMARY SOURCES

Adenet le Roi. *Cleomadés.* In *Les Oeuvres d'Adenet le Roi.* Ed. Albert Henry. Vol. 5, 2 pts. Brussels: Université de Bruxelles, 1971.

Aelfric. *Aelfric's Lives of the Saints.* Ed. Walter W. Skeat. E.E.T.S., o.s., 76, 82, 94, 114. London: Trübner, 1881, 1885, 1890, 1900.

[The Medieval French "Roman d'] Alexandre". Vol. 2. *Version of Alexander de Paris.* Ed. E. C. Armstrong et al. Elliot Monographs, no. 37. Princeton: Princeton University Press, 1937.

[Kyng] Alisaunder. Ed. G. V. Smithers. 2 vols. E.E.T.S., o.s., 227, 237. London: Oxford University Press, 1952, 1957.

Amadas et Ydoine. Ed. John R. Reinhard. C.F.M.A. 51. Paris: Champion, 1926.

Amis and Amiloun. Ed. MacEdward Leach. E.E.T.S., o.s., 203. London: Oxford University Press, 1937.

Bacon, Roger. *The "Opus Majus" of Roger Bacon.* Ed. John Henry Bridges. 2 vols. Oxford: Clarendon, 1897.

Bennett, J.A.W., ed. *The Knight's Tale.* By Geoffrey Chaucer. 2d ed. London: Harrap, 1958.

Benoit de Sainte-Maure. *Le Roman de Troie.* Ed. Léopold Constans. 6 vols. S.A.T.F. 50. Paris: Firmin-Didot, 1904–1912.

[The Romance of Sir] Beues of Hamtoun. Ed. Eugen Kölbing. E.E.T.S., e.s., 46, 48, 65. London: Trübner, 1885, 1886, 1894.

Boccaccio, Giovanni. *Chaucer's Boccaccio: Sources of "Troilus" and the "Knight's" and "Franklin's Tales."* Trans. N. R. Havely. Cambridge: D. S. Brewer, 1980.

Boccaccio, Giovanni. *Decameron*. Ed. Vittore Branca. In *Tutte le Opere di Giovanni Boccaccio*. Gen. ed. Vittore Branca. Vol. 4. Verona: Mondadori, 1976.

———. *Filocolo*. Ed. Antonio Enzo Quaglio. In *Tutte le Opere di Giovanni Boccaccio*. Gen. ed. Vittore Branca. Vol. 1. Verona: Mondadori, 1967.

———. *Teseida delle nozze d'Emilia*. Ed. Alberto Limentani. In *Tutte le opere di Giovanni Boccaccio*. Gen. ed. Vittore Branca. Vol. 2. Verona: Mondadori, 1964.

Boethius, Anicius Manlius Severinus. *De consolatione philosophiae libri quinque*. Ed. George D. Smith. Hildesheim: Georg Olms, 1976.

[Der anglonormannische] Boeve de Haumtone. Ed. Albert Stimming. Bibliotheca normannica, no. 7. Halle: Niemeyer, 1899.

Chaucer, Geoffrey. *The Canterbury Tales: A Facsimile and Transcription of the Hengwrt Manuscript, with Variants from the Ellesmere Manuscript*. Ed. Paul G. Ruggiers. Norman: University of Oklahoma Press, 1979.

———. *The Ellesmere Manuscript of Chaucer's Canterbury Tales: A Working Facsimile*. Introd. Ralph Hanna III. Cambridge: D. S. Brewer, 1990.

———. *The Riverside Chaucer*. Gen. ed. Larry D. Benson. 3d ed. Boston: Houghton, 1987.

———. *A Variorum Edition of the Works of Geoffrey Chaucer*. Vol. 2. *The Canterbury Tales*. Pt. 12. *The Squire's Tale*. Ed. Donald C. Baker. Norman: University of Oklahoma Press, 1990.

———. *A Variorum Edition of the Works of Geoffrey Chaucer*. Vol. 5. *The Minor Poems*. Ed. George B. Pace and Alfred David. Norman: University of Oklahoma Press, 1982.

Chestre, Thomas. *Sir Launfal*. In *Middle English Metrical Romances*. Ed. Walter Hoyt French and Charles Brockway Hale. 2 vols. New York: Russell, 1964. 343–80.

Chrétien de Troyes. *Le Chevalier au Lion (Yvain)*. Ed. Mario Roques. C.F.M.A. 89. Paris: Champion, 1960.

———. *Le Chevalier de la Charrette*. Ed. Mario Roques. C.F.M.A. 86. Paris: Champion, 1965.

———. *Cligés*. Ed. Alexandre Micha. C.F.M.A. 84. Paris: Champion, 1970.

———. *Erec et Enide*. Ed. Mario Roques. C.F.M.A. 80. Paris: Champion, 1977.

Christine de Pisan. *Oeuvres Poétiques*. Ed. Maurice Roy. 3 vols. S.A.T.F. 79–81. Paris: Firmin Didot, 1886, 1891, 1896.

[Sir] Degare. In *Middle English Metrical Romances*. Ed. Walter Hoyt

PRIMARY SOURCES   207

French and Charles Brockway Hale. 2 vols. New York: Russell, 1964.
287–320.

Eneas, roman du XIIᵉ siècle. Ed. J.-J. Salverda de Grave. C.F.M.A. 44, 62.
Paris: Champion, 1925, 1929.

Etienne de Fougères. *Le Livre des manières.* Ed. R. Anthony Lodge.
Textes littéraires français, 275. Geneva: Droz, 1979.

Floriant et Florete. Ed. Harry F. Williams. Ann Arbor: University of Michigan Press, 1947.

[The Middle English Lai le] Freine. Ed. Margaret Wattie. *Smith College
Studies in Modern Languages* 10, no. 3 (April 1929).

Froissart, Jean. *Méliador.* Ed. Auguste Longnon. 3 vols. S.A.T.F. 35. Paris:
Firmin Didot, 1895, 1895, 1899.

Gautier d'Arras. *Ille et Galeron.* Ed. Yves Lefèvre. C.F.M.A. 109. Paris:
Champion, 1988.

Gautier de Tournay. *L'Histoire de Gille de Chyn.* Ed. Edwin B. Place.
Northwestern University Studies in the Humanities, 7. Evanston, Ill.:
Northwestern University, 1941.

[Sir] Gawain and the Green Knight. Ed. J.R.R. Tolkien and E. V. Gordon.
2d ed. rev. Norman Davis. Oxford: Clarendon, 1967.

Geoffrey de la Tour Landry. *The Book of the Knight of the Tower.* Trans.
William Caxton. Ed. M. Y. Offord. E.E.T.S., s.s., 2. London: Oxford University Press, 1971.

———. *Le Livre du Chevalier de la Tour Landry.* Ed. Anatole de Mon-
taiglon. Paris: Jannet, 1854.

Geoffrey of Monmouth. *Historia Regum Brittaniae.* Ed. Jacob Hammer.
Cambridge: Medieval Academy of America, 1951.

Gerbert de Montreuil. *La Continuation de Perceval.* Ed. Mary Williams
and Marguerite Oswald. C.F.M.A. 28, 50, 101. Paris: Champion, 1922–
1975.

Girard d'Amiens. *Le Roman du cheval de fust, ou de Meliacin.* Ed. Paul
Aebischer. Geneva: Droz, 1974.

Gower, John. *Confessio Amantis.* In *The Complete Works of John
Gower.* Ed. G. C. Macaulay. Vol. 2. Oxford: Clarendon, 1901.

———. *Vox Clamantis.* In *The Complete Works of John Gower.* Ed. G. C.
Macaulay. Vol. 4. Oxford: Clarendon, 1902.

Gui de Warewic. Ed. Alfred Ewert. C.F.M.A. 74, 75. Paris: Champion,
1932, 1933.

Guillaume de Lorris and Jean de Meun. *Le Roman de la Rose.* Ed. Félix
Lecoy. 3 vols. C.F.M.A. 92, 95, 98. Paris: Champion, 1973, 1975, 1976.

*[The Romance of] Guy of Warwick: The First or Fourteenth-Century Ver-
sion.* Ed. Julius Zupitza. E.E.T.S., e.s., 42, 49, 59. London: Oxford University Press, 1883, 1887, 1891.

Hanning, Robert W., and Joan Ferrante, ed. and trans. *The Lais of Marie de France*. New York: Dutton, 1978.

Havelok. Ed. G. V. Smithers. Oxford: Clarendon, 1987.

Heldris de Cornuälle. *Le Roman de Silence: A Thirteenth-Century Arthurian Verse-Romance*. Ed. Lewis Thorpe. Cambridge: Heffer, 1972.

[King] Horn. Ed. Joseph Hall. Oxford: Clarendon, 1901.

Hue de Rotelande. *Ipomedon*. Ed. A. J. Holden. Paris: Klincksieck, 1979.

Ipomadon. In *Hue de Rotelande's Ipomedon in drei englischen Bearbeitungen*. Ed. Eugen Kölbing. Breslau: Koebner, 1889. 3–253.

Jean d'Arras. *Mélusine, roman du XIVᵉ siècle*. Ed. Louis Stouff. Publications de l'Université de Dijon, no. 5. Dijon: Bernigaud et Privat, 1932.

Jean de Condé. "Ch'est li dis des estas dou monde." In *Gedichte von Jehan de Condet nach der casanatensischen Handschrift*. Ed. Adolf Tobler. Bibliothek des Litterarischen vereins in Stuttgart, 54. Stuttgart: Litterarischer verein, 1860. 177–85.

———. "Li dis dou Levrier." In *Dits et contes de Badouin de Condé et de son fils Jean de Condé*. Ed. August Scheler. 3 vols. Brussels: Victor Devaux, 1866–1867. 2:303–53.

Jean de Meun. "Boethius' *De Consolatione* by Jean de Meun." Ed. V. L. Dedeck-Héry. *Mediaeval Studies* 14 (1952): 165–275.

Jehan le Fèvre. *Les Lamentations de Matheolus et le livre de leesce*. Ed. Anton-Gerard van Hamel. 2 vols. Paris: Bouillon, 1892, 1905.

John of Salisbury. *Policraticus: Of the Frivolities of Courtiers and the Footprints of Philosophers*. Ed. and trans. Cary J. Nederman. Cambridge: Cambridge University Press, 1990.

Lancelot do Lac: The Non-cyclic Old French Prose Romance. Ed. Elspeth Kennedy. 2 vols. Oxford: Clarendon, 1980.

Lybeaus Desconus. Ed. Maldwyn Mills. E.E.T.S., o.s., 261. London: Oxford University Press, 1969.

Lydgate, John. *Lydgate's Fall of Princes*. Ed. Henry Bergen. E.E.T.S., e.s., 121, 122. London: Oxford University Press, 1924.

Manly, John M., and Edith Rickert, eds. *The Text of the "Canterbury Tales."* By Geoffrey Chaucer. 8 vols. Chicago: University of Chicago Press, 1940.

Mannyng, Robert. *The Story of England by Robert Manning of Brunne*. Ed. F. J. Furnivall. 2 vols. Rolls Series, 87. London: Eyre and Spottiswoode, 1887.

Marie de France. *Les Lais de Marie de France*. Ed. Jean Rychner. C.F.M.A. 93. Paris: Champion, 1983.

The Marriage of Sir Gawaine. In *SA*. 235–41.

Melusine [Middle English]. Ed. A. K. Donald. E.E.T.S., e.s., 68. London: Kegan Paul, 1895.

Orderic Vitalis. *The Ecclesiastical History of Orderic Vitalis.* Ed. and trans. Marjorie Chibnall. 6 vols. Oxford: Clarendon, 1968–1980.

[Sir] Orfeo. Ed. A. J. Bliss. 2d ed. Oxford: Clarendon, 1966.

[The Middle-English Versions of] Partonope of Blois. Ed. A. Trampe Bödtker. E.E.T.S., e.s., 109. London: Kegan Paul, 1912.

The Peasants' Revolt of 1381. Ed. R. B. Dobson. 2d ed. London: Macmillan, 1983.

Piramus, Denis. *La Vie Seint Edmund le Rei.* Ed. Hilding Kjellman. Göteborg: Elanders, 1935.

Reliquae antiquae. Ed. Thomas Wright and J. O. Halliwell. 2 vols. London: J. R. Smith, 1841, 1843.

Renaut de Beaujeu. *Le Bel Inconnu.* Ed. G. Perrie Williams. C.F.M.A. 38. Paris: Champion, 1929.

[Der mittelenglische Versroman über] Richard Löwenherz. Ed. Karl Brunner. Wiener Beiträge zur englischen Philologie 42. Vienna: Braumüller, 1913.

Sources and Analogues of Chaucer's "Canterbury Tales." Ed. W. F. Bryan and Germaine Dempster. Atlantic Highlands, N.J.: Humanities Press, 1941; rpt. 1958.

Spearing, A. C., ed. *The Franklin's Prologue and Tale.* By Geoffrey Chaucer. Cambridge: Cambridge University Press, 1966.

———, ed. *The Knight's Tale.* By Geoffrey Chaucer. Cambridge: Cambridge University Press, 1966.

Statius. *P. Papini Stati Thebaidos libri XII.* Ed. D. E. Hill. Leiden: Brill, 1983.

Sumner, Laura, ed. *The Weddynge of Sir Gawen and Dame Ragnell.* *Smith College Studies in Modern Languages* 5, no. 4 (July 1924).

[Le Roman de] Thèbes. Ed. Léopold Constans. 2 vols. S.A.T.F. 30. Paris: Firmin-Didot, 1890.

[Le Roman de] Thèbes. Ed. Guy Raynaud de Lage. C.F.M.A. 94, 96. Paris: Champion, 1966, 1967.

Thomas of Kent. *The Anglo-Norman "Alexander" ("Le Roman de toute chevalerie").* Ed. Brian Foster and Ian Short. A.N.T.S. 29–31, 32–33. London: Anglo-Norman Text Society, 1976, 1977.

Tyrwhitt, Thomas, and Charles Cowden Clarke, eds. *The Canterbury Tales.* By Geoffrey Chaucer. 3 vols. Edinburgh: Nimmo, 1868.

Virgil. *Aeneid.* Ed. and trans. H. Rushton Fairclough. Loeb Classical Library. 2 vols. Cambridge: Harvard University Press, 1915–1916. Rev. ed. 1934.

Wace. *Le Roman de Brut de Wace.* Ed. Ivor Arnold. 2 vols. Paris: S.A.T.F., 1938, 1940.

The Weddynge of Sir Gawen and Dame Ragnell. In *SA.* 242–64.

William of Palerne, an Alliterative Romance. Ed. G.H.V. Bunt. Groningen: Bouma, 1985.

Wyclif, John. *Select English Works of John Wyclif.* Ed. Thomas Arnold. 3
vols. Oxford: Clarendon, 1869–1871.

Yunck, John A., trans. *Eneas: A Twelfth-Century French Romance.* New
York: Columbia University Press, 1974.

Ywain and Gawain. Ed. Albert B. Friedman and Norman T. Harrington.
E.E.T.S., o.s., 254. London: Oxford University Press, 1964.

SECONDARY SOURCES

Adler, A. "Eneas and Lavine: *Puer et Puella Senes.*" *Romanische For-
schungen* 71 (1959): 73–91.

Aebischer, Paul. "Paléozoologie de l'*Equus Clavileñus*, Cervant." *Etudes
de Lettres,* ser. 2, 5 (1962): 93–130.

Aers, David. *Chaucer, Langland and the Creative Imagination.* London:
Routledge, 1980.

Ahl, Frederick. *Metaformations: Soundplay and Wordplay in Ovid and
Other Classical Poets.* Ithaca: Cornell University Press, 1985.

Alcoff, Linda. "Cultural Feminism versus Poststructuralism: The Identity Crisis in Feminist Theory." *Signs* 13 (1987–1988): 405–36.

Allen, Prudence. *The Concept of Woman: The Aristotelian Revolution,
750 B.C.–A.D. 1250.* Montreal: Eden Press, 1985.

Anderson, David. *Before the Knight's Tale: Imitation of Classical Epic in
Boccaccio's "Teseida."* Philadelphia: University of Pennsylvania Press,
1988.

Auerbach, Erich. *Mimesis: The Representation of Reality in Western Literature.* Trans. Willard R. Trask. Princeton: Princeton University
Press, 1953.

Bakhtin, Mikhail M. *The Dialogic Imagination: Four Essays.* Trans.
Caryl Emerson and Michael Holquist. Austin: University of Texas
Press, 1981.

———. *Rabelais and His World.* 1965. Trans. Helene Iswolsky. Bloomington: Indiana University Press, 1984.

Barron, W.R.J. *English Medieval Romance.* London: Longman, 1987.

Batany, Jean. "Les 'estats' au féminin: un problème de vocabulaire sociale
du XIIe au XVe siècle." In *Mélanges de langue et de littérature médiévales offerts à Alice Planche.* Ed. Maurice Accarie and Ambroise
Queffelec. Annales de la Faculté des Lettres et Sciences Humaines de
Nice, 48. Nice: Centre d'Etudes Médiévales, 1984. 51–59.

Beauvoir, Simone de. *The Second Sex.* Trans. and ed. H. M. Parshley.
New York: Knopf, 1953.

Bennett, Michael J. *Community, Class and Careerism: Cheshire and*

Lancashire Society in the Age of "Sir Gawain and the Green Knight." Cambridge: Cambridge University Press, 1983.

Benson, Larry D. "Courtly Love and Chivalry in the Later Middle Ages." In *Fifteenth-Century Studies: Recent Essays*. Ed. R. F. Yeager. Hamden, Conn.: Archon, 1984. 237–57.

———. *Malory's "Morte Darthur."* Cambridge: Harvard University Press, 1976.

———. "The 'Queynte' Punnings of Chaucer's Critics." In *Studies in the Age of Chaucer, Proceedings*. No. 1. *Reconstructing Chaucer*. Ed. Paul Strohm and Thomas J. Heffernan. Knoxville, Tenn: New Chaucer Society, 1985. 23–47.

Berger, Harry, Jr. "The F-Fragment of the *Canterbury Tales*." *Chaucer Review* 1 (1966–1967): 88–102, 135–56.

Bernheimer, Richard. *Wild Men in the Middle Ages: A Study in Art, Sentiment, and Demonology*. New York: Octagon, 1970.

Beston, John. "How Much Was Known of the Breton Lai in Fourteenth-Century England?" In *The Learned and the Lewed: Studies in Chaucer and Medieval Literature*. Ed. Larry D. Benson. Cambridge: Harvard University Press, 1974. 319–36.

Blamires, Alcuin. "Chaucer's Revaluation of Chivalric Honor." *Mediaevalia* 5 (1979): 245–69.

Blanch, Robert J., and Julian N. Wasserman. "White and Red in the *Knight's Tale*: Chaucer's Manipulation of a Convention." In *Chaucer in the Eighties*. Ed. Robert J. Blanch and Julian N. Wasserman. Syracuse: Syracuse University Press, 1986. 175–91.

Bloch, R. Howard. *Etymologies and Genealogies: A Literary Anthropology of the French Middle Ages*. Chicago: University of Chicago Press, 1983.

———. *Medieval French Literature and Law*. Berkeley and Los Angeles: University of California Press, 1977.

———. *Medieval Misogyny and the Invention of Western Romantic Love*. Chicago: University of Chicago Press, 1991.

Bloomfield, Morton W. "Episodic Motivation and Marvels in Epic and Romance." In *Essays and Explorations: Studies in Ideas, Language, and Literature*. Cambridge: Harvard University Press, 1970. 97–128.

Boitani, Piero. *Chaucer and Boccaccio*. Medium Aevum Monographs, n.s., 8. Oxford: Society for the Study of Mediaeval Languages and Literature, 1977.

Boswell, John. *Christianity, Social Tolerance, and Homosexuality: Gay People in Western Europe from the Beginning of the Christian Era to the Fourteenth Century*. Chicago: University of Chicago Press, 1980.

Braddy, Haldeen. "The Genre of Chaucer's *Squire's Tale*." *Journal of English and Germanic Philology* 41 (1942): 279–90.

Braswell, Mary Flowers. "The Magic of Machinery: A Context for Chaucer's *Franklin's Tale*." *Mosaic* 18 (1985): 101–10.

Brewer, Derek. "Class Distinction in Chaucer." *Speculum* 43 (1968): 290–305.

———. "Honour in Chaucer." *Essays and Studies*, n.s., 26 (1973): 1–19.

———. "The Relationship of Chaucer to the English and European Traditions." In *Chaucer and Chaucerians: Critical Studies in Middle English Literature*. Ed. D. S. Brewer. London: Thomas Nelson, 1966. 1–38.

———. *Symbolic Stories: Traditional Narratives of the Family Drama in English Literature*. Cambridge: D. S. Brewer, 1980.

Brooks, Douglas, and Alastair Fowler. "The Meaning of Chaucer's *Knight's Tale*." *Medium Aevum* 39 (1970): 123–46.

Bruckner, Matilda Tomaryn. *Narrative Invention in Twelfth-Century French Romance: The Convention of Hospitality (1160–1200)*. French Forum Monographs 17. Lexington, Ky.: French Forum, 1980.

Brundage, James A. *Law, Sex, and Christian Society in Medieval Europe*. Chicago: University of Chicago Press, 1987.

Bullough, Vern L. "The Sin against Nature and Homosexuality." In *Sexual Practices and the Medieval Church*. Ed. Vern L. Bullough and James Brundage. Buffalo, N.Y.: Prometheus, 1982. 55–71.

Bumke, Joachim. *The Concept of Knighthood in the Middle Ages*. Trans. W.T.H. Jackson and Erika Jackson. New York: AMS Press, 1982.

Burgwinkle, William. "Knighting the Classical Hero: Homo/Hetero Affectivity in *Eneas*." *Exemplaria* 5 (1993): 1–43.

Burrow, J. A. "The *Canterbury Tales* I: Romance." In *The Cambridge Chaucer Companion*. Ed. Piero Boitani and Jill Mann. Cambridge: Cambridge University Press, 1986. 109–24.

———. *Essays on Medieval Literature*. Oxford: Clarendon, 1984.

———. *Ricardian Poetry: Chaucer, Gower, Langland and the "Gawain" Poet*. London: Routledge, 1971.

Butler, Judith. *Gender Trouble: Feminism and the Subversion of Identity*. New York and London: Routledge, 1990.

Carasso-Bulow, Lucienne. *The Merveilleux in Chrétien de Troyes' Romances*. Geneva: Droz, 1976.

Charnes, Linda. "'This Werk Unresonable': Narrative Frustration and Generic Redistribution in Chaucer's *Franklin's Tale*." *Chaucer Review* 23 (1988–1989): 300–315.

Cixous, Hélène, and Catherine Clément. *The Newly Born Woman*. Trans. Betsy Wing. Minneapolis: University of Minnesota Press, 1986.

Clogan, Paul M. "Criseyde's Book of the Romance of Thebes." *Hebrew University Studies in Literature and the Arts* 13 (1985): 18–28.

Coleman, Janet. *Medieval Readers and Writers*. New York: Columbia University Press, 1981.

Cook, Jon. "Carnival and *The Canterbury Tales*." In *Medieval Literature*. 169–91.

Cooper, Helen. *The Canterbury Tales*. Oxford: Clarendon, 1989.

———. "Magic That Does Not Work." *Medievalia et Humanistica* 7 (1976): 131–46.

Cormier, Raymond J. *One Heart One Mind: The Rebirth of Virgil's Hero in Medieval French Romance*. Romance Monographs, no. 3. University, Miss.: Romance Monographs, Inc., 1973.

Cormier, Raymond J., and Harry J. Kuster. "Old Views and New Trends: Observations on the Problem of Homosexuality in the Middle Ages." *Studi medievali*, ser. 3, 25, no. 2 (1984): 587–610.

Crane, Susan. "Alison's Incapacity and Poetic Instability in the Wife of Bath's Tale." *PMLA* 102 (1987): 20–28.

———. "Brotherhood and the Construction of Courtship in Arthurian Romance." *The Arthurian Yearbook* 3 (1993): 191–99.

———. "The Franklin as Dorigen." *Chaucer Review* 24 (1989–1990): 236–52.

———. *Insular Romance: Politics, Faith, and Culture in Anglo-Norman and Middle English Literature*. Berkeley and Los Angeles: University of California Press, 1986.

———. "Medieval Romance and Feminine Difference in the *Knight's Tale*." *Studies in the Age of Chaucer* 12 (1990): 47–63.

———. "The Writing Lesson of 1381." In *Chaucer's England: Literature in Historical Context*. Ed. Barbara Hanawalt. Minneapolis: University of Minnesota Press, 1992. 201–21.

Crosby, Ruth. "Chaucer and the Custom of Oral Delivery." *Speculum* 13 (1938): 420–32.

Culler, Jonathan. "The Call of the Phoneme: Introduction." In *On Puns: The Foundation of Letters*. Ed. Jonathan Culler. Oxford: Blackwell, 1988. 1–16.

David, Alfred. "Recycling *Anelida and Arcite*: Chaucer as a Source for Chaucer." In *Studies in the Age of Chaucer, Proceedings*. No. 1. *Reconstructing Chaucer*. Ed. Paul Strohm and Thomas J. Heffernan. Knoxville, Tenn: New Chaucer Society, 1985. 105–15.

Davidson, Harriet. " 'I Say I Am There': Siting/Citing the Subject of Feminism and Derridean Deconstruction." In *Critical Encounters: Reference and Responsibility in Deconstructive Writing*. Ed. Cathy Caruth. London: Routledge, forthcoming, 1994.

Davis, Natalie Zemon. *Society and Culture in Early Modern France*. Stanford: Stanford University Press, 1965.

De Lauretis, Teresa. *Alice Doesn't: Feminism, Semiotics, Cinema.* Bloomington: Indiana University Press, 1984.

———. "Eccentric Subjects: Feminist Theory and Historical Consciousness." *Feminist Studies* 16 (1990): 115–50.

———. "Feminist Studies/Critical Studies: Issues, Terms, and Contexts." In *Feminist Studies/Critical Studies.* Ed. Teresa de Lauretis. Bloomington: Indiana University Press, 1986. 1–19.

———. *Technologies of Gender: Essays on Theory, Film, and Fiction.* Bloomington: Indiana University Press, 1987.

Delany, Sheila. "Sexual Economics: Chaucer's Wife of Bath and the Book of Margery Kempe." *Minnesota Review,* n.s., 5 (1975): 104–15.

Dellamora, Richard. *Masculine Desire: The Sexual Politics of Victorian Aestheticism.* Chapel Hill: University of North Carolina Press, 1990.

Dempster, Germaine. "Chaucer at Work on the Complaint in the *Franklin's Tale.*" *Modern Language Notes* 52 (1937): 16–23.

———. "A Further Note on Dorigen's *Exempla.*" *Modern Language Notes* 54 (1939): 137–38.

Dinshaw, Carolyn. *Chaucer's Sexual Poetics.* Madison: University of Wisconsin Press, 1989.

Doane, Mary Ann. "Film and the Masquerade: Theorising the Female Spectator." *Screen* 23, no. 2 (1982): 74–87.

———. "Masquerade Reconsidered: Further Thoughts on the Female Spectator." *Discourse* 11 (1988–1989): 42–54.

Donovan, Mortimer. *The Breton Lay: A Guide to Varieties.* Notre Dame: University of Notre Dame Press, 1969.

Dressler, Alfred. *Der Einfluss des altfranzösischen Eneas-Romanes auf die altfranzösische Literatur.* Leipzig: Noske, 1907.

duBois, Page. *Centaurs and Amazons: Women and the Pre-History of the Great Chain of Being.* Ann Arbor: University of Michigan Press, 1982.

Duby, Georges. "Dans la France du Nord-Ouest au XIIᵉ siècle: les 'Jeunes' dans la société aristocratique." *Annales: Economies, Sociétés, Civilisations* 19 (1964): 835–46.

———. *Medieval Marriage: Two Models from Twelfth-Century France.* Trans. Elborg Forster. Baltimore: Johns Hopkins University Press, 1978.

———. *The Three Orders: Feudal Society Imagined.* Trans. Arthur Goldhammer. Chicago: University of Chicago Press, 1980.

———. *William Marshal, the Flower of Chivalry.* Trans. Richard Howard. New York: Pantheon, 1985.

Dumézil, Georges. *Jupiter, Mars, Quirinus.* Paris: Gallimard, 1941.

Dumont, Louis. *Homo Hierarchicus: The Caste System and Its Implications.* Trans. Mark Sainsbury, Louis Dumont, and Basia Gulati. Rev. ed. Chicago: University of Chicago Press, 1980.

Eade, J. C. "'We ben to lewed or to slowe': Chaucer's Astronomy and Audience Participation." *Studies in the Age of Chaucer* 4 (1982): 58–69.

Everett, Dorothy. "Chaucer's 'Good Ear.'" *Review of English Studies* 23 (1947): 201–8.

Faral, Edmond. *Recherches sur les sources latines de contes et romans courtois du Moyen Age.* Paris: Champion, 1913.

Farmer, Sharon. "Persuasive Voices: Clerical Images of Medieval Wives." *Speculum* 61 (1986): 517–43.

Feminism and Foucault: Reflections on Resistance. Ed. Irene Diamond and Lee Quinby. Boston: Northeastern University Press, 1988.

Ferrante, Joan. *The Conflict of Love and Honor: The Medieval Tristan Legend in France, Germany and Italy.* The Hague: Mouton, 1973.

———. "The Conflict of Lyric Conventions and Romance Form." In *In Pursuit of Perfection: Courtly Love in Medieval Literature.* Ed. Joan M. Ferrante and George D. Economou. Port Washington, N.Y.: Kennikat Press, 1975. 135–78.

———. "Male Fantasy and Female Reality in Courtly Literature." *Women's Studies* 11 (1984): 67–97.

———. *Woman as Image in Medieval Literature: From the Twelfth Century to Dante.* New York: Columbia University Press, 1975.

Ferster, Judith. "Interpretation and Imitation in Chaucer's Franklin's Tale." In *Medieval Literature: Criticism, Ideology and History.* Ed. David Aers. New York: St. Martin's, 1986. 148–68.

Fetterley, Judith. *The Resisting Reader: A Feminist Approach to American Fiction.* Bloomington: Indiana University Press, 1978.

Fewster, Carol. *Traditionality and Genre in Middle English Romance.* Cambridge: D. S. Brewer, 1987.

Fisher, John H. "Animadversions on the Text of Chaucer, 1988." *Speculum* 63 (1988): 779–93.

Fisher, Sheila. "Taken Men and Token Women in *Sir Gawain and the Green Knight.*" In *Seeking the Woman in Late Medieval and Renaissance Writings.* Ed. Sheila Fisher and Janet E. Halley. Knoxville: University of Tennessee Press, 1989. 71–105.

Foucault, Michel. *Discipline and Punish: The Birth of the Prison.* Trans. Alan Sheridan. New York: Pantheon, 1977.

———. *The History of Sexuality.* Vol. 1. *An Introduction.* Trans. Robert Hurley. New York: Random, 1980.

———. "The Subject and Power." In *Michel Foucault: Beyond Structuralism and Hermeneutics.* Ed. Hubert L. Dreyfus and Paul Rabinow. 2d ed. Chicago: University of Chicago Press, 1983. 208–26.

Fourrier, Anthime. *Le Courant réaliste dans le roman courtois en France au moyen âge.* Vol. 1. *Les Débuts (XIIe siècle).* Paris: Nizet, 1960.

Fowler, Alastair. *Kinds of Literature: An Introduction to the Theory of Genres and Modes*. Cambridge: Harvard University Press, 1982.

Fradenberg, Louise O. *City, Marriage, Tournament: Arts of Rule in Late Medieval Scotland*. Madison: University of Wisconsin Press, 1991.

———. "The Wife of Bath's Passing Fancy." *Studies in the Age of Chaucer* 8 (1986): 31–58.

Frank, Robert Worth, Jr. *Chaucer and the Legend of Good Women*. Cambridge: Harvard University Press, 1972.

Fraser, Nancy. *Unruly Practices: Power, Discourse and Gender in Contemporary Social Theory*. Minneapolis: University of Minnesota Press, 1989.

Freeman, Michelle A. "Marie de France's Poetics of Silence: The Implications for a Feminine *Translatio*." *PMLA* 99 (1984): 860–83.

Freud, Sigmund. "The Taboo of Virginity." Trans. Angela Richards. *The Standard Edition of the Complete Psychological Works of Sigmund Freud*. Gen. ed. James Strachey. London: Hogarth, 1957. 11:191–208.

———. "The 'Uncanny.'" Trans. Alix Strachey. In *The Standard Edition of the Complete Psychological Works of Sigmund Freud*. Gen. ed. James Strachey. London: Hogarth, 1955. 17:217–56.

Friedman, Albert B. "'When Adam Delved . . .': Contexts of a Historic Proverb." In *The Learned and the Lewed: Studies in Chaucer and Medieval Literature*. Ed. Larry D. Benson. Cambridge: Harvard University Press, 1974. Pp. 213–30.

Frost, William. "An Interpretation of Chaucer's Knight's Tale." *Review of English Studies* 25 (1949): 289–304.

Frye, Northrop. *The Secular Scripture: A Study of the Structure of Romance*. Cambridge: Harvard University Press, 1976.

Fuss, Diana. *Essentially Speaking: Feminism, Nature and Difference*. New York and London: Routledge, 1989.

Fyler, John M. "Domesticating the Exotic in the *Squire's Tale*." *ELH* 55 (1988): 1–26.

———. "Man, Men, and Women in Chaucer's Poetry." In *The Olde Daunce: Love, Friendship, Sex, and Marriage in the Medieval World*. Ed. Robert R. Edwards and Stephen Spector. Albany: SUNY Press, 1991. 154–76.

Ganim, John M. "Bakhtin, Chaucer, Carnival, Lent." In *Studies in the Age of Chaucer, Proceedings*. No. 1. *Reconstructing Chaucer*. Ed. Paul Strohm and Thomas J. Heffernan. Knoxville, Tenn.: New Chaucer Society, 1985. 59–71.

Gash, Anthony. "Carnival against Lent: The Ambivalence of Medieval Drama." In *Medieval Literature*. 74–98.

Gaunt, Simon. "From Epic to Romance: Gender and Sexuality in the *Roman d'Enéas*." *Romanic Review* 83 (1992): 1–27.

Godefroy, Frédéric Eugène. *Dictionnaire de l'ancienne langue française.* 10 vols. Paris: Vieweg, 1881–1902.

Goodich, Michael. *The Unmentionable Vice: Homosexuality in the Later Medieval Period.* N.p.: Dorset, 1979.

Goodman, Jennifer R. "Chaucer's *Squire's Tale* and the Rise of Chivalry." *Studies in the Age of Chaucer* 5 (1983): 127–36.

Gradon, Pamela. *Form and Style in Early English Literature.* London: Methuen, 1971.

Green, Dennis Howard. *Irony in the Medieval Romance.* Cambridge: Cambridge University Press, 1979.

Green, Richard Firth. "Chaucer's Victimized Women." *Studies in the Age of Chaucer* 10 (1988): 3–21.

———. "The *Familia Regis* and the *Familia Cupidinis.*" In *English Court Culture in the Later Middle Ages.* Ed. V. J. Scattergood and J. W. Sherbourne. New York: St. Martin's, 1983. 87–108.

———. *Poets and Princepleasers: Literature and the English Court in the Late Middle Ages.* Toronto: University of Toronto Press, 1980.

———. "Women in Chaucer's Audience." *Chaucer Review* 18 (1983): 146–54.

Greenberg, David F. *The Construction of Homosexuality.* Chicago: University of Chicago Press, 1988.

Haidu, Peter. *Aesthetic Distance in Chrétien de Troyes: Irony and Comedy in "Cligès" and "Perceval."* Geneva: Droz, 1968.

Halperin, David M. *One Hundred Years of Homosexuality, and Other Essays on Greek Love.* New York and London: Routledge, 1990.

Halverson, John. "Aspects of Order in the Knight's Tale." *Studies in Philology* 57 (1960): 606–21.

Hanning, Robert W. "The Audience as Co-Creator of the First Chivalric Romances." *Yearbook of English Studies* 11 (1981): 1–28.

———. "'I Shal Finde It in a Maner Glose': Versions of Textual Harassment in Medieval Literature." In *Medieval Texts and Contemporary Readers.* Ed. Laurie A. Finke and Martin B. Shichtman. Ithaca: Cornell University Press, 1987. 27–50.

———. *The Individual in Twelfth-Century Romance.* New Haven: Yale University Press, 1977.

Hansen, Elaine Tuttle. *Chaucer and the Fictions of Gender.* Berkeley and Los Angeles: University of California Press, 1992.

Harf-Lancner, Laurence. *Les Fées au Moyen Age: Morgane et Mélusine: La Naissance des fées.* Paris: Champion, 1984.

Harrison, Joseph. "'Tears for Passing Things': The Temple of Diana in the *Knight's Tale.*" *Philological Quarterly* 63 (1984): 108–16.

Heng, Geraldine. "Feminine Knots and the Other *Sir Gawain and the Green Knight.*" *PMLA* 106 (1991): 500–514.

Heng, Geraldine. "A Woman Wants: The Lady, *Gawain*, and the Forms of Seduction." *Yale Journal of Criticism* 5, no. 3 (1992): 101–34.

Hernadi, Paul. *Beyond Genre: New Directions in Literary Classification*. Ithaca: Cornell University Press, 1972.

Hidden from History: Reclaiming the Gay and Lesbian Past. Ed. Martin Bauml Duberman, Martha Vicinus, and George Chauncey, Jr. New York: NAL Books, 1989.

A History of Private Life. Vol. 2. *Revelations of the Medieval World*. Ed. Georges Duby, Trans. Arthur Goldhammer. Cambridge: Harvard University Press, 1988.

Hornstein, Lillian Herlands. "Composites of Courtly Romance." In *A Manual of the Writings in Middle English, 1050–1500*. Gen. ed. J. Burke Severs. Vol. 1. *Romances*. New Haven: Connecticut Academy of Arts and Sciences, 1967. 147–58.

Howard, Donald. *The Idea of the "Canterbury Tales."* Berkeley and Los Angeles: University of California Press, 1976.

Huchet, Jean-Charles. "Nom de femme et écriture féminine au Moyen Age: Les *Lais* de Marie de France." *Poétique*, no. 48 (November 1981): 407–30.

———. "Psychanalyse et littérature médiévale: rencontre ou méprise? (A propos de deux ouvrages récents)." *Cahiers de civilisation médiévale* 28 (1985): 223–33.

———. *Le Roman médiéval*. Paris: Presses Universitaires de France, 1984.

Hudson, Harriet. "Middle English Popular Romances: The Manuscript Evidence." *Manuscripta* 28 (1984): 67–78.

Hult, David F. *Self-Fulfilling Prophecies: Readership and Authority in the First "Roman de la Rose."* Cambridge: Cambridge University Press, 1986.

Hume, Kathryn. "Why Chaucer Calls the *Franklin's Tale* a Breton Lai." *Philological Quarterly* 51 (1972): 365–79.

Irigaray, Luce. *Speculum of the Other Woman*. Trans. Gillian C. Gill. Ithaca: Cornell University Press, 1985.

———. *This Sex Which Is Not One*. Trans. Catherine Porter with Carolyn Burke. Ithaca: Cornell University Press, 1985.

Jacquart, Danielle, and Claude Thomasset. *Sexuality and Medicine in the Middle Ages*. Trans. Matthew Adamson. Princeton: Princeton University Press, 1988.

Jaeger, C. Stephen. "L'Amour des rois: Structure sociale d'une forme de sensibilité aristocratique." Trans. Jean-François Sené. *Annales: Economies, Sociétés, Civilisations* 46 (1991): 547–71.

———. *The Origins of Courtliness: Civilizing Trends and the Formation of Courtly Ideals, 939–1210*. Philadelphia: University of Pennsylvania Press, 1985.

Jameson, Fredric. "Magical Narratives: Romance as Genre." *New Literary History* 7 (1975): 135–63.

——. *The Political Unconscious: Narrative as a Socially Symbolic Act.* Ithaca: Cornell University Press, 1981.

Jauss, Hans Robert. "Negativität und Identifikation: Versuch zur Theorie der ästhetischen Erfahrung." In *Positionen der Negativität*. Ed. Harald Weinrich. Poetik und Hermeneutik, no. 6. Munich, 1975. 263–339.

——. *Towards an Aesthetic of Reception*. Trans. Timothy Bahti. Minneapolis: University of Minnesota Press, 1982.

Johnson, Barbara. *The Critical Difference: Essays in the Contemporary Rhetoric of Reading*. Baltimore: Johns Hopkins University Press, 1980.

Jordan, Robert. "The Question of Genre: Five Chaucerian Romances." In *Chaucer at Albany*. Ed. Rossell Hope Robbins. New York: Burt Franklin, 1975. 77–103.

Kaplan, Cora. "Pandora's Box: Subjectivity, Class and Sexuality in Socialist Feminist Criticism." In *Making a Difference: Feminist Literary Criticism*. Ed. Gayle Greene and Coppélia Kahn. London: Methuen, 1985. 146–76.

Kaske, Robert E. "Chaucer's Marriage Group." In *Chaucer the Love Poet*. Ed. Jerome Mitchell and William Provost. Athens: University of Georgia Press, 1973. 45–65.

Kay, Sarah. *Subjectivity in Troubadour Poetry*. Cambridge: Cambridge University Press, 1990.

Keen, Maurice. *Chivalry*. New Haven: Yale University Press, 1984.

Kelly, Douglas. *The Art of Medieval French Romance*. Madison: University of Wisconsin Press, 1992.

Kennedy, Elspeth. "The Quest for Identity and the Importance of Lineage in Thirteenth-Century French Prose Romance." In *The Ideals and Practice of Medieval Knighthood, II: Papers from the Third Strawberry Hill Conference, 1986*. Ed. Christopher Harper-Bill and Ruth Harvey. Woodbridge, Suffolk: Boydell, 1988. 70–86.

Kieckhefer, Richard. *Magic in the Middle Ages*. Cambridge: Cambridge University Press, 1990.

Kittredge, George Lyman. *Chaucer and His Poetry*. Cambridge: Harvard University Press, 1915.

Knapp, Peggy. *Chaucer and the Social Contest*. New York and London: Routledge, 1990.

Knight, Stephen. "The Social Function of the Middle English Romances." In *Medieval Literature*. 99–122.

Köhler, Erich. *Ideal und Wirklichkeit in der höfischen Epik: Studien zur Form der frühen Artus- und Gralsdichtung.* 2d ed. Tübingen: Niemeyer, 1970.

Kolve, V. A. *Chaucer and the Imagery of Narrative: The First Five Canterbury Tales.* Stanford: Stanford University Press, 1984.

Kovetz, Gene H. "Canterbury Tales, A 2349–52." *Notes and Queries,* n.s., 5 (1958): 236–37.

Krueger, Roberta. *Women Readers and the Ideology of Gender in Old French Verse Romance.* Cambridge: Cambridge University Press, 1993.

Kurath, Hans, et al. *Middle English Dictionary.* Ann Arbor: University of Michigan Press, 1952–.

Lacan, Jacques. *Feminine Sexuality: Jacques Lacan and the "école freudienne."* Ed. Juliet Mitchell and Jacqueline Rose. Trans. Jacqueline Rose. New York: Norton, 1982.

Lamphere, Louise. "Strategies, Cooperation, and Conflict among Women in Domestic Groups." In *Woman, Culture, and Society.* Ed. Michelle Zimbalist Rosaldo and Louise Lamphere. Stanford: Stanford University Press, 1974. 97–112.

Laqueur, Thomas. *Making Sex: Body and Gender from the Greeks to Freud.* Cambridge: Harvard University Press, 1990.

Lawton, David. *Chaucer's Narrators.* Chaucer Studies 13. Woodbridge, Suffolk: D. S. Brewer, 1985.

Le Goff, Jacques. *La Civilisation de l'occident médiéval.* Paris: Arthaud, 1964.

———. "L'Occident médiéval et l'océan indien: un horizon onirique." In *Mediterraneo e Oceano Indiano.* Ed. Manlio Cortelazzo. Florence: Olschki, 1970. 243–63.

———. *Time, Work, and Culture in the Middle Ages.* Trans. Arthur Goldhammer. Chicago: University of Chicago Press, 1980.

Lee, Ann Thompson. "'A Woman True and Fair': Chaucer's Portrayal of Dorigen in the *Franklin's Tale.*" *Chaucer Review* 19 (1984–1985): 169–78.

Leicester, H. Marshall, Jr. *The Disenchanted Self: Representing the Subject in the "Canterbury Tales."* Berkeley and Los Angeles: University of California Press, 1990.

Lewis, C. S. *The Allegory of Love.* Oxford: Oxford University Press, 1936.

Loomis, Laura Hibbard. "Chaucer and the Breton Lays of the Auchinleck MS." *Studies in Philology* 38 (1941): 14–33.

———. "Secular Dramatics in the Royal Palace, Paris, 1378, 1389, and Chaucer's 'Tregetoures.'" *Speculum* 33 (1958): 242–55.

Loomis, Roger Sherman. *Wales and the Arthurian Legend.* Cardiff: University of Wales Press, 1956.

Luecke, Janemarie. "Dorigen: Marriage Model or Male Fantasy." *Journal of Women's Studies in Literature* 1 (1979): 107–21.

Luengo, Anthony E. "Magic and Illusion in *The Franklin's Tale*." *Journal of English and Germanic Philology* 77 (1978): 1–16.

MacDonald, Alison. *The Figure of Merlin in Thirteenth-Century French Romance*. Lewiston, N.Y.: Mellen, 1990.

McKeon, Michael. *The Origins of the English Novel, 1600–1740*. Baltimore: Johns Hopkins University Press, 1987.

MacKinnon, Catharine A. "Desire and Power: A Feminist Perspective." In *Marxism and the Interpretation of Culture*. Ed. Cary Nelson and Lawrence Grossberg. Urbana: University of Illinois Press, 1988. 105–16.

———. "Feminism, Marxism, Method, and the State: An Agenda for Theory." *Signs* 7 (1982): 515–44.

———. "Feminism, Marxism, Method, and the State: Toward a Feminist Jurisprudence." *Signs* 8 (1983): 635–58.

Maclean, Ian. *The Renaissance Notion of Woman: A Study in the Fortunes of Scholasticism and Medical Science in European Intellectual Life*. Cambridge: Cambridge University Press, 1980.

Mann, Jill. "Chance and Destiny in *Troilus and Criseyde* and the *Knight's Tale*." In *The Cambridge Chaucer Companion*. Ed. Piero Boitani and Jill Mann. Cambridge: Cambridge University Press, 1986. 75–92.

———. *Chaucer and Medieval Estates Satire: The Literature of Social Classes and the "General Prologue" to the "Canterbury Tales."* Cambridge: Cambridge University Press, 1973.

———. *Geoffrey Chaucer*. New York: Harvester, 1991.

———. "Now Read On: Medieval Literature." *Encounter*, no. 55 (July 1980): 60–64.

———. "'Taking the Adventure': Malory and the *Suite du Merlin*." In *Aspects of Malory*. Ed. Toshiyuki Takamiya and Derek Brewer. Cambridge: D. S. Brewer, 1981. 71–91.

Marchello-Nizia, Christiane. "Amour courtois, société masculine et figures du pouvoir." *Annales: Economies, Sociétés, Civilisations* 36 (1981): 969–82.

Mathew, Gervase. *The Court of Richard II*. London: John Murray, 1968.

Medieval Literature: Criticism, Ideology, and History. Ed. David Aers. New York: St. Martin's, 1986.

Meindl, Robert J. "'For Drye as Whit as Chalk': Allegory in Chaucer and Malory." *Studia Mystica* 6, no. 1 (Spring 1983): 45–58.

Méla, Charles. "Romans et merveilles." In *Précis de littérature française du Moyen Age.* Ed. Daniel Poirion. Paris: Presses Universitaires de France, 1983. 214–35.

Ménard, Philippe. "Chrétien de Troyes et le merveilleux." *Europe,* no. 642 (October 1982): 53–60.

―――. *Les Lais de Marie de France: Contes d'amour et d'aventure du Moyen Age.* Paris: Presses Universitaires de France, 1979.

Metlitzki, Dorothee. *The Matter of Araby in Medieval England.* New Haven: Yale University Press, 1977.

Middleton, Anne. "Chaucer's 'New Men' and the Good of Literature in the *Canterbury Tales.*" In *Literature and Society: Selected Papers from the English Institute, 1978.* Ed. Edward W. Said. Baltimore: Johns Hopkins University Press, 1980. 15–56.

―――. "War by Other Means: Marriage and Chivalry in Chaucer." In *Studies in the Age of Chaucer, Proceedings.* No. 1. *Reconstructing Chaucer.* Ed. Paul Strohm and Thomas J. Heffernan. Knoxville, Tenn.: New Chaucer Society, 1985. 119–33.

Miles, Margaret R. "The Virgin's One Bare Breast: Female Nudity and Religious Meaning in Tuscan Early Renaissance Culture." In *The Female Body in Western Culture.* Ed. Susan Rubin Suleiman. Cambridge: Harvard University Press, 1986. 193–208.

Miller, Robert P. "Chaucer's Rhetorical Rendition of Mind: *The Squire's Tale.*" In *Chaucer and the Craft of Fiction.* Ed. Leigh A. Arrathoon. Rochester, Mich.: Solaris, 1986. 219–40.

Minnis, A. J. *Chaucer and Pagan Antiquity.* Cambridge: D. S. Brewer, 1982.

Mohl, Ruth. *The Three Estates in Medieval and Renaissance Literature.* New York: Columbia University Press, 1933.

Morgan, Gerald. "Boccaccio's *Filocolo* and the Moral Argument of the *Franklin's Tale.*" *Chaucer Review* 20 (1985–1986): 285–306.

Morris, Colin. *The Discovery of the Individual, 1050–1200.* New York: Harper and Row, 1972.

Morris, Meaghan. "The Pirate's Fiancée: Feminists and Philosophers, or maybe tonight it'll happen." In *Feminism and Foucault: Reflections on Resistance.* Ed. Irene Diamond and Lee Quinby. Boston: Northeastern University Press. 21–42.

Muscatine, Charles. *Chaucer and the French Tradition.* Berkeley and Los Angeles: University of California Press, 1957.

―――. *The Old French Fabliaux.* New Haven: Yale University Press, 1986.

Nelson, Deborah. "Eliduc's Salvation." *The French Review* 55 (1981–1982): 37–42.

Nerlich, Michael. *Ideology of Adventure: Studies in Modern Consciousness, 1100–1750.* Trans. Ruth Crowley. 2 vols. Minneapolis: University of Minnesota Press, 1987.

New French Feminisms. Ed. Elaine Marks and Isabelle de Courtivron. Amherst: University of Massachusetts Press, 1980.

Niccoli, Ottavia. *I sacerdoti, i guerrieri, i contadini: Storia di un'immagine della società.* Turin: Einaudi, 1979.

Nichols, Stephen G. "Amorous Imitation: Bakhtin, Augustine, and *Le Roman d'Enéas.*" In *Romance: Generic Transformation from Chrétien de Troyes to Cervantes.* Ed. Kevin Brownlee and Marina Scordilis Brownlee. Hanover, N.H.: University Press of New England, 1985. 47–73.

Nolan, Barbara. *Chaucer and the Tradition of the "Roman Antique."* Cambridge: Cambridge University Press, 1992.

Nykrog, Per. *Les Fabliaux.* Copenhagen: Ejnar Munksgaard, 1957.

Ortner, Sherry B. "Gender and Sexuality in Hierarchical Societies: The Case of Polynesia and Some Comparative Implications." In *Sexual Meanings: The Cultural Construction of Gender and Sexuality.* Ed. Sherry B. Ortner and Harriet Whitehead. Cambridge: Cambridge University Press, 1981. 359–409.

Owst, Gerald Robert. *Literature and Pulpit in Medieval England.* Cambridge: Cambridge University Press, 1933.

Paris, Gaston. "Etudes sur les romans de la Table Ronde: Lancelot du Lac, II, Le *Conte de la Charrette.*" *Romania* 12 (1883): 459–534.

Parker, Patricia A. *Inescapable Romance: Studies in the Poetics of a Mode.* Princeton: Princeton University Press, 1979.

Patch, Howard R. *The Goddess Fortuna in Mediaeval Literature.* Cambridge: Harvard University Press, 1927.

Pater, Walter. *The Renaissance: Studies in Art and Poetry, the 1893 Text.* Ed. Donald L. Hill. Berkeley and Los Angeles: University of California Press, 1980.

Paton, Lucy Allen. *Studies in the Fairy Mythology of Arthurian Romance.* 2d ed. New York: Burt Franklin, 1970.

Patterson, Lee. *Chaucer and the Subject of History.* Madison: University of Wisconsin Press, 1991.

———. "'What Man Artow?': Authorial Self-Definition in *The Tale of Sir Thopas* and *The Tale of Melibee.*" *Studies in the Age of Chaucer* 11 (1989): 117–75.

Pearcy, Roy J. "Chaucer's Franklin and the Literary Vavasour." *Chaucer Review* 8 (1973–1974): 33–59.

Pearsall, Derek. *The Canterbury Tales.* London: Allen and Unwin, 1985.

Pearsall, Derek. "The Development of Middle English Romance." *Mediaeval Studies* 27 (1965): 91–116.

———. "Middle English Romance and Its Audiences." In *Historical and Editorial Studies in Medieval and Early Modern English for Johan Gerritsen*. Ed. Mary-Jo Arn and Hanneke Wirtjes. Groningen: Wolters-Noordhoff, 1985. 37–47.

Perret, Michèle. "Travesties et transsexuelles: Yde, Silence, Grisandole, Blanchandine." *Romance Notes* 25 (1984–1985): 328–40.

Peters, Edward. *The Magician, the Witch, and the Law.* [Philadelphia]: University of Pennsylvania Press, 1978.

Petit, Aimé. "La Reine Camille dans le *Roman d'Enéas.*" *Lettres Romanes* 36 (1982): 5–40.

———. "Le Traitement courtois du thème des Amazones d'après trois romans antiques: *Enéas, Troie* et *Alexandre.*" *Le Moyen Age* 89 (1983): 63–84.

Playing with Gender: A Renaissance Pursuit. Ed. Jean R. Brink, Maryanne C. Horowitz, and Allison P. Coudert. Urbana: University of Illinois Press, 1991.

Poirion, Daniel. *Le Poète et le Prince: l'évolution du lyrisme courtois de Guillaume de Machaut à Charles d'Orléans.* Paris: Presses Universitaires de France, 1965.

Post, J. B. "Sir Thomas West and the Statute of Rapes, 1382." *Bulletin of the Institute of Historical Research* (University of London) 53 (1980): 24–30.

Pratt, Robert A. "Conjectures Regarding Chaucer's Manuscript of the *Teseida.*" *Studies in Philology* 42 (1945): 745–63.

Rey-Flaud, Henri. *La Névrose courtoise.* Paris: Seuil, 1983.

Ribard, J. "Des lais au XIVᵉ siècle? Jean de Condé." In *Mélanges de langue et de littérature du moyen âge et de la renaissance offerts à Jean Frappier.* Geneva: Droz, 1970. 2:945–55.

Riley, Denise. *Am I That Name? Feminism and the Category of "Women" in History.* Minneapolis: University of Minnesota Press, 1988.

Riviere, Joan. "Womanliness as a Masquerade." In *Psychoanalysis and Female Sexuality.* Ed. Hendrik M. Ruitenbeek. New Haven: College and University Press, 1966. Essay reprinted from *International Journal of Psychoanalysis* 10 (1929): 201–20.

Robertson, D. W., Jr. *A Preface to Chaucer: Studies in Medieval Perspectives.* Princeton: Princeton University Press, 1962.

Rosmarin, Adena. *The Power of Genre.* Minnneapolis: University of Minnesota Press, 1985.

Rubin, Gayle. "The Traffic in Women: Notes on the 'Political Economy' of Sex." In *Toward an Anthropology of Women*. Ed. Rayna R. Reiter. New York: Monthly Review Press, 1975. 157–210.

Russo, Mary. "Female Grotesques: Carnival and Theory." In *Feminist Studies/Critical Studies*. Ed. Teresa de Lauretis. Bloomington: Indiana University Press, 1986. 213–29.

Said, Edward W. *Orientalism*. New York: Pantheon, 1978.

Salter, Elizabeth. *Fourteenth-Century English Poetry: Contexts and Readings*. Oxford: Clarendon, 1983.

Sargent-Bauer, Barbara Nelson. "Belle Enide, bonne Enide." In *Mélanges de langue et de littérature médiévales offerts à Pierre le Gentil*. Paris: SEDES, 1973. 767–71.

Scaglione, Aldo. *Knights at Court: Courtliness, Chivalry, and Courtesy from Ottonian Germany to the Italian Renaissance*. Berkeley and Los Angeles: University of California Press, 1991.

Sedgwick, Eve Kosofsky. *Between Men: English Literature and Male Homosocial Desire*. New York: Columbia University Press, 1985.

Seeking the Woman in Late Medieval and Renaissance Writings: Essays in Feminist Contextual Criticism. Ed. Sheila Fisher and Janet E. Halley. Knoxville: University of Tennessee Press, 1989.

Sherwood, Merriam. "Magic and Mechanics in Medieval Fiction." *Studies in Philology* 44 (1947): 567–92.

Shoaf, R. A. "Chaucer and Medusa: The *Franklin's Tale*." *Chaucer Review* 21 (1986–1987): 274–90.

———. "The Play of Puns in Late Middle English Poetry: Concerning Juxtology." In *On Puns: The Foundation of Letters*. Ed. Jonathan Culler. Oxford: Blackwell, 1988. 44–61.

Sienaert, Edgard. *Les Lais de Marie de France: Du conte merveilleux à la nouvelle psychologique*. Paris: Champion, 1978.

Smith, Paul. *Discerning the Subject*. Minneapolis: University of Minnesota Press, 1988.

Southern, Robert W. *Western Views of Islam in the Middle Ages*. Cambridge: Harvard University Press, 1962.

Spearing, A. C. "Marie de France and Her Middle English Adapters." *Studies in the Age of Chaucer* 12 (1990): 117–56.

———. *Medieval to Renaissance in English Poetry*. Cambridge: Cambridge University Press, 1985.

Stallybrass, Peter, and Allon White. *The Politics and Poetics of Transgression*. Ithaca: Cornell University Press, 1986.

Stevens, John. *Medieval Romance: Themes and Approaches*. London: Hutchinson, 1973.

Stillwell, Gardiner. "Chaucer in Tartary." *Review of English Studies* 24 (1948): 177–88.

Stock, Lorraine Kochanske. "The Two Mayings in Chaucer's *Knight's Tale*: Convention and Invention." *Journal of English and Germanic Philology* 85 (1986): 206–21.

Strohm, Paul. *Hochon's Arrow: The Social Imagination of Fourteenth-Century Texts*. Princeton: Princeton University Press, 1992.

―――. "The Origin and Meaning of Middle English *Romaunce*." *Genre* 10 (1977): 1–28.

―――. *Social Chaucer*. Cambridge: Harvard University Press, 1989.

―――. "*Storie, Spelle, Geste, Romaunce, Tragedie*: Generic Distinctions in the Middle English Troy Narratives." *Speculum* 46 (1971): 348–59.

Taylor, Andrew. "The Myth of the Minstrel Manuscript." *Speculum* 66 (1991): 43–73.

Thiébaux, Marcelle. *The Stag of Love: The Chase in Medieval Literature*. Ithaca: Cornell University Press, 1974.

Thompson, John J. "The Compiler in Action: Robert Thornton and the 'Thornton Romances' in Lincoln Cathedral MS 91." In *Manuscripts and Readers in Fifteenth-Century England*. Ed. Derek Pearsall. Cambridge: D. S. Brewer, 1983. 113–24.

Thorndike, Lynn. *A History of Magic and Experimental Science during the First Thirteen Centuries of Our Era*. 2 vols. New York: Macmillan, 1923.

Tyrrell, W. Blake. *Amazons: A Study in Athenian Mythmaking*. Baltimore: Johns Hopkins University Press, 1984.

Vale, Malcolm. *War and Chivalry*. London: Duckworth, 1981.

Van Hamel, A. G. "Cligès et Tristan." *Romania* 33 (1904): 465–89.

Vance, Eugene. "Le combat érotique chez Chrétien de Troyes." *Poétique* 12 (1972): 544–71.

Wack, Mary. *Lovesickness in the Middle Ages: The "Viaticum" and Its Commentaries*. Philadelphia: University of Pennsylvania Press, 1990.

Watt, Ian. *The Rise of the Novel: Studies in Defoe, Richardson, and Fielding*. Berkeley and Los Angeles: University of California Press, 1957.

Weiss, Judith. "The Wooing Woman in Anglo-Norman Romance." In *Romance in Medieval England*. Ed. Maldwyn Mills, Jennifer Fellows, and Carol M. Meale. Woodbridge, Suffolk: D. S. Brewer, 1991. 149–61.

Whiting, B. J. "Gawain: His Reputation, His Courtesy and His Appearance in Chaucer's *Squire's Tale*." *Mediaeval Studies* 9 (1947): 189–234.

Wilmotte, M. "Observations sur le *Roman de Troie*." *Le Moyen Age* 27 (1914): 93–119.

Wimsatt, James. *Chaucer and His French Contemporaries: Natural Music in the Fourteenth Century*. Toronto: University of Toronto Press, 1991.

Wise, Boyd Ashby. *The Influence of Statius upon Chaucer.* Baltimore: Furst, 1911.

Wurtele, Douglas J. "Chaucer's Franklin and the Truth about 'Trouthe.'" *English Studies in Canada* 13 (1987): 359–74.

Zink, Michel. "Bel-Aceuil le travesti." *Littérature,* no. 47 (October 1982): 31–40.

INDEX

꧁꧂